Praise for *The Sacrament of Mercy*

The Sacrament of Mercy is unique, a comprehensive study of its subject. It is logical and well-organized; a scholarly work that employs a scholarly methodology and achieves an in-depth analysis. The author is not only a scholar of canon law but a man immersed in the practicalities (both pastoral and pedagogical) of his subject.

The Sacrament of Penance, also commonly called the Sacrament of Reconciliation or Confession, is in fact the sacrament of mercy because in the act of Confession, God forgives man's guilt. The sacramental reality studied here involves the mysterious action of God. And man, in preparing for this sacrament, examines his conscience and decides to improve himself in order to be in constant communion with God, to live in sanctifying grace, and at the same time to remain in peaceful communion with other people, forgiving them if they are guilty.

The Sacrament of Penance must be based upon the foundation of canon law so that it is not distorted in its practice. The granting of the sacrament should be of great importance in the life of each parish community. Religious pedagogy indicates the need for education in deepening a person's religious life — this includes the use of the sacramental ministry.

The contents of this book show us how we can live a mature religious life, which has above all a vertical direction (searching for and finding God) and thus a salvific direction. At the same time one cannot fail to notice the horizontal direction of a mature religious life, which can be reflected in both the moral and the mental health of a person.

The Sacrament of Mercy is recommended above all to those who recognize the value of the sacramental life and seek God through it.

— **Professor Rev. Waldemar Woźniak**, Associate Professor of the Institute of Psychology, the Faculty of Christian Philosophy, the Cardinal Stefan Wyszyński University, Warsaw, Poland

THE SACRAMENT OF MERCY

Welcoming with the Love of God

Law — Theology — Education

Msgr. Krzysztof Nykiel
Regent of the Apostolic Penitentiary

Preface by Cardinal Pietro Parolin
Foreword by Cardinal Mauro Piacenza

First published in 2019 as *Il Sacramento della Miseriocrdia: Accogliere con l'Amore di Dio*, by Libreria Editrice Vaticana.

English translation by Matthew Fforde.

Available from:
Marian Helpers Center
Stockbridge, MA 01263

Prayerline: 1-800-804-3823
Orderline: 1-800-462-7426

Websites:
Marian.org
TheDivineMercy.org
DivineMercyPlus.org
ShopMercy.org

Library of Congress Control Number: 2023951496
ISBN: 978-1-59614-607-5

Imprimi Potest:
Very Rev. Chris Alar, MIC
Provincial Superior, Blessed Virgin Mary, Mother of Mercy Province
Marian Fathers of the Immaculate Conception of the B.V.M.
January 1, 2024
Solemnity of Mary, the Holy Mother of God

Nihil Obstat:
Robert A. Stackpole, STD
Censor Deputatus
January 1, 2024

Note: The *Nihil Obstat* and corresponding *Imprimi Potest* are not a certification that those granting it agree with the contents, opinions, or statements expressed in the work. Instead, they merely confirm that the work contains nothing contrary to faith and morals.

Copy editors: Susan Gamer and Rachel Salvetti

Layout and Cover Design: Kathy Szpak

TABLE OF CONTENTS

PREFACE

"Love is not something that one can teach but it is the most important thing to learn." This seems to be one of the most known and remembered aphorisms of St. John Paul II. And rightly so because from the history of salvation we learn that everything that God says and does, in Christ and in the Spirit, is a manifestation of His being, which is Love. God is love, as the Apostle John declares (cf. 1 Jn 4:8), and love is seen, touched and experienced: for this reason one can behold, love and imitate love. Holy Scripture and Tradition are the "signs" of the Word of God through which one can experience the love of God. God who is love, indeed, manifests Himself as "mercy" towards those who are poor, suffering and sinners. The manifestations of His mercy are the tangible signs of His love.

There are many passages in Holy Scripture that reveal the love of God as mercy towards the people of the covenant, just as there are very many terms that describe it and define its meaning. How can we not mention the term "*rahamim*" which refers to the deeply felt love that a mother feels for her child, a love characterized by a strong intensity of sensitive emotions, a love freely given and often not deserved, a love that springs from a happily "obliged" heart: "Can a mother forget her infant, be without tenderness for the child of her womb? Even should she forget, I will never forget you" (Is 49:15). The word "*hesed*" refers to the paternal love of God, a love of pure goodness that continuously takes the initiative and is constantly poured over men: "Yet it was I who taught Ephraim to walk, who took them in my arms; I drew them with human cords, with bands of love; I fostered them like one who raises an infant to his cheeks; Yet, though I stooped to feed my child, they did not know that I was their healer" (Hos 11:3-4). Especially intense in meaning is the term "*emet*" which expresses the absolute faithfulness of God to His people, even if that people lives in unfaithfulness and transgressions of the covenant: "How could I give you up, O Ephraim, or deliver you up, O Israel?... I will not give vent to my blazing anger, I will not destroy Ephraim again; For I am God and not man, the Holy One present among you; I will not let the flames consume you" (Hos 11:8-9). These are only some of the terms that express the riches of the merciful love of God that is continuously poured over the history of many centuries of His people.

At a literal level, in Holy Scripture the phrase "merciful love" does not appear explicitly. However, it can be well substituted by St. Paul's phrase "merciful Father." Indeed, St. Paul, when addressing the Corinthians, begins his Letter with a typically Jewish formula of blessing: "Blessed be the God and Father of our Lord Jesus Christ, the Father of compassion and God of all encouragement" (2 Cor 1:3). And the mercy of the Father, the founding element of the whole Christian experience, is fully revealed in the Son. As St. John Paul II observed:

> Christ, then, reveals God who is Father, who is "love," as St. John will express it in his first letter (1 Jn 4:8,16); Christ reveals God as "rich in mercy," as we read in St. Paul (Eph 2:4) This truth is not just the subject of a teaching; it is a reality made present to us by Christ. Making the Father present as love and mercy is, in Christ's own consciousness, the fundamental touchstone of His mission as the Messiah.[1]

From the testimony of the Gospels — and especially of the fourth Gospel — we know that nobody has ever seen God and that Jesus, His only begotten Son, who is God and is in the bosom of the Father, has revealed Him (cf. Jn 1:18). Divine mercy, therefore, becomes fully and perfectly audible, visible and palpable in Jesus:

> [I]n Christ and through Christ, God also becomes especially visible in His mercy; that is to say, there is emphasized that attribute of the divinity which the Old Testament, using various concepts and terms, already defined as "mercy." Christ confers on the whole of the Old Testament tradition about God's mercy a definitive meaning. Not only does He speak of it and explain it by the use of comparisons and parables, but above all He Himself makes it incarnate and personifies it. He Himself, in a certain sense, is mercy. To the person who sees it in Him — and finds it in Him —

[1] John Paul II, Encyclical Letter *Dives in misericordia* (30 November 1980) (hereafter *DM*), n. 3.

> God becomes "visible" in a particular way as the Father who is "rich in mercy."[2]

The living and working presence of God the Father is the fundamental theme of the preaching of Jesus, beginning with the synagogue of Nazareth. But it is in the death on the cross and the resurrection of the Son that the mercy of God for men as sinners is expressed in a full and perfect way. Indeed, the cross of Jesus is the most profound and humanly unthinkable moment of the submissiveness of God and His bending down to man — the "program" of the merciful love of God towards a humanity that is fallen, poor, suffering, imprisoned, oppressed and distant from God. Crucified love is a love that reconciles God and man; man and man.

> With our eyes fixed on the mystery of Golgotha we should be reminded always of that "vertical" dimension of division and reconciliation concerning the relationship between man and God, a dimension which in the eyes of faith always prevails over the "horizontal" dimension, that is to say, over the reality of division between people and the need for reconciliation between them.[3]

Crucified and merciful love, the divine love that foresees every expectation of man, attests not only that sin and death no longer have the last word about the destiny of man but also that "The favors of the Lord are not exhausted, his mercies are not spent" (Lam 3:22). Indeed, as the *Magnificat* reminds us, from generation to generation the mercy of God is bestowed on those who fear Him, on those who through the preaching and the work of the Church accept the ancient and always contemporary invitation to allow themselves to be reconciled with God. It is essential to understand that the prophetic words expressed in the Spirit by the Mother of God do not refer to a more or less remote past, to a story to be remembered but which now no longer exists. On the contrary, they relate to the whole future of the people of God on earth and to our generation which, with its contradictions, perceives the need to be touched by the mercy of God.

"We implore you on behalf of Christ, be reconciled to God" (2 Cor 5:20) is the fervent appeal of Saint Paul that still today echoes

---

[2] Ibid., n. 2.

[3] John Paul II, Post-Synodal Apostolic Exhortation *Reconciliatio et Paenitentia* (2 December 1984), n. 7.

in the Church and from the Church because by divine mandate the Church carries on the proclaiming and the work of reconciliation that characterized the mission of Christ, inviting every man to convert and to believe in the salvific power of the Gospel. In this proclaiming it appears evident that:

> Christ, in revealing the love-mercy of God, at the same time demanded from people that they also should be guided in their lives by love and mercy. This requirement forms part of the very essence of the Messianic message and constitutes the heart of the Gospel ethos.[4]

Mercy and reconciliation, therefore, constitute an inseparable tandem whose terms are completely interdependent. This also applies to the words "reconciliation" and "conversion," forgiveness and peace. Pope Francis emphasizes this well in his apostolic letter *Misericordia et misera*, highlighting how mercy is first of all a divine initiative, love that always precedes us and accompanies us, despite the limitations and the sins of man. God in Jesus Christ and in the Holy Spirit forgives us, reconciles us with Him and in doing this reconciles us with our ourselves and with the creation. It is God "who has reconciled us to himself through Christ and given us the ministry of reconciliation" (2 Cor 5:18). "We were the first to be forgiven in view of this ministry, made witnesses at first hand of the universality of God's forgiveness."[5]

Mercy, reconciliation, conversion and forgiveness are not, however, words without meaning: the Church, in proclaiming them and celebrating them, must be very careful to avoid them being perceived only as the words of a song of love with a pleasant sound but not put into practice (cf. Ez 33:32). Mercy, observes Pope Francis, "is this concrete action of love that, by forgiving, transforms and changes our lives."[6]

Hence the concern of the Pope to invite the whole of the Church and every man and woman of good will to celebrate the mercy of God above all in the liturgy and in a particular way in the Sacrament of Reconciliation where it "is not only repeatedly evoked, but is truly received and experienced."[7] The Supreme Pontiff identifies the

---

[4] *DM*, n. 3.

[5] Pope Francis, Apostolic Letter *Misericordia et misera* (20 November 2016), n. 11.

[6] Ibid., n. 2.

[7] Ibid., n. 5.

theological-pastoral summary of this mystery of love, which from the heart of God is transfused into the heart of man, in the formula of absolution spoken by a confessor: "God, the Father of mercies, through the death and resurrection of his Son has reconciled the world to himself and sent the Holy Spirit among us for the forgiveness of sins; through the ministry of the Church may God give you pardon and peace." In this formula we can see not only the unity and the complementariness of the tandem referred to above but also, and above all, the fact that every reference to mercy is "highly *performative*, which is to say that as we invoke mercy with faith, it is granted to us, and as we confess it to be vital and real, it truly transforms us."[8]

We need, therefore, the Sacrament of Mercy to find once again a central place in our lives as believers so that everyone is offered the opportunity of experiencing the greatness of the mercy of God and the liberating power of forgiveness, in the awareness that there is nothing that "can prevent God from once more embracing the son who returns to him, admitting that he has done wrong but intending to start his life anew."[9]

Lastly, I would like to repeat the heartfelt appeal of Pope Francis to develop and advance a culture of mercy that starts with the conversion of our hearts to the Word of the Lord and calls us every day to move out of indifference to the love of God towards us and thus from individualism and insensitivity towards our brothers and sisters. For a culture of mercy to be built, a mentality of faith should be formed which, following the example of Christ who was humble, poor and faithful to the Father, defines our lives as believers through concrete works and acts for those who live in need and suffering. It is not licit for us to turn our gaze elsewhere when we encounter the suffering of our brothers and sisters,[10] nor can we allow ourselves to fall into the temptation of finding that we are "theoreticians of mercy." This is because this shows that our hearts are not really open and meek to the action of the Spirit. Let us therefore make ours the teaching of the Apostle John: "Children, let us love not in word or speech but in deed and truth" (1 Jn 3:18).

I keenly congratulate Msgr. Krzysztof Nykiel on this book, whose subjects of mercy, reconciliation, and forgiveness are broadly

---

[8] Ibidem.

[9] Ibid., n. 11.

[10] Cf. ibid., n. 20.

addressed and suitably located in a theological, pastoral and educational approach. There is always a need for this. This text can be seen as good fruit borne by a tree of thought and personal experience, and corroborated recently by the healthy wind that blew strongly during the Jubilee Year of Mercy. Already in the title, *The Sacrament of Mercy: Welcoming with the Love of God*, one perceives the purpose of this work which seeks to be, in a certain sense, a response to the difficulties at the level of pastoral care that the celebration of the Sacrament of Reconciliation has encountered in the recent past and still encounters in the lives of believers. This is a sacrament which more than the others is often diminished and undervalued, being seen as a reality that one can easily do without. Every crisis that weakens the presence and the celebration of a sacrament is before anything else a consequence of a lack of faith in the Word of God, a sign that faith has lost its pathway in truth. Let us hope, therefore, that this text finds the greatest resonance possible as a precious expression of a valuable service of the Church.

Cardinal Pietro Parolin
Secretary of State of His Holiness

FOREWORD

The first information on reconciliation granted for sins committed after Baptism is to be found in *The Shepherd of Hermas*. In this work it is stated that the only reconciliation granted to men is that received at Baptism, whereas in a totally exceptional way one could grant a second reconciliation during a person's life (*Mandata*, IV, 1, 8). In *De Poenitentia* Tertullian also affirmed that penance was not repeatable. Thus this great writer from Carthage stated that in the case of grave sins a second penance was possible but only once (*De Poenitentia*, 7, 9, 10). Although it was a part of the great ecclesial Tradition of the first centuries, during which the discipline of penance was certainly rigid but always organized and elaborated starting with concrete cases, this practice has undergone down the centuries various variations, until arriving at the system that we know today and the penitential renewal that it proposes. The gradual renewal of the discipline of penance finds its wellspring in that "fontal" Reconciliation to which the Church always goes back because she "feels an obligation to go to the roots of that original wound of sin in order to bring healing and to re-establish, so to speak, an equally original reconciliation which will be the effective principle of all true reconciliation."[1] One thus understands why Reconciliation truly becomes necessary, because there was the break of sin, from which are derived all the other forms of fracture in the innermost part of man and around him. Reconciliation, therefore, to be full necessarily requires liberation from sin, rejected at its deepest roots. Thus a close internal tie links conversion and reconciliation: it is impossible to disjoin these two realities or to speak about one but keep silent about the other.

I am grateful to Msgr. Nykiel, certainly for the shared feelings of priestly fraternity and in a special way for this book, because from its first pages it expresses the view that the pathway of Reconciliation

[1] John Paul II, Post-Synodal Apostolic Exhortation *Reconciliatio et Paenitentia* (2 December 1984), n. 4.

is a complex and fascinating pathway that begins with an "encounter" that unfolds substantially in time for all the years of the life of a believer. This is an encounter between two realities or better of two hearts: the heart of God who foresees and calls man unceasingly to communion with Him, and the heart of man who perceives in his innermost being the need to allow himself to be embraced by the Father, God-Love. To employ a terminology that is not new to the Magisterium of the Church, borrowed from the revelation of the economy of revelation, it is the encounter between the *mysterium iniquitatis*, which holds that sin is the victor and the protagonist of history, and the *mysterium pietatis*, the design of merciful God who in Christ and for Christ, in the dynamism of history, proclaims and realizes that the sin of man is not only cancelled but even taken on and removed through the sacrifice of Jesus on the cross.

The teachings of the recent Supreme Pontiffs have often paid great attention to the Sacrament of Reconciliation, to its subjects and, in a certain sense, also to its "settings." To the Church has been entrusted the ministry and the word of Reconciliation (cf. *2* Cor 5:18-19) and she, like a loving Mother, with the Word, prayer and the celebration of the sacraments, proclaims the message of Reconciliation to the whole world. As St. John Paul II observed:

> The church ... shows man the paths and offers the means for reaching this fourfold reconciliation. The paths are precisely those of conversion of heart and victory over sin, whether this latter is selfishness or injustice, arrogance or exploitation of others, attachment to material goods or the unrestrained quest for pleasure. The means are those of faithful and loving attention to God's word; personal and community prayer; and in particular the sacraments, true signs and instruments of reconciliation, among which there excels, precisely under this aspect, the one which we are rightly accustomed to call the sacrament of reconciliation or penance.[2]

As the temptation to underestimate the grave character of sin with its personal and social consequences, to the point of even cancelling its meaning from the conscience of the believer, always emerges, Benedict XVI hoped that in all the Churches a pedagogy

---

[2] Ibid., n. 8.

of conversion would be fostered in order to sustain the wish to have recourse to sacramental Confession amongst the faithful.[3] For this reason, the fact that the Pope Emeritus saw confessionals as theological-pastoral "settings" that express the profound meaning of the Sacrament of Reconciliation does not seem strange in the least. To these farsighted phrases are added those of Pope Francis who has called on the whole of the Church to internalize that in the whole of sacramental life mercy is given to us in abundance. For this reason, there is an urgent need for the people of God, ordained ministers and the lay faithful, to become attached to the celebration of the mercy of God which "takes place in a very particular way in the *Sacrament of Penance and Reconciliation*. Here we feel the embrace of the Father, who comes forth to meet us and grant us the grace of being once more his sons and daughters. We are sinners and we bear the burden of contradiction between what we wish to do and what we do in fact (cf. Rm 7:14-21). Yet grace always precedes us and takes on the face of the mercy that effects our reconciliation and pardon. God makes us understand his great love for us precisely when we recognize that we are sinners. Grace is stronger than sin: it overcomes every possible form of resistance, because love conquers all (cf. 1 Cor 13:7)."[4]

This book by Msgr. Nykiel expresses the canonical-sacramental and theological-educational dimensions of the Sacrament of Reconciliation. From it emerges a harmonious summary of the pronouncements of the Magisterium of the Church on Reconciliation, as well as the fact that it is the outcome of a great deal of personal experience of service to the Sacrament of Mercy. Worthy of note, *inter alia*, is the subject of the confessional which is present throughout the text in a transversal way. The confessional is presented not only as a physical space and it must not be transformed into a setting for torture. It is above all else a "theological space," a setting in which the penitent really encounters the merciful heart of God the Father. A setting for the proclaiming of truth and understanding, a setting for faith and encouragement, a setting where the joy of a return of a penitent heart to the welcoming and loving heart of the Father is experienced. This aspect could only be present given the generous dedication of Msgr. Nykiel to the Sacrament of Forgiveness and this can be seen both in his daily work at the Apostolic Penitentiary and in the world of

[3] Cf. Benedict XVI, Post-Synodal Apostolic Exhortation *Sacramentum caritatis* (22 February 2007), nn. 20-21.

[4] Pope Francis, Apostolic Letter *Misericordia et misera* (20 November 2016), n. 8.

pastoral care. In addition, only a man "impassioned" of this Sacrament could have brought together in an analysis, with simplicity of language and clarity of exposition, almost in a symbiosis, the Magisterium, theology, pastoral care, and experience in the field.

Cardinal Mauro Piacenza
Major Penitentiary

INTRODUCTION

During my years of priestly ministry — when the Lord has granted to me and continues to grant to me the grace of being a minister of His merciful love, in particular through the celebration of the Sacrament of Reconciliation — the gaze of my spirit has often turned to what in my judgment is the profound, mysterious, and at the same time accessible, reason that inspired the writing and the publication of this book. The encounter between the welcoming and vivifying love of God, and the wish for forgiveness and reconciliation that animates the troubled heart of man, has its wellspring in the fact that the "desire for God is written in the human heart, because man is created by God and for God; and God never ceases to draw man to himself. Only in God will he find the truth and happiness he never stops searching for."[1] With other words this truth was affirmed as long ago as Irenaeus of Lyons who asserted that the glory of God is man fully alive and that the life of man consists of taking part in the life itself of God and enjoying His goodness (cf. *Against Heresies*, 4, 20, 5). However, this intimate and living link with God can not only be forgotten about by man himself — it can also be rejected by him. This is the sad experience of sin as disobedience and detachment from the love of God, an abuse and distortion of that freedom that God has given to the human person so that he may love God, and in Him, his neighbor.

From Biblical revelation, however, we know that the heart of the Father has not abandoned His children. On the contrary, He has always called them to communion with Him through the mystery of Christ and the mission of the Church. Reconciliation and forgiveness are a gift of God and His initiative, and this last "takes concrete form in the mystery of Christ the redeemer, the reconciler and the liberator of man from sin in all its forms ... the Church ... grasps her mission of working, in imitation of the Lord, for the conversion of hearts and for

[1] *Catechism of the Catholic Church* (Vatican City, 1992) (hereafter *CCC*), n. 27.

the reconciliation of people with God and with one another — these being two realities that are intimately connected."[2]

The Church herself, to whom has been entrusted the word and the ministry of reconciliation by the Lord, is defined by Pope Francis not as a tollhouse but as a house of the Father that is always open; a fatherly house but one with the heart of a mother where there is a place for everyone with their difficult lives.[3] Daily experience, of which we are all after a certain fashion the leading figures, above all at a young age, tells us about the importance of the open heart of a mother who generates, nourishes, looks after and intercedes for her children with their father, especially when they have made themselves the sad agents of errors and failings. This, indeed, is what the Mother Church does with her children through the Sacrament of Reconciliation. She takes by the hand and lovingly accompanies her children who have been caught up in the painful experience of sin so that they may allow themselves to encounter the merciful heart of the Father who is already waiting for them and always precedes them in love. One thus understands that the Sacrament of Mercy is a privileged "setting" for the encounter of God with man, for the flow of new life and unconditional love that is poured by the heart of God into the heart of man.

In essential terms, the pages of this book seek to narrate, within the limits of what is possible, the inestimable value of forgiveness and reconciliation received from God the Father in Christ through the ministry of the Church. But they also aim to describe the responsibility and joy of being ministers (who are certainly inadequate) of this mysterious encounter between the tenderness of God, who awaits us and offers Himself with love to the prodigal son, and the yearning for hope and joy towards which man the sinner is directed. The two icons referred to by the Holy Father Francis in his apostolic letter *Misericordia et misera* are beautiful and particularly touching. They are living images that tell us how great is both the merciful love of the Lord and the joyous resurrection that this love generates in people's hearts. The episodes of the adulteress and the woman sinner in the house of the Pharisee: two stories like very many others, experienced in the sadness and loneliness of those who know the situation of their

---

[2] John Paul II, Post-Synodal Apostolic Exhortation *Reconciliatio et Paenitentia* (2 December 1984) (hereafter *RP*), nn. 7-6.

[3] Cf. Pope Francis, Apostolic Exhortation *Evangelii gaudium* (24 November 2013) (hereafter *EG*), n. 47.

hearts before the holiness of God and, in a certain sense, experience shame, abandonment and marginalization by men. These are stories of melancholy and spiritual emptiness that can lead to forms of hopelessness that one cannot even imagine. Despite this, the encounter with the mercy of God, in Jesus Christ, really goes beyond what their hearts dare to hope:

> What great joy welled up in the heart of these two women: the adulteress and the sinner! Forgiveness made them feel free at last and happy as never before. Their tears of shame and pain turned into the smile of a person who knows that he or she is loved. Mercy gives rise to *joy*, because our hearts are opened to the hope of a new life. The joy of forgiveness is inexpressible, yet it radiates all around us whenever we experience forgiveness. Its source is in the love with which God comes to meet us, breaking through walls of selfishness that surround us, in order to make us in turn instruments of mercy.[4]

Since nothing of what a penitent sinner places in front of the mercy of God can remain without the embrace of His forgiveness, and mercy is a concrete action of love that in forgiving transforms, liberates and changes a person's life, the Church through her ministers and in a special way confessors has to proclaim in one voice with the Lord: "Has no one condemned you?...Neither do I condemn you. Go, (and) from now on do not sin any more" (Jn 8:10-11); "her many sins have been forgiven; hence, she has shown great love" (Lk 7:47).

I would like to recall what Pope Francis wrote for priests and confessors in his *Misericordia et misera*:

> I invite priests once more to prepare carefully for the ministry of Confession, which is a true priestly mission. I thank all of you from the heart for your ministry, and I ask you to be *welcoming* to all, *witnesses* of fatherly tenderness whatever the gravity of the sin involved, *attentive* in helping penitents to reflect on the wrong they have done, *clear* in presenting moral principles, *willing* to walk patiently beside the faithful on their penitential journey, *far-sighted*

[4] Pope Francis, Apostolic Letter *Misericordia et misera* (20 November 2016) (hereafter *MM*), n. 3.

> in discerning individual cases and *generous* in dispensing God's forgiveness. Just as Jesus chose to remain silent in order to save the woman caught in adultery from the sentence of death, so every priest in the confessional should be open-hearted, since every penitent is a reminder that he himself is a sinner, but also a minister of mercy.[5]

Taking to heart these words of the Holy Father, I hope that this text can be of help to very many brothers in the priesthood who every day live the experience of received and given forgiveness. Since one should never ignore the fact that because of the first sin man has a wounded nature that is inclined to evil — this would be an error at the level of education, I also hope that this book will fraternally help confessors to educate themselves continuously and permanently in the beauty and importance of penance, which finds its fullness in the Sacrament of Reconciliation, and at the same time dedicate themselves lovingly to the celebration of this sacrament — an instrument of conversion, new life and energy of grace for the whole of the Church. I also hope that these thoughts of mine can help all the faithful to draw near to the Sacrament of Mercy with faith and joy, in order to experience the strength of forgiveness which raises us up and restores enthusiasm to us, allowing us to look to the future with hope.

Post scriptum: the original edition of this volume, which was published in Italian in 2019, was written before the reform of Book VI of the Code of Canon Law which came into force on 8 December 2021. For this reason, although the subject-matter has substantially remained the same, the numbers of some canons do not correspond to the new updated numeration of Book VI of the Code of Canon Law.

---

[5] Ibid., n. 10.

PART ONE

THE SACRAMENT OF PENANCE AND RECONCILIATION:
CANONICAL-SACRAMENTAL ASPECTS

THE APOSTOLIC PENITENTIARY: A DICASTERY OF THE ROMAN CURIA AT THE SERVICE OF CONFESSORS AND PENITENTS

When people hear the Apostolic Penitentiary talked about, it is not surprising that some of them ask themselves — because of its appellation — whether it is not perhaps a detention center, that is to say a sort of prison of the Church. In reality, the Apostolic Penitentiary is the oldest dicastery of the Roman Curia. Indeed, the historical sources attest as far back as the twelfth century to the existence of a Cardinal who was delegated by the Supreme Pontiff with taking his place in hearing the confessions of penitents. In addition, it is the first of the Apostolic Tribunals whose competence is exclusively of the internal forum, namely the intimate area of the relationship between God and the sinner. The other two Tribunals, the Apostolic Signatura and the Roman Rota, instead, engage in activity whose functions are typically judicial and thus of the external forum.

The Apostolic Penitentiary engages in a purely spiritual service that is directly connected with the ultimate purpose of the entire existence of the Church — *salus animarum*. In reality, all the institutions of the Roman Curia perform a role directed towards the salvation of souls, but the Penitentiary does so in a more direct and immediate way. The purpose of the Apostolic Penitentiary is to help the faithful on their journey of reconciliation with God and the Church, aware that reconciliation, achieved by Christ and implemented by the Holy Spirit, ordinarily takes place through the mediation of the Church. This is because she herself acts, in time and in history, exclusively as a Body united to, and dependent on, her Head — the Lord Jesus Christ.

Unfortunately, this is a truth that many Catholics ignore. The action of the Church in the forgiveness of sins forms a part of the will of God. This is not a practice that developed with the passing of time nor is it a form of action whose intention is to centralize or bureaucratize forgiveness.

The Apostolic Penitentiary, as Pope Francis has defined it, is that "'tribunal of mercy,' to which one turns to obtain that indispensable medicine for our soul, which is Divine Mercy!"[1] Being a tribunal of mercy, it is in the front line, at the service of confessors and penitents, and its competence relates to matters of the sacramental and extra-sacramental internal forum, according to whether activity takes place during confession or during spiritual direction.

1. The Notion of the Internal Forum

The internal forum is the internal complex of the relationships between a member of the faithful and God where the mediation of the Church acts not to regulate directly the social consequences of such relationships but to provide for the supernatural good of that person as regards their friendship with God, that is to say a state of grace, and thus — in terms of ultimate ends — eternal life. It is evident that an upright relationship between a soul and God, re-established through the mediation of the Church, also has consequences for the social lives of the faithful. The Sacrament of Penance, a privileged setting and an instrument to the utmost of the internal forum, offers a very clear example of these concepts. This sacrament above all else reconciles a soul with God and re-establishes an upright relationship between a soul and God. Yet in doing this it also reconciles the penitent with the Church and eliminates the *vulnus* that sin inflicts on ecclesial communion. In addition to the sacramental internal forum, a non-sacramental internal forum also exists: the expression of their conscience that a member of the faithful can make to the Church outside confession but no less in secret. The classic example of this is spiritual direction, which takes place through activity that is distinct and separate from sacramental confession. There is also the expression of their conscience of religious to their Superiors, or a request for consultation, or the pointing out of grave facts to ecclesiastical Superiors, with a mutual commitment to secrecy.

[1] Pope Francis, Address to those Taking Part in the Course Organized by the Apostolic Penitentiary, 17 March 2017.

1.1. *The Internal Forum in Canon Law*

The *Code of Canon Law*[2] sub-divides the power of governance in the Church into an external forum and an internal forum (cf. *CIC*, can. 130). These are not two powers of jurisdiction in the Church, one of the internal forum and the other of the external forum, but, rather, a single power that can be exercised both in the internal forum and in the external forum. Only the juridical effects, consequent upon the exercise of this single power, are different. The difference, therefore, lies only in the sphere of the exercise of this power.[3]

In the external forum, the Church exercises her power of governance in order to pursue the common and public good and to set in order the social relationships of the faithful. The power of governance in the external forum is exercised with the juridical effects of public order. To the external forum, therefore, belongs everything relating to discipline, order, and the social relationships of the faithful with each other and with the various authorities.

In the internal forum, on the other hand, the Church exercises her power of governance to attend to all of the spiritual and private good of the individual faithful; she sets in order the relationships of the faithful with God in order to lead them to the way of salvation. To the internal forum belongs, therefore, everything that takes place in the intimate realm of consciences and has a direct relationship with God. Since the exercise of the power of governance of the internal forum is for the spiritual and private good of the faithful, the effects that it produces at times are not recognized in the external forum because of a lack of external proof of what has taken place in the internal forum. This does not mean that there are not effects in the external forum — only that they are not recognized in the external forum. Thus, the faithful can have peace of mind both in their consciences and before the ecclesial community.[4] This is why the term "internal forum" in a broad sense is employed both to designate the idea of "privacy," namely the domain of personal autonomy and non-subjection to

---

[2] *Codex Iuris Canonici auctoritate Ioanni Pauli PP. II promulgatus* (Vatican City, 1983) (hereafter *CIC*).

[3] Cf. V. De Paolis, "Il Libro I del Codice," in *Il diritto nel mistero della Chiesa*, 1, *Il diritto nella realtà umana e nella vita della Chiesa*, edited by the *Gruppo Italiano Docenti di Diritto Canonico* (Rome, 1988, second edition), pp. 374-401; here the reference is to pp. 387-390.

[4] Cf. ibidem; F. D'Ostilio, *Prontuario del Codice di Diritto Canonico* (Vatican City, 1995), p. 109.

external laws, and the intimate realm of the personal conscience and matters relating to morality and ethics. In a strict sense, we can define the "internal forum" as an action — which for pastoral or spiritual reasons remains hidden and not openly expressed — of the ecclesiastical power of jurisdiction which works through its own and original juridical powers (cf. *CIC*, *potestas regiminis*, can. 129).

Given that this is a jurisdictional activity of the Church, the agents that can engage in decisions of the internal forum are the Holy See, for the universal Church, and the Ordinary of the place concerned for the faithful placed under him for matters not reserved to the Holy See. The Apostolic Penitentiary is the dicastery of the Roman Curia whose sphere of competence refers to matters that concern the internal forum. However, the Penitentiary is not a "tribunal" in the strict sense of the term, like, for example, the Roman Rota or the Apostolic Signatura, because its "jurisdictional" activity does not involve disputes but is of a voluntary character, and it does not work publicly but in the internal forum.

The origins of the notion of internal forum and its distinction from the notion of external forum underwent a long process in the history of law. The Code of 1917[5] held the concept of internal forum with a juridical meaning to be equivalent to the concept of "forum of the conscience," which has a moral dimension, thereby generating a significant confusion: "*alia est fori externi alia fori interni, seu conscientiae, sive sacramentalis sive extrasacramentalis*" (*CIC* 1917, can. 196). This equivalence created confusion between the juridical, moral and sacramental spheres. This equivalence and thus confusion was overcome by the *Code of Canon Law* of 1983 where canon 130 makes clear that one is dealing with a single power of jurisdiction in the Church which is generally exercised in the external forum but at times also in the internal forum: "Of itself, the power of governance is exercised for the external forum; sometimes, however, it is exercised for the internal forum alone, so that the effects which its exercise is meant to have for the external forum are not recognized there, except insofar as the law establishes it in determined cases." Canon 130 of the *CIC* defines the external forum as the specific domain of the *potestas regiminis*, albeit admitting that concrete circumstances can occur envisaged by law where this *potestas* can be exercised in the sacramental or non-sacramental internal forum. We find a similar

[5] *Codex Iuris Canonici Pii X Pontificis Maximi iussu digestus Benedicti Papae XV auctoritate promulgatus*, Romae 1917 (hereafter *CIC* 1917).

description for the Eastern Churches in canon 980, §2 of the *Code of Canons of the Eastern Churches.*[6]

1.2. *The Principal Characteristics of the Internal Forum*

An initiative of the faithful. Jurisdiction in the internal forum is defined by canon law as a paradigm of voluntary jurisdiction and not one relating to disputes: only the member of the faithful who is involved is able to set in motion the jurisdiction of the internal forum, self-evidently because only they are able to demonstrate the truth of the facts that have taken place.

An "occult juridical decision." The decision that is required of the authority is an occult (hidden) decision of jurisdiction that derives both from the secret nature of the facts on which it is based and on the confidential way in which the jurisdiction was activated by the interested party. One is not dealing here with two types of jurisdiction, as the Code of 1917 might lead one to suppose, but to a single power of jurisdiction which acts with full effect yet not in a public way.

A remissive juridical measure. Jurisdiction in the internal forum has a necessarily remissive nature, one of forgiveness. Juridical decisions involving required obedience are not allowed in the internal forum. All the jurisdictional commands involving authority relate to the external forum and thus can be the subject of an administrative appeal. Exercising jurisdiction in the internal forum is not a kind of "optional" in the hands of the ecclesiastical authority so as not to be subject to the rules established for the exercise of the power of governance, imposing, for example, a precept in an occult form on someone. The principle, instead, is specifically the inverse: the implementation of ecclesiastical jurisdiction through the internal forum is activated and "established" by the member of the faithful when in a spontaneous way they have recourse to this authority.

Juridical certainty and the question of proof. A jurisdictional decision of the internal forum is effective in juridical terms and it is not necessary to repeat it in the external forum. However, being occult it raises the problem of juridical security and being known about publicly, which is related essentially to the probative aspect. Therefore, to prevent possible public knowledge subsequent to a question being

[6] *Codex Canonum Ecclesiarum Orientalium auctoritate Ioanni Pauli PP. II promulgatus* (Vatican City, 1990) (hereafter *CCEO*).

resolved in the internal (non-sacramental) forum, juridical development has consolidated discreet and anonymous forms in order to be able to certify externally — if necessary — the granting of suitable dispensations etc., such as that indicated in canon 1082 of the *CIC.*

Incommunicability between the external forum and the internal forum. The incommunicability of the two forums is a general principle of canon law and exists to assure the freedom and the dignity of the person involved. However, this principle has some exceptions. A case begun in the external forum can never be subsequently taken to the internal forum, with the exception of some special cases envisaged by canon 64 of *CIC. Vice versa*, cases made in the internal forum can at times be transferred to the external forum, with the evidence of dispensation, for example, or because the ecclesiastical authority, for the good of the faithful, sees that it should prevent scandal and publicly declare that a given situation is of the internal forum (the suspension of a priest or the excommunication of an individual, etc.).

2. The Special Characteristics of the "Tribunal of Mercy"

The Apostolic Penitentiary is defined in ecclesiastical terms as a "Tribunal" because in it individual cases of conscience are called to be judged. However, it has specific characteristics that determine the way in which it is different from other Tribunals of the Church. These characteristics, to summarize, are the following: absolute confidentiality, the absence of a dispute, and celerity.

Confidentiality. The Apostolic Penitentiary deals with matters of absolute confidentiality. It performs its functions exclusively through confessors. This, for that matter, does not prohibit any of the faithful from having recourse to the Penitentiary directly. It is however preferable for such recourse to be done by a confessor priest. This assures greater clarity and doctrinal exactitude in the exposition, the objectivity and impartiality of the judgment and, lastly, the possibility of providing psychological data and data relating to the character, the social situation, the reputation and so forth of the interested party, which only with difficulty could they give about themselves. If the confessor in this recourse should refer to the name of the penitent, the first task of the Penitentiary is to cancel that name from the proceedings. Thus in presenting cases the confessors must always use fictitious names: James, John, Pater, N.N., X.Y, etc. It should be made clear that the rescripts of the Apostolic Penitentiary have validity only for the internal forum and the confessors are, according to the rules, obliged to destroy them after executing them.

Absence of disputes. In this Tribunal there is no conflict between parties who defend their rights and also no libel. Nobody addresses this dicastery asking for the infliction of a canonical punishment or the issuing of a disciplinary measure.

Celerity. The matters for which this Tribunal are responsible are of such importance for the salvation of souls that no delays as regards answers or decisions are permitted.

3. The Structure of the Dicastery

Still today the Apostolic Penitentiary is governed in an overall sense by the rules of the Apostolic Constitution *Quae divinitus* of Pius XI of 25 March 1935 and by the small changes introduced by the Apostolic Constitution *Regimini Ecclesiae universae* of 15 August 1967. The subsequent Apostolic Constitution *Pastor bonus* of John Paul II (28 June 1988) changed practically nothing as regards the provisions of the previous two documents.[7]

The head of the Apostolic Penitentiary is the Cardinal Major Penitentiary who embodies all the faculties of the dicastery. It is difficult to list these faculties given that it is impossible to catalogue all the cases of conscience that can arise. Therefore, to safeguard and provide juridical certainty to the faculties belonging to the Penitentiary, Pope Benedict XVI, at the beginning of his pontificate, confirmed in a specific way and laid down that "the Apostolic Penitentiary, in order to be able to perform its tasks in the internal forum, possesses all the necessary authorizations, with the sole exception of those that the Holy Father has expressly communicated to the Cardinal Penitentiary as wanting to reserve to himself."[8] As a consequence, the Penitentiary can do in the internal forum everything that the other offices of the Roman Curia address in the external forum. If the solution to a problem goes beyond the habitual faculties of the

[7] It should be noted that *Quae divinitus* was explicitly confirmed in the Apostolic Constitution *Universi dominici gregis* of John Paul II of 22 February 1996 which lays down rules for when the Apostolic See is vacant and for the election of the Supreme Pontiff.

[8] *Rescriptum ex Audientia SS.mi* of 16 June 2005.

Apostolic Penitentiary, this acts *ex Audientia SS.mi*, that is to say after addressing the case with the Holy Father and receiving from him the necessary authorization.

The Cardinal Major Penitentiary is received every so often in audience by the Holy Father and reports on the work done by the dicastery as well as its development.

The Cardinal Major Penitentiary also appoints, and bestows relevant faculties on, the Minor Penitentiaries of the Papal Basilicas of Rome after they have passed the examination laid down by the pontifical rules for their role. He also bestows due faculties on the confessors proposed as replacements for the Minor Penitentiaries.

Another task of the Cardinal Major Penitentiary is to sign the public documents of the dicastery, the rescripts and letters of greater importance, such as, for example, general decrees, decrees of indulgence and rescripts that provide a definitive solution to cases of the internal forum.

I would also like to observe that the Cardinal Major Penitentiary, specifically because of the nature of his activity for the good of souls, continues to hold his post even when there is a vacancy of the Holy See. Indeed, the Apostolic Constitution *Pastor bonus*,[9] at article 6, renewed this rule which had been established for the first time at the Council of Vienna (1311-12). The Apostolic Penitentiary is allowed to communicate in a confidential way with its head when he is taking part in a conclave to elect the new Pope.

After the Cardinal Major Penitentiary comes the "Regent" who is a Superior Prelate. As his name in Latin indicates, he "supports" the Penitentiary and is directly responsible for the smooth running of the dicastery. He organizes and directs the normal handling of office work. He is present every day in the offices and when the Cardinal Major Penitentiary is absent he takes his place. In addition, he exercises other faculties that are delegated to him by the Cardinal Major Penitentiary. He has to be especially competent in moral theology and canon law.

Then there is the Council of the Cardinal Major Penitentiary (called the "Signature of the Apostolic Penitentiary") which is made up of the Regent and another five prelates. They are the Theologian, who by custom since the reform of St. Pius V has always been chosen from the Society of Jesus,[10] the Canonist and three other Councillors

---

[9] John Paul II, Apostolic Constitution *Pastor bonus* (28 June 1988) (hereafter *PB*).

[10] Even during the period when the Society of Jesus was suppressed the "Theologians" were always chosen from former Jesuits.

who are experts in canon law and moral theology.[11] They share in the power of jurisdiction in the internal forum. The Officials of this dicastery are priests who take part in the daily meetings ("congresses") chaired by the Regent for the study of cases. The solutions that emerge in these congresses are submitted to the Cardinal Major Penitentiary for his decision.

4. The Tasks of the Dicastery

The tasks of the Apostolic Penitentiary are described in articles 117-120 of the above-mentioned Constitution *Pastor bonus*. Articles 117 and 118 set out its areas of competence, namely everything connected with the internal forum, whether sacramental or non-sacramental. Indeed, the Apostolic Penitentiary grants graces, absolutions, dispensations, commutations, validations and condonations. Equally, it examines and resolves cases of conscience that are submitted to it. The phrase "cases of conscience" covers a variety of questions that are difficult to define. In that very broad gamut, the Apostolic Penitentiary has the task of directing, with papal authority, concrete individual cases, whereas the resolving of questions *sub specie universalitatis* is the task of the Congregation for the Doctrine of the Faith (when one is dealing in particular with questions that are specifically doctrinal). The Apostolic Penitentiary does not perform the role of a professor of moral theology or canon law, even if, in answering concrete cases, it does not fail to offer recommendations and authoritative guidelines. The answers provided by the Apostolic Penitentiary, therefore, have an authoritative value (which according to the case involve prescriptive instructions or remissions) only for concrete cases and the real circumstances that are submitted to it for examination but not for other cases. It is evident, however, that the doctrinal and disciplinary orientation included in the resolutions themselves can be applied by the priest who presented the recourse as a prudential criterion in a wider area as well. In no case is disclosing these answers allowed.

[11] Since 1969 they have been called "Councillors" in place of the ancient titles that up to that point were held by three of the five prelates: "Dater," "Sealer," and "Corrector," titles that no longer corresponded to specific tasks. The title of "Councillor" was more in harmony with what was said in n. 111 of *Regimini Ecclesiae universae*: "*Sacrae Paenitentiariae Apostolicae praeficitur Cardinalis Paenitentiarius Maior, qui adiuvatur a Regente aliisque Praelatis qui eiusdem Paenitentiarii Maioris Consilium efficiunt.*"

In virtue of article 119 of this Constitution, the Apostolic Penitentiary is also entrusted with the Penitentiaries of the patriarchal basilicas of Rome who are called Minor Penitentiaries.

Lastly, the Apostolic Penitentiary is charged by article 120 of the same Constitution with everything relating to the granting and use of indulgences, without prejudice to the tasks of the Congregation for the Doctrine of the Faith as regards dogmatic teaching relating to them.

5. The Most Frequent Matters Covered by the Tasks of the Dicastery

5.1. *Reserved Censures*

The *Code of Canon Law* of 1983 mentioned five delicts that are punished with the penalty of excommunication *latae sententiae* reserved to the Apostolic See. The excommunication *latae sententiae* is a kind of punishment that is automatically incurred because of the sole fact of committing certain delicts (*ipso facto*), without there being a need to impose it through a canonical process or a decree. Some censures can be remitted by a diocesan Ordinary or by major religious Superiors as regards those under them. The five delicts mentioned by the *Code of Canon Law* in force, for which *ipso facto* the above-mentioned censure is incurred, reserved to the Holy See, are the following:

- — The profanation of the holy consecrated species (cf. *CIC*, can. 1367).
- — The direct violation of the sacramental seal (cf. *CIC*, can. 1388 §1).
- — The absolution of an accomplice in a sin against the sixth commandment of the Decalogue (cf. *CIC*, can. 1378).
- — The use of physical force against the person of the Roman Pontiff (cf. *CIC*, can. 1370 §1).
- — The consecration of a bishop without a pontifical mandate (cf. *CIC*, can. 1382).

A new delict has recently been introduced into canon law, namely the attempted sacred ordination of a woman. This is punishable with excommunication *latae sententiae* reserved to the Apostolic See.[12]

We may now consider in summarizing form the particular figures responsible for those delicts that share the penalty of excommunication which, if they have not been the subject of a judicial sentence or a declaration, are addressed in the internal forum of the Tribunal of the Apostolic Penitentiary.

5.1.1. *Profanation of the Holy Consecrated Species*

The profanation of the holy consecrated species is a very grave delict by which one directly offends God, the Supreme Good, who is worthy of being loved above everything. It involves the undue retention of the consecrated species for sacrilegious, superstitious or obscene ends, or, more in general, any voluntary action of grave contempt for the Most Holy Sacrament, whether individually or in the presence of other people. Many profanations are committed during satanic rites.

To commit the delict of profanation of the consecrated species, a person must have an *animus profanandi*, that is to say a real sacrilegious intention.

On this point, canon 1367 of the *CIC* (cf. *CCEO*, can. 1442 which envisages the penalty of major excommunication and, for clerics, other penalties as well, not excluding dismissal from the clerical state) lays down that a person who throws away the consecrated species, or takes or retains it for a sacrilegious purpose, incurs *ipso facto* excommunication *latae sentententiae*. Given that this is a censure reserved to the Apostolic See, it can be remitted or absolved only by the Apostolic Penitentiary in the internal forum or by the Congregation for the Doctrine of the Faith in the external forum, as well as by any priest, in the internal forum, when the life of the person who has committed the delict is in danger, with the obligation of the penitent to have recourse to the external authority if they recover or their lives cease to be in danger.

---

[12] John Paul II, Apostolic Letter in the form of a motu proprio *Sacramentorum sanctitatis tutela* (30 April 2001) (hereafter *SST*), art. 5, n. 1; with an updating by Benedict XVI on 21 May 2010.

5.1.2. *Direct Violation of the Sacramental Seal*

The direct violation of the sacramental seal is a delict that is punished with excommunication *latae sententiae* reserved to the Apostolic See (cf. *CIC*, can. 1388 §1). However, an unspecific penalty *ferendae sententiae* is imposed for an indirect violation.

This is a delict that can be committed only by a priest who has acted as a confessor, even when he may not have given sacramental absolution. For there to have been a direct violation of the sacramental seal, the confessor must have with malice disclosed a sin heard in confession, as well as the identity of the penitent who has confessed. These two elements are fundamental for the delict of direct violation of the sacramental seal to have taken place.

The reason for the existence of the penalty of excommunication for this delict lies in wanting to protect the holiness of the Sacrament of Penance, the only means by which the faithful ordinarily obtain forgiveness for their sins. If the faithful did not have the guarantee of the secrecy of their confessions, probably they would not draw near to this sacrament.

The inviolability of the sacramental seal does not allow of exceptions or dispensations. Even after the death of the penitent, the confessor is anyway required to observe the sacramental seal.

According to canon 1456 §1 of the *CCEO*, a confessor who has directly violated the sacramental seal is punished by major excommunication, although canon 728 §1 n. 1 of the *CCEO* remains in force. This canon lays down that the absolution of this sin is reserved to the Apostolic See. The direct violation of the sacramental seal in the *Code of Canons of the Eastern Churches*, therefore, is considered a "sin reserved" to the Apostolic See. In the *motu proprio Sacramentorum Sanctitatis tutela*, at articles 4 and 5, reference is made to the grave delict against the holiness of the Sacrament of Penance which is reserved to the Congregation for the Doctrine of the Faith, naturally if the case is of the external forum. In the internal forum, it belongs to the competence of the Apostolic Penitentiary.

5.1.3. *Absolution of an Accomplice in the Sin against Chastity*

The delict of absolution of an accomplice is a very grave delict that can be committed by a priest who acts as confessor and "absolves" a penitent of a sin against chastity in which both have participated.

In this case, in reality, the confessor does not absolve validly, except in danger of death, as is envisaged by canon 977 of the *CIC*.

The gravity of this delict is not specifically the sin against chastity that the confessor has committed with the penitent but, rather, having given them an invalid absolution. The confessor does not have the faculty to absolve this kind of sin when his accomplice is involved in it.

This delict includes all the external sins committed with an accomplice against chastity, even if the sin took place before his ordination as a priest. Unfortunately, it happens that at times priests think that they can absolve when they have not committed a "complete conjugal act."

Through the penalty of excommunication, the Church protects the holiness of the Sacrament of Penance and seeks the effective amends of the guilty parties. If the absolution of the accomplice in such a matter were valid, the sin would be converted into routine.

Logically, to commit this delict the confessor must realize that he is absolving a person of a sin committed by both parties. If the confessor does not recognize the penitent, he does not commit this delict.

If the accomplice does not confess a sin against chastity committed with the confessor, because this person has already been absolved by another confessor, in this case as well a delict does not take place. However, it would be a good rule not to listen to the confession of a person with whom the confessor has committed a sin against chastity.

What happens if the confessor is unaware that the penalty of excommunication exists when he "absolves" the accomplice of a sin against chastity? In this case, lack of awareness does not exonerate him from the penalty. All confessors enabled to exercise the ministry of confession must know about the canonical rules relating to this sacrament.

According to canon 1457 of the *CCEO*, the priest who has absolved the accomplice of the sin against chastity should be punished with major excommunication, with canon 728 §1, n. 2 still in operation. This canon lays down that the absolution of this sin is reserved to the Apostolic See. Examination of a case of this kind in the external forum (in the public domain) comes under the judgment of the Congregation for the Doctrine of the Faith (cf. *SST*, art. 4, n. 1), but for the internal forum it remains the exclusive competence of the Apostolic Penitentiary.

Canon 729, 1 and 2, of the *CCEO* should be borne in mind both as regards the violation of the sacramental seal and with respect to absolution of the accomplice. This canon lays down that any case of absolution reserved to the Apostolic Penitentiary does not apply when the person engaging in confession is sick and cannot leave their house, or when, in the prudent judgment of the confessor, the faculty to absolve cannot be asked from the competent authority without grave inconvenience to the penitent or without danger of exposing the sacramental seal to violation.

It should also be emphasized that the absolution of the accomplice, except when that person's life is in danger, is also invalid for the faithful of the Eastern Churches because of canon 730 of the CCEO.

5.1.4. *The Use of Physical Force Against the Person of the Roman Pontiff*

The committing of such a delict requires the use of physical violence with the intention of killing or injuring the Roman Pontiff.

5.1.5. *The Consecration of a Bishop Without a Pontifical Mandate*

This involves conferring on a member of the faithful the sacrament of the sacred order at the level of the episcopate without due pontifical authorization. This can be committed only by a Catholic bishop when he carries out an episcopal ordination without the authorization of the Roman Pontiff. This ordination is valid but illicit. He who confers the sacred order and he who receives it incur the censure of excommunication *latae sententiae*, the remission of which is reserved to the Apostolic Penitentiary where there is an occult case. If the delict committed is in the public domain, this remission is the competence of the Congregation for the Doctrine of the Faith.

5.1.6. *The Attempted Sacred Ordination of a Woman*

A new delict has been recently introduced into canon law, namely the attempted sacred ordination of a woman. This is punishable with excommunication *latae sententiae* reserved to the Apostolic See (*SST*, art. 5, n. 1): to the Congregation for the Doctrine of the Faith in the external forum and to the Apostolic Penitentiary in the internal forum. This ordination is not valid and for the committing of this delict both the minister who has attempted the conferring, and the woman who has sought to receive the sacred order, are punished. If, then, he who attempts the conferring of the sacred order, or the woman who seeks to receive it, are members of the faithful subject to the *Code of Canons of the Eastern Churches*, although the provision of cannon 1443 of the same code still applies, he is punished with major excommunication whose remission is also reserved to the Apostolic See (cf. *SST*, art. 5, n. 2).

6. The Absolution of Censures

All the delicts to which reference has been made are self-evidently very grave sins and for this reason canon law has established the gravest penalties for them. The gravest canonical penalty is excommunication: this prohibits a person from receiving the sacraments or administering them. The competent authority in the internal forum in the above-mentioned cases is the Apostolic Penitentiary. This Tribunal, by apostolic authority, grants absolution in these cases. Naturally, if one of these delicts becomes of the public domain then it falls under the competence of the Congregation for the Doctrine of the Faith.

The censures are considered medicinal penalties inasmuch they are conceived to obtain the amends of the person who has committed the delict. They seek to break contumacy, that is to say the persistent disobedience to the authority and its decisions manifested by the author of the delict. The principal purpose of medicinal penalties is to correct contumacy and obtain the conversion of the member of the faithful. Thus, they cannot be imposed for a specific period of time and one cannot leave the absolution to the will of the Superior. Once the contumacy has ceased, absolution cannot be denied because the member of the faithful has the right to be absolved.[13]

Who in general can absolve a member of the faithful from the penalty of excommunication? Only the authority that by ecclesiastical law has this faculty can do this or he who has received a corresponding mandate. In the case of excommunications reserved to the Apostolic See for the delicts referred to above, the competent authority is the Apostolic Penitentiary, as long as one is dealing with occult cases and the excommunication has not been declared in the external forum.

When a censure has been declared in the external forum, the Apostolic Penitentiary cannot intervene. To obtain the absolution one must therefore have recourse to the competent authority.

---

[13] Cf. *CIC*, can. 1358 §1.

How should a confessor behave towards a member of the faithful who has incurred a censure reserved to the Apostolic See? The confessor has two possibilities before him.

The first possibility is to explain to the penitent their canonical status, instructing them in the obligation to present a recourse in order to obtain absolution of the censure. The penitent can have recourse themselves to the Apostolic Penitentiary, but it is always advisable for the confessor himself to make himself available and present the recourse. In this case, the confessor should fix an appointment with the penitent or agree an address, if the penitent is prevented from presenting themselves personally, to which the decision of the Apostolic Penitentiary can be sent. In the recourse — presented in a confidential way and without mentioning the person's name — the facts that occurred should be well described and authorization should be asked to be able to absolve the penitent of the censure that has been incurred, as well as indications about the penance that should be imposed on the penitent. Once the answer of the Apostolic Penitentiary has arrived, the penitent who presents himself again to the confessor will be absolved of the censure and the sins and the related penitence will be indicated to him.

The second possibility is the so-termed "urgent case absolution" which, in a certain sense, is the most advisable for a properly disposed penitent because they will be able to begin to receive the sacraments immediately. Recourse is made to this possibility when it is truly difficult for the member of the faithful to remain in a state of mortal sin, without being able to receive the sacraments, while waiting for their confessor to obtain permission to absolve them of the censure that has been incurred, and they really repent of the delict that they have committed. In this circumstance the confessor, in virtue of canon 1357 of the *CIC*, can absolve the member of the faithful from the censure and their sins and ask them to return after a few weeks, on a date that is convenient for both parties, to receive the indication regarding the penance. In this case, the confessor has the duty to have recourse within thirty days to the Apostolic Penitentiary to refer the case and ask what the penance should be. This Tribunal will examine the case, ratify the absolution, give certain instructions on the matter, and impose the penance.

With respect to censures applied to holy ministers, one should bear in mind canon 1335 of the *CIC*, in virtue of which one can exercise ministry despite a censure when this is necessary for the spiritual needs of a member of the faithful whose life is in danger. The same canon also allows the exercise of ministry if there is no danger of death when a censure *latae sententiae* has not been declared.

7. Recourse to the Apostolic Penitentiary

Such recourse is a letter in which the confessor, omitting the name of the penitent and any circumstance that could identify them, asks from the Apostolic Penitentiary the faculty to absolve the penitent who has committed a delict of a censure or the ratification of an absolution that has already been given to the penitent, attaining in this case to the provision of canon 1357. In this letter, the confessor must try to expound objectively what has happened in a summarizing way, by making reference to all the circumstances of the delict, whether aggravating or attenuating (age, social position, etc.).

The recourse must always be made by letter. Neither fax nor e-mail are allowed because, given that we are dealing here with matters usually protected by the sacramental seal, it is believed that a letter assures the inviolability of the *sigillum* in a better way.

One can write the recourse to this Tribunal in any current language but to facilitate the work of the staff and obtain a more rapid answer one of the following languages is advised: Italian, English, German, French, Spanish, Portuguese, Polish or Latin.

To avoid the Tribunal of the Apostolic Penitentiary asking for a clarification of the case, in drawing up the recourse it is important to mention some of the information listed below.

In the case of the delict of profanation of the consecrated species, it is necessary to refer in the recourse to:

— The approximate age of the penitent and their mental health.

— When they committed the delict.

— How many times they committed it.

— In what way they committed it.

— What the reasons were that induced them into profanation.

— If the delict was committed on their own or with other people.

— If the penitent committed the delict at the instigation of a sect and if they have ended contact with it.

In the case of the delict of the direct violation of the sacramental seal, reference should be made to:

— The approximate age of the penitent.

— When the delict was committed.

— How often it was committed.

— In what circumstances it was committed.

— If it was committed deliberately or if it was an act of imprudence.

— If it led to damage being caused to the penitent.

— If the penitent is a confessor who is habitually prudent in such matters.

In the case of the delict of absolution of an accomplice of a sin against the sixth commandment of the Decalogue, one should specify:

— The approximate age of the penitent.

— The approximate age of the accomplice.

— The sex of the accomplice

— The state of the accomplice: unmarried, married, religious or priest.

— How many times the "absolution" took place.

— The last time the person was "absolved."

— Whether the sinful relations with the person who was an accomplice have ended.

— Whether the penitent leads a life worthy of the priestly ministry: daily celebration of the Holy Mass, liturgical prayers of the hours, etc.

The indication of these facts in the recourse makes possible a more complete assessment of the case that has been submitted to the Apostolic Penitentiary and it is useful in deciding the penance that will be imposed on the penitent and establishing the length of the granting of ministerial faculties. These elements allow the Apostolic

Penitentiary to give instructions that are really useful for a penitent who is absolved from a censure.

How should the confessor communicate the contents of the answer of the Apostolic Penitentiary to the penitent absolved from the censure? The most suitable way is to make everything known in a subsequent confession. Thus, it is advisable for the confessor to agree with the penitent on a date that is convenient for both parties. The penitent has the right not to be recognized and not to be seen. Thus, the new meeting with the confessor can take place in a confessional equipped with a grill. The penitent communicates to the penitent the contents of the answer of the Apostolic Penitentiary and the number of the protocol and destroys the relative document as soon as possible. It is advisable for the penitent to conserve the number of the protocol in the event of the presentation of a new recourse. In this case, indeed, the above-mentioned number must be explicitly indicated in the document in question so that the Tribunal can easily identify the case.

8. Irregularities

The Apostolic Penitentiary can grant dispensations in occult cases of irregularity. An irregularity is a perpetual canonical prohibition that impedes the licit receiving of Holy Orders or the exercise of Holy Orders already received unless a dispensation from the relevant authority has been obtained. Irregularities can have their origins in the committing of a delict; however, they are not canonical penalties. Therefore a member of the faithful can be absolved of a delict that they have committed or of all of their sins and remain in their irregular condition until they obtain a dispensation. Irregularities safeguard the reverence due to the dignity of holy ministry. Given that irregularities do not have a penal character, the fact of being unaware of them does not exempt the individual from them (cf. *CIC*, can. 1045).

The Apostolic Penitentiary can grant dispensations from irregularities to receive Holy Orders, and to exercise them once they have been received, when their cause is not a fact of public knowledge (cf. *CIC*, canons 1041 n. 4 and 1044 §1 n. 3). This Tribunal is competent to dispense from irregularities in the internal forum where the dispensation is reserved to the Holy See, in particular those that derive from committing or positively cooperating in the crime of murder or abortion where effected (cf. *CIC*, can. 1398 and *CCEO*, can. 1450).

To the Holy See are also reserved those irregularities whose original case was assigned to the judicial forum, but it is evident that here one is dealing with the external forum and thus it does not belong to the responsibilities of the Apostolic Penitentiary.

Although it is certain that not all irregularities are reserved to the Holy See and that in many cases the diocesan bishop has the faculty to give a dispensation, the faithful can nonetheless freely choose to have recourse to the Apostolic Penitentiary.

As regards irregularities and the exercise of Holy Orders, one should remember the provision of canon 1048 of the *CIC*: in more urgent cases this allows the exercise of ministry in the case of holy ministers subject to irregularities in occult cases when there is imminent danger of grave harm or infamy. But the irregular person has the duty to make recourse as soon as possible through a confessor who must not indicate the name of the penitent. This applies to the exercise of Holy Orders but not to receiving them.

Dispensation from an irregularity is requested through a letter that the confessor, or spiritual director, of an irregular person writes to the Apostolic Penitentiary. In this request, it is self-evident that one has to omit the name of the person and information that can identify them and describe clearly the fact that was the cause of the irregularity. In the case of a candidate for Holy Orders, the confessor or the spiritual director must not omit to provide a judgment on the person's suitability to receiving the sacrament. In the case of a person who has already been ordained, it is important to refer to their amends.

The request for dispensation from an irregularity when it involves a candidate for Holy Orders is usually not sent before a year prior to the date envisaged for the ordination, and in this request it is important to refer to the suitability of the candidate. The Apostolic Penitentiary, following practice, examines the requests with celerity so that the confessor or the spiritual director of the candidate has the answer available to him in the shortest time possible.

9. Other Situations that Belong to the Domain of the Internal Forum

One can have recourse to the internal forum not only for sins, censures or irregularities but in general also for occult situations which it is not advisable to disclose in the external forum such as, for example:

A dispensation or commutation for both personal and real obligations that derive from vows, canon law, and obligations taken personally (for example the obligation of the Liturgy of the Hours, private vows, public vows, but only as regards validations and not dispensations, and pecuniary obligations towards the Church. The Church can forgo the satisfaction of a certain right but cannot dispense from an obligation of justice that a member of the faithful has towards a third party).

Validations or *sanations* of acts that are invalid but can be sanated (validated retroactively), as long as the cause of their being invalid is occult (hidden). For example, the sanation of religious vows that are invalid because of circumstances known only to the individual involved, or the radical sanation of a marriage when it is advisable to do this in the internal forum: for example when the invalidity of the marriage is known to only one of the parties and the disclosure of the invalidity could cause grave damage. It is evident that a sanation cannot sanate situations of invalidity derived from the invalidity of a sacrament, with the exception of the case involving marriage already indicated. But one can have recourse in the internal forum to the Apostolic Penitentiary in occult cases for a judgment on the validity or otherwise of Baptism, Confirmation, or Holy Orders, both when the doubt relates to subjective conditions (intention, free will) and when it relates to the subject of the sacrament, to its minister or to another person (for example a master of ceremonies who cannot disclose, at least *hinc et nunc*, the facts without creating scandal or grave disadvantages). In these cases, there are two possible solutions. Either the answer makes clear that unfounded doubts are involved, or, where there are certain cases of invalidity or doubts that have foundations, it authorizes the renewal of the sacramental rite, either *absolute* or *sub conditione*.

The dispensation or reduction or commutation of obligations in relation to Holy Masses (cf. *CIC*, can. 945-958 and CCEO, can. 717) that apply to physical persons and could jeopardize the good reputation of a person. If instead one is dealing with obligations that apply to moral entities (diocesan curias, seminaries, religious families, etc.), one must make recourse to the Congregation for the Clergy.

A priest who finds that he is unable to celebrate — either personally or through another — the number of Holy Masses that have been assigned to him, can make a request to the Apostolic Penitentiary, through his own confessor, to be granted a reduction. In this recourse, the confessor, omitting the name of the penitent priest, should indicate:

— The number of Holy Masses that were not celebrated.

— The approximate age of the priest.

— The reason why he did not celebrate them and how he used the money received for them.

— The state of his health and the number of Holy Masses that he could celebrate personally or by assigning them to other priests.

The Apostolic Penitentiary, after assessing all the information contained in the recourse, will proceed to a reduction in the quantity of Holy Masses that have not been celebrated by the penitent priest, imposing the obligation to celebrate or to have celebrated a lesser number; for the rest use will be made of the "treasury of the Church."

The examination of questions of a moral and juridical character. In the internal forum, through recourse to the Apostolic Penitentiary, doubts can be resolved in moral and juridical areas as well when one is dealing with occult circumstances and individual concrete facts. For example, whether a specific individual is suitable or not for marriage; whether a specific biological procedure is simply therapeutic or whether it is contraceptive or abortifacient; whether specific cooperation in an evil is direct or not direct, necessary or not necessary, and so forth. It may be emphasized that the recourse in the internal forum is the suitable means for individual and occult concrete cases. When the questions relate to public cases, the recourse must be made in the external forum, more specifically not to the Apostolic Penitentiary but to another dicastery of the Holy See (the Congregation for the Doctrine of the Faith; the Congregation for Divine Worship and the Discipline of the Sacraments; the Pontifical Council for Legislative Texts, etc.). A typical occasion when recourse in the internal forum for doubts of this kind is advisable is that of problems posed to a confessor priest by the penitent when, either because of a lack of expert people in the locality or because of the needs of caution as regards respect for the sacramental seal, it is not possible to pose questions to people of the local context.

10. Indulgences

The Apostolic Penitentiary is also entrusted with everything relating to the granting and the use of indulgences, except for what is the responsibility of the Congregation of the Doctrine of the Faith concerning what attains to dogmatic doctrine about indulgences themselves.

Pope St. Paul VI, by his Apostolic Constitution *Indulgentiarum doctrina* of 1 January 1967, promoted, in conformity with the recommendations expressed by the Bishops' Conferences and by the Apostolic Penitentiary at the Second Vatican Ecumenical Council, a profound reform of the discipline of indulgences, without, however, changing any of their theological foundations. The reform had the purpose of fostering in members of the faithful a sense of participation in the communion of saints, the fervor of charity (especially towards deceased members of the faithful), and a spirit of prayer, rebirth and sacrifice. The most evident points in the reform of the Blessed Paul VI are the following:

— A plenary indulgence can be obtained only once each day, with the exception of the case of a member of the faithful who obtains it again on the same day *in articulo mortis.*

— The measurement in years and days of a partial indulgence was abolished with the establishment in its place that the gift of the Church (the indulgence) is proportionate to the expiatory spiritual value of the action completed by the member of the faithful.

— The appellations "personal indulgences," "real indulgences" and "local indulgences" were abolished to indicate in a clear way that the gift of the indulgence is given through the action of the member of the faithful, even when connected to a pious place or an object of veneration.

— Diocesan bishops — and ecclesiastical authorities made equivalent to them by law — can grant partial indulgences in favor of their subjects. As regards the granting of plenary indulgences, recourse should be made to the Apostolic Penitentiary. The Roman Pontiff, to whom has been entrusted by Christ the Lord the distribution of all of the spiritual treasury of the Church (cf. *CIC*

> 1917, can. 912), has absolute power over indulgences inasmuch as he has supreme jurisdiction over the universal Church. Thus he has full powers to grant indulgences without having recourse to the Apostolic Penitentiary. In addition, he can also entrust the granting of indulgences to other dicasteries of the Roman Curia when he thinks this is advisable. At the present time — as was observed above — the use and the granting of indulgences are the responsibility of the Apostolic Penitentiary.

All the rules regarding the discipline of indulgences and acts of piety and prayers indicated by the Church for an indulgence, together with the referred to Apostolic Constitution *Indulgentiarum doctrina*, are collected together in *Enchiridion indulgentiarum*, an official text of the Church. This has been published on a number of occasions since 1968 and has been translated into Italian, Spanish, Portuguese, English, German and Dutch by various Bishops' Conferences. The English edition of *Enchiridion* is entitled: *Manual of Indulgences. Norms and Grants.*[14]

In this *Manual* we find to begin with the definition of an indulgence: "An indulgence is a remission before God of the temporal punishment for sins, whose guilt is forgiven, which a properly disposed member of the Christian faithful obtains under certain and clearly defined conditions through the intervention of the Church, which, as the minister of Redemption, dispenses and applies authoritatively the treasury of the expiatory works of Christ and the saints."[15]

Indulgences are divided into the plenary and the partial: "An indulgence is partial or plenary according to whether it removes either part or all of the temporal punishment due sin."[16] A plenary indulgence, therefore, removes all of the temporal punishment due to sins already cancelled as regards guilt and eternal punishment. A partial indulgence is one that removes only a part of this penalty.

To acquire indulgences one must be baptized, not excommunicated, and be in a state of grace at least at the completion of the

[14] *Enchiridion Indulgentiarum. Normae et concessiones* (Vatican City, 1999, fourth edition). For the Italian edition see *Manuale delle Indulgenze. Norme e concessioni* (Vatican City, 1999; reprint 2012) (hereafter *MDI*). For the English edition see *Manual of Indulgences. Norms and Grants*, United States Conference of Catholic Bishops, Washington, D.C., 1994.

[15] *MDI*, *Norme sulle indulgenze*, n. 1.

[16] Ibid., *Norme sulle indulgenze*, n. 2.

prescribed works. In addition, a member of the faithful must have at least the general intention of acquiring the indulgence and must carry out the prescribed works at the stated time and in due fashion, according to the sense of the grant (cf. *CIC*, can. 966, §2): "The faithful can obtain partial or plenary indulgences for themselves, or they can apply them to the dead by way of suffrage."[17]

In addition to the grants present in *Enchiridion*, which concern all of the faithful, the Apostolic Penitentiary gives grants to special groups of the faithful. Indeed, bishops, religious Superiors, rectors of sanctuaries, heads of pious associations or movements implore the Holy Father for the gift of indulgences, often through the good offices of nunciatures.

There are many occasions when plenary indulgences are asked for: a jubilee celebration (at a national, eparchial, diocesan or parish level); the erection of a particular church (for example the twenty-fifth, fiftieth or first centenary of a diocese), of an institute of consecrated life or apostolic life, and of a parish of a (diocesan, national or international) sanctuary, of a religious Province or house, and of a pious association; the dedication of a holy place: the blessing of holy stairs or doors; the crowning of an image of the Blessed Virgin; a special time of prayer or penance (a missionary or Marian year, novena, triduum or day); a community pilgrimage; the indulgence of the Portiuncola or a titular feast day for churches that are not parish churches; the birthdays on this earth and births to heaven of famous patron saints, etc.

The Apostolic Penitentiary is always ready to answer — respecting current practice — all questions because the use of indulgences according to the *sensus Ecclesiae* stimulates the faithful to the fervor of charity and thus to the worthy receiving of the sacraments and to works of mercy and penance. In addition, it is an admirable sign of ecclesial communion.

Before sending in the plea — when this is not personally addressed by the diocesan ordinary or religious Superior — it is useful to verify that there is the necessary commendation of the local bishop. The Apostolic Penitentiary, in each case, appreciates the opinion of the representative of the Roman Pontiff on the matter. Therefore, it is hoped that the requests will be presented through nunciatures. However, individual bishops can freely approach the Apostolic Penitentiary directly or endorse the requests drawn up by the interested parties, their subjects.

[17] Ibid., *Norme sulle indulgenze*, n. 3.

The rescript of the Apostolic Penitentiary contains a first part — the expository part — which is short but dense with spiritual and historical contents, and a second part — the enacting part — which, according to the case, limits the grant only to the time of the commemorative event or to a period of some years (for example *ad septennium*), or lays down its perpetual duration (*in perpetuum*).

It may be observed that the granting of indulgences is done without there being payment.

In illustrating the structure, responsibilities and tasks, and the practice of the Apostolic Penitentiary, an attempt has been made here to provide a more accessible picture of the oldest dicastery of the Roman Curia, which is a Tribunal of mercy, an organ at the service of confessors and penitents. All those to whom priestly ministry has been, or will be, entrusted should never neglect the Sacrament of Penance, an instrument of Divine Mercy and lymph of the evangelization of people. Let us not forget the words spoken by our Lord Jesus: "there will be more joy in heaven over one sinner who repents than over ninety-nine righteous people who have no need of repentance" (Lk 15:7).

THE GOOD CONFESSOR IN THE LIGHT OF THE APOSTOLIC LETTER *MISERICORDIA ET MISERA* OF POPE FRANCIS

The Apostolic Letter *Misericordia et misera* of Pope Francis is a treasure of spiritual, pastoral, moral, ecclesial and social subjects that all Christians should turn to. Pope Francis teaches us how to celebrate and live mercy; he shows us that forgiveness is a visible sign of the love of the Father. There is no limit to Divine Mercy, which generates joy and distances all sadness from the heart. The pathway of the Church is to celebrate the mercy of God, to communicate with certainty that God loves us and forgives us, through listening to and offering His Word. The Sacrament of Penance is indispensable and central in all of this. In this sacrament, the priest is the minister of welcome and a witness to the tenderness of God. All of this leads to a culture of mercy, obviously under the guidance of the Virgin Mary — the high road of Divine Mercy. Pope Francis writes in *Misericordia et misera*:

> A woman and Jesus meet. She is an adulteress and, in the eyes of the Law, liable to be stoned. Jesus, through his preaching and the total gift of himself that would lead him to the Cross, returned the Mosaic Law to its true and original intent. Here what is central is not the law or legal justice, but the love of God, which is capable of looking into the heart of each person and seeing the deepest desire hidden there; God's love must take primacy over all else … Jesus looked that woman in the eye and read in her heart a desire to be understood, forgiven and set free. The misery of sin was clothed with the mercy of love (*MM*, n. 1).

Jesus through the offer of forgiveness, of reconciliation and of peace led back men and women from spiritual death to new life in God, making them taste how sweet experience of the mercy of God the Father was.

Let us now draw near to two episodes in the Bible that are paradigms of the expression of mercy of God, who forgives, reconciles to Himself and saves.

"Neither do I condemn you. Go, (and) from now on do not sin any more" (Jn 8:11). In my view, this phrase deserves special attention because it is a synthesis of the encounter of the infinite breadth of the mercy of God and the reality that Divine Mercy can produce abundant fruit of grace and the conversion of hearts. This phrase means that something has happened that goes beyond the thinkable. Jesus works justice but he goes beyond justice because he goes beyond the Law. Since Holy Scripture prophesies repentance and conversion, expressing a broader and perfect vision of the heart of God, Jesus forgives the woman but goes beyond forgiveness because he places her anew before God and men, and points out to her the way for the reconstruction of her authentic humanity.[1] For this reason, this lapidary phrase reminds us that the mercy of the Lord always takes place with a view to repentance and the conversion of hearts to the gospel.

"So I tell you, her many sins have been forgiven; hence, she has shown great love" (Lk 7:47). When reading with care this passage from the gospel which contains this expression of the forgiveness and the mercy of the Lord, we notice that this woman, aware of her own condition, goes infinitely beyond what it was fitting to do. She engages in a gesture of very great love for Jesus and this is a sign of a repentance that was radically changing her life and projecting her into the arms of the merciful love of God that does not delay in expressing itself. The words of forgiveness of Jesus, indeed, give to the life of the woman a new scent which had already begun the moment she went to the Teacher to ask for forgiveness, knowing who he was and what he could do for her. The words of the Teacher give redemption to the woman; her heart can now go in peace.

Here we have, then, the authentic image to which every confessor should turn and by which he should allow himself to be shaped: a confessor according to the heart of God at the service of our brothers

[1] Cf. Pope Francis, Morning Meditation in the Chapel of *Domus Sanctae Marthae,* 7 April 2014.

and sisters. For these reasons, I will give to this section a theological-pastoral approach, thereby illustrating how a priest who is a confessor and former of consciences, in the light of the Word of God and the recent Magisterium of the Church, especially *Misericordia et misera*, should live the ministry of mercy through the Sacrament of Reconciliation as a privileged experience of the merciful love of God.

1. The Importance of the Ongoing Formation of a Priest in the Sacrament of Penance

"I invite priests once more to prepare carefully for the ministry of Confession, which is a true priestly mission" (*MM*, n. 10).

In addition to this clear and direct invitation of Pope Francis, we can cite here the words of St. John Paul II when, in one of his very many messages addressed to the Apostolic Penitentiary, he invited priests-confessors to "return to the experience of the Cenaculum to rediscover their profound reason for their formation as ministers of the mercy of God and administrators of the Sacrament of Reconciliation."[2] Where theology emphasizes that a holy minister acts *in persona Christi*,[3] the outpouring of the Spirit in the Cenaculum was foreshadowed for the apostles, after the resurrection of Christ, specifically in relation to the ministry of the forgiveness of sins. Saint John Paul II observed: "We priests, in imparting to the faithful grace and forgiveness in the Sacrament of Penance, perform the highest act, after the celebration of the Eucharist, of our priesthood, and in it we achieve, one can say, the very purpose of the incarnation."[4] Thus in absolving in what is to the utmost the ministry of mercy, the priest-confessor goes beyond the forgiveness of sins, and moves towards reaching almost a mystical identification with Jesus Christ.

> The Sacrament of Reconciliation must regain its central place in the Christian life. This requires priests capable of putting their lives at the service of the "ministry of reconciliation" (2 Cor 5:18), in such a way that, while no sincerely

[2] John Paul II, Address to the Penitentiaries of the Patriarchal Basilicas of Rome, 20 March 1989.

[3] Cf. Congregation for the Clergy, *Directory for the Ministry and the Life of Priests* (Vatican City, 2013), n. 10.

[4] John Paul II, Address to the Penitentiaries of the Patriarchal Basilicas of Rome, 20 March 1989.

> repentant sinner is prevented from drawing near to the love of the Father who awaits his return, everyone is afforded the opportunity of experiencing the liberating power of forgiveness (*MM*, n. 11).

Although, on the one hand, it is important and urgent to educate the priest-confessor in a continuous and ongoing way in the beauty of penance, which finds its fullness in the Sacrament of Reconciliation, it is equally urgent to educate him in loving dedication to this sacrament, aware that this passion will be truly involving where that personal experience is made up of Divine Mercy. This is the reason why the Magisterium lays emphasis on educating us as priests not only in a theological-sacramental knowledge of the Sacrament of Reconciliation and its health-inducing effects, but also by dedicating "time and energy to hearing the confessions of the faithful, who, as experience demonstrates, come freely to receive this sacrament as long as there are priests available."[5]

2. The Art of Accompanying Those Who Draw Near to the Sacrament of Forgiveness

> I thank all of you from the heart for your ministry, and I ask you to be *welcoming* to all, *witnesses* of fatherly tenderness whatever the gravity of the sin involved, *attentive* in helping penitents to reflect on the wrong they have done, *clear* in presenting moral principles, *willing* to walk patiently beside the faithful on their penitential journey, *far-sighted* in discerning individual cases and *generous* in dispensing God's forgiveness. Just as Jesus chose to remain silent in order to save the woman caught in adultery from the sentence of death, so every priest in the confessional should be openhearted, since every penitent is a reminder that he himself is a sinner, but also a minister of mercy (*MM*, 10).

It seems to me that the various aspects emphasized in this phrase constitute a true and clear pathway of spiritual accompanying of the faithful to the encounter with the mercy of God. But even more specifically they highlight the various and important stages of

[5] Congregation for the Clergy, *Directory*, n. 52.

an educational process relating to the Sacrament of Reconciliation to which every priest-confessor must permanently refer.

The other great aspect that I would like to emphasize with respect to the priest-confessor is the art of accompanying spiritually those who draw near to the sacrament of forgiveness. The relationship of nearness through the reality of pastoral accompanying is the challenge that makes the proclaiming of the mercy of the Church credible. I would like to dwell for a moment on the mission of accompanying pastorally our fellow men as a special expression of the ministry of mercy.

The maternal mercy of the Church is not a dimension or a "sector" of the work of evangelization — it is the founding attitude and motivation of all pastoral activity. It is characteristic of a mother to slow down, to put worries to one side to look at her child in the eyes and listen, to forgo what she sees as pressing needs, in order to accompany to the encounter with the merciful Jesus those who have been left behind at the side of the road of history.[6] It is important to take seriously every person and the project that the Lord has for them, just as it is of fundamental importance not to fall into that pastoral apathy that generates a lack of accompanying of the poorest and of all those who ask to be reconciled with God and the Church. The appeal of the Holy Father is clear and strong. He asks us to enter the "art of accompanying" which involves, first of all, always learning to take off one's sandals in front of the holy ground of the other and then, with the health-giving rhythms of nearness, to begin to be close, respectful and full of mercy so as to behold, be moved and stop in front of one's brothers and sisters whenever this is needed.[7] As an attentive pastor, Pope Francis also points to some ways that can be followed by which the art of accompanying finds specific concrete expression. The proclaiming of mercy cannot take place in an inexperienced way and thus be exposed to uselessness. Accompanying, according to what Pope Francis indicates, requires a journey in certain virtues, such as prudence, mutual listening and seeing the mystical dimension of life.[8]

So that accompanying may involve telling the truth about personal relationships under the heading of service, the Supreme Pontiff provides the example of the Good Shepherd in order to be

---

[6] Cf. ibid., n. 46; *EG*, n. 31.

[7] Cf. *EG*, n. 169.

[8] Cf. ibid., nn. 171-172.

a witness to the living experience of mercy in the encounter with Christ. In his magisterium and in daily life, the poor and those in need, of all kinds and ranks, listened and saw that the God of Jesus Christ is not a pitiless judge or a Lord unable to understand the limits and the suffering of living, hardness of hearts, and the difficulties of human relationships.

For this reason, the Pope invites priests who are confessors not to feel that they are the owners of the sacrament of forgiveness but, rather, its servants and administrators, welcoming the faithful like the father in the parable of prodigal son. A father who waits, goes out to meet, clasps, forgives, forgets and re-establishes; a father who knows how to receive from the heart of the other the plea for help and forgiveness.[9]

The Church, and in her each one of us, is called to be a setting for gratuitous mercy where everybody can feel welcomed, loved, forgiven and encouraged to live according to the good life of the gospel.[10] But also a setting in which people take care of one another, as an expression of respect, union and fraternal communion. The Church is the setting from which, and in which, the invitation to allow ourselves to be reconciled with God (cf. 2 Cor 5:20) must continuously echo forth and where we abandon ourselves to the arms of His mercy through the Sacrament of Reconciliation. This sacrament of healing — suitably prepared and celebrated — expresses through the mediation of the Church the tender face of the mercy of God, the compassion of the love of Christ in the Spirit, because it makes us be born again from spiritual death, creates a new life, tends to and relieves the wounds of a heart offended by sin, bandages that heart and cares for it through the mercy that is received.[11] The *Catechism of the Catholic Church*, taking up *Lumen Gentium* n. 11, also states that: "Those who approach the sacrament of Penance obtain pardon from God's mercy for the offence committed against him, and are, at the same time, reconciled with the Church which they have wounded by their sins and which by charity, by example, and by prayer labors for their conversion."[12] One draws near to this sacrament so that, through grace, one becomes aware of one's own abject state, one sees the days of humiliation and shame provoked by sin, and thus one feels

[9] Cf. ibid., n. 67.

[10] Cf. ibid., n. 114.

[11] Cf. Pope Francis, Bull *Misericordiae vultus* (11 April 2015) (hereafter *MV*), n. 15.

[12] *CCC*, n. 1422.

the desire to return to communion with the heavenly Father and the nostalgia to share in His merciful tenderness in His home.[13]

a. I ask you to be *welcoming* to all.

Welcoming everybody, far from being a simple human habit should be seen in its aspect of faith and thus in its transcendental dimension. One must not forget that Abraham thought that he would welcome men but, in reality, he welcomed the very angels of God. Thus the young Tobias, welcoming as a travelling companion a young man like himself, welcomed in reality the Archangel Raphael. In the context of the challenges that the Sacrament of Penance poses, the priestly ministry of confession is a demanding service, one that is difficult but exalting, in which welcoming, as the initial moment, involves the confessor and the penitent in a unique moment of faith and love: the other, who is welcomed and respected by me, is the other with me, and the bearer of a mystery that goes beyond me. In this spirit, rendering visible the merciful love of God the Father in the confessional is one of the most gripping aspects of the priestly ministry. However, it is also a responsibility.

In the exercise of the ministry of reconciliation, priests must seek to perform their mission as fathers, advisers, "judges" and animators in harmony with the doctrine of the Magisterium of the Church, obtaining the learning that is necessary for this task and proceeding with prudence, discretion, patience, discernment and goodness. What should be avoided is the danger of creating an "anxiety" of sin or a "guilt complex" in penitents who, instead, need to be encouraged to place all of their trust in the infinite mercy of God. Penitents often do not need only forgiveness. They can also need light by which to illuminate some "dark areas" of their conscience. They can need strong stimuli or an authentic shake-up so as not to continue to remain rooted in sin. They can need some words of encouragement that give them peace of mind and help them to believe that with the help of God they can manage to change their lives. They may need some words of comfort during moments of pain or a friendly presence that provides them with security and consolation at a moment of hopelessness ... And a confessor can transmit all of this only if he has achieved his own human maturity, a good moral and Christian formation, and if he cultivates a healthy spiritual and priestly life.

---

[13] Cf. *RP*, n. 5.

b. I ask you to be *witnesses* of fatherly tenderness whatever the gravity of the sin.

The priest-confessor must also try to be what Jesus was for the sinners that he encountered on his journey. The penitent has the right to see in him not only the powers but also the Heart of Jesus. The confessor must have a great capacity for welcome and fatherly love towards every penitent and above all else towards "lost" sons who return from very far away. He must be a true father because he regenerates and increases the life of grace in the soul of the penitent. This fatherhood of his, which is like a shadow of the paternity of God, must emerge clearly from his way of doing things. The confessor is fully a "father" if he regenerates the repentant members of the faithful not only with the grace that comes from on high but also through his contribution of setting a good example — of prayer and of expiation.

c. I ask you to be *attentive* in helping penitents to reflect on the wrong they have done.

A sign of gospel care in the sacrament of forgiveness is a confessor who in performing his mission as a judge and a father always tries to find a further reason to love and to grant forgiveness. He finds such a reason on the basis of his own experience as a forgiven man who is reconciled with God, with the Church and with himself, having in front of his eyes the icon of the loving care of the Mother of God for her cousin Elizabeth. Care is love and love does not lose an opportunity to love. The confessor must not be like the judges of this world who ascertain whether in the accused there is guilt to be punished by a sentence. He must be a judge who discerns if in a soul there are the conditions to receive the forgiveness of the Lord; a judge who works according to the justice of God by applying mercy. Pope Francis has observed:

> The ministers of the Church must be merciful, take responsibility for people, accompanying them like the Good Samaritan who washes, cleans and raises up his neighbor. This is pure Gospel. God is greater than sin. Organizational and structural reforms are secondary, that is to say they come afterwards. The first reform must be that of the approach. The ministers of the Gospel must be people who are capable of warming the hearts of people, to walk in the night with them, to know how to engage in dialogue and also to descend into their nights, into their darkness without

getting lost. The people of God want pastors and not state functionaries or clerics.[14]

d. I ask you to be *clear* in presenting moral principles.

We are all called to "make disciples of all nations ... teaching them to observe all that I have commanded you" (Mt 28:19-20). Thus a priest is, and must be, a teacher of virtue in the confessional as well, a teacher who proposes anew the teaching of Jesus about what is good and what is bad, without any power of interpreting gospel truth according to his own way of seeing things. Perhaps, believing that they were serving the truth and doing good to souls, some confessors have used an overly severe language without justification, forgetting that confession is essentially the Sacrament of Mercy. A certain harshness is useful and necessary with the falsely repentant, with those who more than converting would like to "convert" the priest and convince him that their vices ... are not vices but virtues. This is a situation that is increasingly experienced today in the confessional. But with those who sin because of weakness, recognize their own sin, and have a wish to free themselves of it, all the goodness, understanding and encouragement that is possible is needed. For that matter, often one can find in the confessor an excessive "sweetness," a kind of honeyed goodness that is not real goodness and does not come from a "zeal" to administer mercy but from a fear of being forced to clash with the penitent. And thus "tranquillisers" are handed out, even to those who need some strong words; the assessment of the situation of a soul in all its aspects is avoided, even if it would be appropriate to do this, and the goodness of the Lord is emphasized in a disproportionate and erroneous way. This approach of the confessor not only does not bring any spiritual benefits to penitents — it also, in contrary fashion, deforms their conscience.

e. I ask you to be *willing* to walk patiently beside the faithful on their penitential journey, keeping in step with them with patience.

When administering the Sacrament of Penance, the confessor performs the delicate task of forming and illuminating the conscience of the penitent. An approach of willingness to accompany the faithful on their penitential journey, according to the witness of St. Peter, finds light in a sensitivity to taking care — willingly and not as an

[14] "Intervista a Papa Francesco," edited by A. Spadaro, in *La Civiltà Cattolica*, 3918 (2013/III), pp. 449-477; quotation p. 462.

obligation — of those hearts that ask for mercy and reconciliation, at the same time educating them according to the rectitude of conscience required by the Gospel. There come to mind those intense words that St. Pope John Paul II used in his Apostolic Exhortation *Reconciliatio et Paenitentia* to emphasize the human and spiritual qualities of a confessor who is always also an educator of consciences:

> the confessor must necessarily have human qualities of prudence, discretion, discernment and a firmness tempered by gentleness and kindness. He must likewise have a serious and careful preparation, not fragmentary but complete and harmonious, in the different branches of theology, pedagogy and psychology, in the methodology of dialogue and above all in a living and communicable knowledge of the word of God. But it is even more necessary that he should live an intense and genuine spiritual life. In order to lead others along the path of Christian perfection the minister of penance himself must first travel this path. More by actions than by long speeches he must give proof of real experience of lived prayer, the practice of the theological and moral virtues of the Gospel, faithful obedience to the will of God, love of the church and docility to her magisterium (*RP*, n. 29).

At a practical level, some confessors may give penitents the impression of being elsewhere with their thoughts. In this case, the person engaging in confession senses a detachment, almost indifference, on the part of the priest; they feel that they are treated more as a "number" than as a person and this certainly does not facilitate openness. In addition, the Christian community needs to know when, how and where to find a priest for confessions, yet there are rather few parishes who provide precise indications as to place and time so that the faithful can go and find a confessor who is available. And thus people who need, and wish, to "unload" their burden remain with their "raft" and their interior suffering, for who knows how long.

f. I ask you to be *far-sighted* in discerning individual cases.

In the confessional, particular cases can present themselves that require, for example, a suitable knowledge of bioethics. The priest, therefore, can find himself in difficulty. In this case, he can ask for a little time before expressing an opinion on the question and consult the Apostolic Penitentiary, which enters the picture in situations where the priest does not have the faculty to absolve and in cases where he may lack a suitable grounding or feel ill at ease. The doctrinal training of a confessor must be such as to allow him at least to perceive the possible existence of a problem. In this case, pastoral prudence, united to humility, taking into account the urgency of the matter or otherwise, and of the anxiety or otherwise of the penitent, will lead him to choose whether to send the penitent to another confessor or whether to fix an appointment for a new meeting and, in the meantime, expand his own knowledge of the question. Always with absolute respect for the sacramental seal, recourse is advised, in the meantime, to priests with greater experience and in particular to the Apostolic Penitentiary, which is always ready, in concrete and therefore individual cases, to offer its service of consultation — a service that is endowed with an authoritative value.

g. I ask you to be *generous* in dispensing God's forgiveness.

> Just as Jesus chose to remain silent in order to save the woman caught in adultery from the sentence of death, so every priest in the confessional should be open-hearted, since every penitent is a reminder that he himself is a sinner, but also a minister of mercy (*MM*, n. 10).
>
> We were the first to be forgiven in view of this ministry, made witnesses at first hand of the universality of God's forgiveness. No law or precept can prevent God from once more embracing the son who returns to him, admitting that he has done wrong but intending to start his life anew. Remaining only at the level of the law is equivalent to thwarting faith and divine mercy (*MM*, n. 11).

How can we not remember here the other important words that Pope Francis pronounced during his meeting with the parish priests and the priests of the clergy of Rome of 6 March 2014? The Holy Father, in addition to remembering the perception of St. John Paul II that for the whole of the Church "this was the time of mercy," emphasized that:

> The priest reveals a heart especially in administering the Sacrament of Reconciliation; he reveals it by his whole attitude, by the manner in which he welcomes, listens, counsels and absolves.... But this comes from how he experiences

> the Sacrament firsthand, from how he allows himself to be embraced by God the Father in Confession and remains in this embrace … . If one experiences this in one's own regard, in his own heart, he can also give it to others in his ministry. And I leave you with the question: How do I confess? Do I allow myself to be embraced?...If one experiences this in his own regard in Confession, in his own heart, he is able to give it to others … The priest is called to learn this, to have a heart that is moved … Neither the laxist nor the rigorist bears witness to Jesus Christ, for neither the one nor the other takes care of the person he encounters. The rigorist washes his hands of them: in fact, he nails the person to the law, understood in a cold and rigid way; and the laxist also washes his hands of them: he is only apparently merciful, but in reality he does not take seriously the problems of that conscience, by minimizing the sin. True mercy *takes the person into one's care*, listens to him attentively, approaches the situation with respect and truth, and accompanies him on the journey of reconciliation.[15]

h. The *responsibility* of acts and words that can reach the depths of the heart of the penitent.

Exercising the ministry of confession is one of the most difficult and tiring tasks of a priest. This is because, albeit with all the influences that come to him from his history and his present, he has to relate to people who most of the time are unknown to him and are different; frequently he only has a few minutes to solve complex situations and very often the penitents themselves do very little to help him see things as they really are. He must have sensitive antennae to perceive situations of frailty, of anxiety, of pain, or situations of shallowness, of arrogance, of pride … which the penitent often does not express clearly. In addition, with each person whom he listens to the priest must know how to leave behind his own personal state of mind or that absorbed from the person whose confession he has just heard. This constant emptying and filling of himself, this moving from one state of mind to another, requires a human and psychological elasticity that nobody possesses as a gift of nature and that easily leads to an internal tiredness. Those priests who regularly and for hours face up

[15] Pope Francis, Address to the Parish Priests of Rome, 6 March 2014.

to the "hard work" of the confessional thus deserve great esteem and gratitude.

Understanding should also be extended to those priests who at times, without wanting it, allow some sign of tiredness or tension to be detected from a word or their tone of voice. In this case, it is not so much readiness to help or generosity that are lacking — perhaps it is just a matter of "run-down batteries," namely, tiredness and nothing else.

Making known more effectively how important the Sacrament of Reconciliation and Penance is in the life of the Church and of each member of the faithful, thanks to the light offered by the Apostolic Letter *Misericordia et misera* as well, is of notable importance. As regards our pastoral activity, especially in the context of confession, one is dealing with behaving like "true pastors," avoiding all ambiguity that creates confusion. The insistent emphasis placed upon mercy by the Holy Father Pope Francis, the urgent need for today's ecclesial community to care for every wound, and the commitment to making confession a setting for reconciliation where the Lord stimulates every penitent to do their best, in their concrete situation, here and now, must not be interpreted as forgoing the objective requirements of the Sacrament of Penance or encouragement to engage in ambiguous behavior in pastoral care. No confessor must ever see himself as being the owner of the sacrament that he is administering; nor must he induce the faithful into error as regards the doctrine or the current juridical practice of the Church. The office of confession, which probably more than the other sacraments highlights all of the humanity, the doctrinal training and the priestly personhood of ministry, requires a high sense of loyalty towards the Magisterium of the Church and great balance. Merciful, therefore, in the light of the only Truth which is Christ himself!

THE SACRAMENTS: CHRIST WITH THE HOLY SPIRIT WORKING IN THE CHURCH

I now want to enter and explore the rich reality of the subject of sacraments in the Church in order to contemplate and perceive the salvific presence of Christ working in them within his mystical body. I also want thereby to manage to savor the splendid salvific experience that is deposited in them and that bursts out for every believer in the Lord who was crucified and rose again and is the giver of the Spirit of sanctification.

I believe that it is right and necessary, in engaging in an analysis of the sacraments of the Church as the signs of the new Covenant, to clarify at the outset the meaning of the terms that will be the subject of this analysis.

1. Sacrament

Etymologically "sacrament" means the action that is engaged in through a means/instrument to make something or somebody sacred. Indeed, in Latin *sacra-mentum* is made up of the word *sacrare* (= the action to make sacred) and the word *mentum* (= the means to reach a certain goal).

In the *Vulgata*, the Latin term *sacramentum* translates the Greek word *mysterion*, which refers to the salvific plan of God, His intention to save man.

Saint Paul in *Ephesians* 3:3-12 defines himself as a "minister of the mystery of Christ" and for this reason he was committed to making known the mystery that had been hidden to the previous generations but was now revealed by means of the Spirit (cf. also 1 Cor 2:7-10; for the Old Testament cf. Dan 2:18-19).

In practical terms, Christ himself, who was born, died and rose again, and his mission, are the first and great *sacramentum* of salvation: "Undeniably great is the mystery of devotion, Who was manifested in the flesh, vindicated in the spirit, seen by angels, proclaimed to the Gentiles, believed in throughout the world, taken up in glory" (1 Tim 3:16).

The gift of salvation, in the current "economy" willed and established by God, comes to man through Christ and in Christ (Sacrament of God), through the Church (Sacrament of Christ), and through the Sacraments-Signs (the Sacraments of Christ and of the Church).

1.1. *Christ: Sacrament of God*

"Sacrament" means revelation-gift of the salvation of God in and through an external-visible form and Christ with his Incarnation (cf. Jn 1:14) is the first great Sacrament: "there is no other Sacrament of God than Christ";[1] "Christ for us, in his humanity, is the Sacrament of God."[2]

The humanity of Christ is the unique, singular and extraordinary *mystery-sacrament* of the salvific encounter of the Father with men in the Holy Spirit, as the Apostle Paul observes: "God … wills everyone to be saved and to come to knowledge of the truth. For there is one God. There is also one mediator between God and the human race, Christ Jesus, himself human, who gave himself as ransom for all" (1 Tim 2:3-5). Indeed, God wanted to save man through the flesh of Christ taken on by divinity ("*caro salutis cardo*": this flesh is the very condition on which salvation hinges, to employ the definition of Tertullian).[3] This most holy flesh, full of the Holy Spirit, is an expression of the power and the wisdom of the Father.

When speaking about the Word of God made man who came to live amongst us, St. John says: "we saw his glory, the glory as of the Father's only Son, full of grace and truth" (Jn 1:14); his works and his miracles, that is to say the signs that he worked, are an expression of the life that was in him, flashes of the "true light, which enlightens everyone … coming into the world" (Jn 1:4,9; 3:19s; 8:12) — everyone who wants to believe, who wants to discover the meaning of this light.

---

[1] Augustine, *In epistolam Joannis ad Parthos tractatus decem*, 3, 6 (*PL* 35, col. 2000).

[2] H. De Lubac, *Meditazione sulla Chiesa* (Milan, 1993), p. 135.

[3] Tertullian, *De carnis resurrectione*, 8, 3 (*PL* 2, col. 806).

Christ realized in an absolute sense the presence of God amongst us, a personal and full presence, which the dwelling of God in the tent or the temple of the Old Covenant only prefigured (cf. Es 25:9; Jer 7:4-10,12-15; 26:1-9). On this subject, the Constitution *Dei Verbum* expresses itself as follows on divine revelation:

> Jesus Christ, therefore, the Word made flesh, was sent as "a man to men." (3) He "speaks the words of God" (John 3:34), and completes the work of salvation which His Father gave Him to do (see John 5:36; John 17:4). To see Jesus is to see His Father (John 14:9). For this reason Jesus perfected revelation by fulfilling it through his whole work of making Himself present and manifesting Himself: through His words and deeds, His signs and wonders, but especially through His death and glorious resurrection from the dead and final sending of the Spirit of truth. Moreover He confirmed with divine testimony what revelation proclaimed, that God is with us to free us from the darkness of sin and death, and to raise us up to life eternal.[4]

In his humanity, Christ is thus the primordial Sacrament of the Father, the Sacrament of the encounter with God.

1.2. *The Church: Sacrament of Jesus Christ*

After Christ, and inseparably linked to him, the Church is also a mystery-sacrament of salvation for all peoples; she is the chosen, intelligent instrument capable of being perceived by the senses by which God makes His word, His wisdom and His Spirit reach the far ends of the earth.

This enabled St. Augustine to write: "The Church of the baptized is the mystery-sacrament of the ark of salvation"[5] and St. Cyprian to declare: "The Church is the indestructible sacrament of unity."[6]

The Church brings into this world the Word and the Sacraments of salvation. The glorious Christ makes himself present in the Church "always, until the end of the age" (Mt 28:20).

---

[4] Second Ecumenical Vatican Council, Dogmatic Constitution on Divine Revelation *Dei Verbum* (18 November 1965), n. 4.

[5] Augustine, *In Evangelium Ioannis tractatus centum viginti quatuor*, 80, 3 (*PL* 35, col. 1840).

[6] Cyprian, *Epistulae*, 69, 12, (*PL* 4, col. 357).

Animated and supported by the Holy Spirit, the Church holds out, and communicates, to all generations and to all peoples the salvation achieved by her Spouse and Lord. Here on earth she is the Sacrament of Jesus Christ, just as Jesus Christ for us, in his divinized humanity, is the Sacrament of God.

And since nobody knows the Father without passing by he who always and for everyone remains the "way" and "the image of the invisible God" (Jn 14:6; Col 1:15), the whole of the Church, visible and invisible, earthly and eternal, has as her purpose showing Christ, leading people to him, and communicating his grace.[7]

1.3. *The Church: Sacrament of Intimate Union with God*

In *Lumen gentium* we read: "the Church is in Christ like a sacrament or as a sign and instrument both of a very closely knit union with God and of the unity of the whole human race."[8]

Thus the Church is not only a visible sign of salvation — she is also a Sacrament of the glorious Christ. As a Sacrament of the risen Christ, she has the mission of making present the salvation worked by Christ through the proclaiming of the Word, the sacraments, and witness. She must proclaim Christ, give him, show him to everyone: she is always, and in all truth, the Church of Christ.

But what she is in herself, she must become in us. What she is for us, she must also be through us. Christ, through us as well, must continue to be proclaimed, celebrated and borne witness to. Flowing forth as an admirable sacrament from the side of Christ sleeping on the cross (cf. St. Augustine quoted in *Sacrosanctum Concilium*)[9], in virtue of that "blood and water" (Jn 19:34) she makes present and contemporary the paschal mystery of Christ and offers to men the possibility of placing themselves in the living organism of his body.

2. The Sacraments of Christ and the Church

Just as Christ is the Sacrament of God and the Church is a Sacrament of Christ, so the Sacraments of the new Covenant are Sacraments of Christ and the Church. Before returning to the Father, Christ

[7] Cf. Second Ecumenical Vatican Council, Dogmatic Constitution on the Church *Lumen gentium* (21 November 1964) (hereafter *LG*), nn. 1 and 8.

[8] *LG*, n. 1.

[9] Second Ecumenical Vatican Council, Constitution on the Sacred Liturgy *Sacrosanctum Concilium* (4 December 1963) (hereafter *SC*).

exclaimed: "It is finished" (Jn 19:30). Thus, "what was visible in our Savior passed into the Sacraments."[10] In his paschal mystery salvation was acquired once and for all (cf. Heb 9:26; 10;10,12,14). What remains now is to communicate to men, who are his body, what was accomplished in Christ the head.

All the mysteries of his life should reverberate in time and space so that all men who face life can feel that they are present and be placed in these mysteries as well.

This work of sanctification is performed by the Holy Spirit in the Church, as is well expressed by St. Bernard: "We have a dual pledge of salvation, the dual outpouring of the blood and the Spirit: one without the other is worthless ... I would not gain from the fact that Christ died for me if I did not vivify myself with his Spirit."[11]

In the sacraments of the Church it is therefore the Spirit that achieves in us what was accomplished in Christ: he interiorizes his mystery and applies its fruits; he ensures that it becomes "our mystery."[12]

Indeed, the sacraments really contain a virtue that emanates from the Incarnation and the death and resurrection of Christ. The sacraments are nothing else but a prolongation of the mysteries of the incarnated Word.

To employ a phrase of Y. Congar, one can also say that "between the two events of Christ, from the death and resurrection that he did for us and the death and resurrection that we will do with him, the Holy Spirit acts to grow and fructify alpha to omega."[13]

Since the Pentecost, the Holy Spirit has been at work at all levels of the life of the Church and the life of each individual believer. In a completely singular way, however, he is present and effective where the Church reaches the "culmination and the source" of all her life — the activity of the liturgy.[14]

Here in fact "the power of the Holy Spirit acts upon us through sacramental signs";[15] it is here that to the utmost "through the sacraments and the ministries of the Church ... the Holy Spirit sanctifies and leads the people of God and enriches it with virtues."[16]

---

[10] Leo the Great, *Sermones*, 74, 2, (*PL* 54, col. 398).

[11] Bernard of Claivaux, *Sermones in Cantica Canticorum*, 61, 2 (*PL* 183, col. 1071).

[12] Second Ecumenical Vatican Council, Decree on the Mission Activity of the Church *Ad gentes* (7 December 1965), n. 4.

[13] Y. Congar, *Spirito e libertà* (Turin 1969), pp. 33-34.

[14] Cf. *SC*, n. 10.

[15] *LG*, n. 50.

[16] Ibid., n. 12.

If "In the liturgy the sanctification of the man is signified by signs perceptible to the senses, and is effected in a way which corresponds with each of these signs,"[17] this is due specifically to this sanctifying action of the Spirit as an actuator of all the wonders performed by Christ for our salvation.

In his tract *On the Holy Spirit*, St. Basil writes: "It is the Spirit that achieves reintegration in heaven, entrance into the kingdom of heaven, the return of the prodigal son. It is he who gives the holy courage to call God Father, to take part in the grace of Christ, to be called children of the light, *to take part* in eternal glory: in a few words, to be in this century and the future."[18]

It thus emerges clearly that the action of the Holy Spirit in the sacramental economy of the Church makes possible for man that vital communication with Christ whose ultimate fulfillment will be access to the glory of the Father. With St. Ambrose we can well say: "I found You in your mysteries."[19]

As regards Christ (the primordial or fundamental Sacrament of the Church) and the Church, the sacraments are directed towards the sanctification of man (they transmit the efficacy of salvation and communicate grace); they render worship to God; they put us in contact with the salvific plan by incorporating us into Christ; and they build up the Church by structuring her as the Body of Christ. As signs, they also have the function of providing instruction.[20]

If it is true that without the Church there are no sacraments, it is equally true that without the sacraments there would be no Church.

Through the sacraments the Church is generated and sanctified; she grows and spreads; she is reinvigorated, completed and purified; she performs her mission.

2.1. *The Salvific Fecundity of the Sacraments*

The sacraments place those who receive them in the paschal mystery of Jesus Christ who died and rose again and makes them take part in the gift of the Holy Spirit, who directs this basic gift called "grace" because it is freely given, towards achieving the specific goal of every sacrament.

---

[17] *SC*, n. 7.

[18] Basil, *Trattato sullo Spirito Santo*, IX, 22-23 (*Sources Chrétiennes*, n. 17bis, pp. 145-148).

[19] Ambrose, *Apologia Prophetae David*, 58 (*PL* 14, col. 871).

[20] Cf. *SC*, n. 59; *CIC*, can. 840.

The first is called "first grace," the second is called "sacramental grace," and they are experienced through an increase in the paschal participation of the believer in Baptism and Confirmation, until culmination in the Eucharist where Jesus Christ is present in a substantial and personal way.

In three sacraments, more precisely in Baptism, Confirmation, and Holy Orders, according to tradition a sign that defines a person is recognized in virtue of which in a continuous way, and for always, those who receive such signs (*sfraghis*: 2 Cor 1:21-22; Eph 1:13; 4:30) are made capable of the triple action of Christ, namely prophecy, priesthood, regality, which are expressed respectively in a Christian sense in Baptism (= *signum Christianitatis*, according to Innocent III); in witness or representation in Confirmation; and in ministry in Holy Orders. Because of this characteristic the three sacraments should be received only once. They cannot, that is to say, be repeated.

2.2. *What are the Sacraments?*

a. They are signs of faith

1. *They express the faith of the Church.* The Church believes in the efficacy of the sacramental signs which she bestows in the name of Christ and with his authority. This is why for a sacrament to be valid what the Church wants to do must always be done.

2. *They express the faith of the person who receives them*: they presuppose such faith (without faith in Christ and in his work of salvation, salvific sacramental action does not exist either: cf. Mk 16:15; *Acts* 8:37ff). It is therefore licit and incumbent to give the anointing of the sick to those who are in a coma, presupposing that if the person had been conscious they would themselves have freely requested it. In the Baptism of infants, the faith of the parents and of the Church herself is presupposed). They express this faith (all the sacraments are a profession-confession of faith in Christ the Lord). They nourish it and they make it more robust ("I do believe, help my unbelief": Mk 9:24).[21]

[21] Cf. *SC*, n. 59.

Without faith, the holy signs do not manage to be read beyond their "earthly" sphere, they cannot indicate detachment from he who is "totally other," always inaccessible in Himself and never fully communicable; without faith, rather than "holy" the sign becomes "magical," almost an attempt to seize divine power and dominate it for one's own ends (cf. the episode of Simon the magician in Acts 8:19-25 and also the episode at Capernaum in Jn 6:26-28).

b. They are signs of grace

In the sacraments God gives Himself totally to man to raise him up, to transform him, to divinize him and to introduce him into the communion of His divine nature.

This grace-gift is thus "unique" (= sanctifying grace), even if bestowed in its "own" way by each sacrament (= sacramental grace).

As "signs" the sacraments have a "three-dimensional" profundity:

— They are an anamnesis-memorial of the death and resurrection of Christ.

— They are an epiclesis-actuation because they fill the soul with grace.

— They are an anticipation-pledge of future glory.

c. They are signs made up of things and words

Just as the invisible God makes Himself visible in the incarnation of Christ because Christ is the *Verbum Caro* (Jn 1:14,18), so in the sacraments this mystery of the salvific incarnation is continued. Saint Augustine in his epoch was already declaring: "Take away the word, and what is the water except water? The word is added to the elemental substance, and it becomes a sacrament ("*Accedit verbum ad elementum et fit sacramentum*")."[22] In the language of the Scholastics reference is also made to "matter" (the thing) and "form" (the word).

2.3. *The Efficacy of the Sacraments and Who Acts in the Sacraments*

"The Church carries out its office of sanctifying in a special way in the sacred liturgy";[23] "In the liturgy the sanctification of the man

[22] Augustine, *In Evangelium Ioannis*, 80, 3 (*PL* 35, col. 1840).

[23] *CIC*, can. 834.

is signified by signs perceptible to the senses, and is effected in a way which corresponds with each of these signs."[24]

The sacraments are effective signs of grace because they are salvific acts of Christ that he performs in the Church and for the Church.

The work of salvation accomplished by Christ once and for all in his paschal mystery (Heb 9:26) continues today to be offered to every believer through the sacraments.

With the Church Fathers we can say: "Peter baptizes? But it is Christ who baptizes ... those baptized by John the Baptist were really baptized by John. Instead those whom Judas baptized, Christ baptized."[25]

The Second Vatican Council observed: "In the bishops, therefore, for whom priests are assistants, Our Lord Jesus Christ, the Supreme High Priest, is present in the midst of those who believe ... through their excellent service He is preaching the word of God to all nations, and constantly administering the sacraments of faith to those who believe."[26]

The sacraments therefore are salvific acts of Christ by which he makes present in the Church and through the Church the mysteries of his death and resurrection.

As he is "the Living One," he who always intercedes for us at the right hand of the Father (Heb 7:25), he is in fact also "the Present One" as regards the Church, and in her and for her (as his Sacrament) he continues to offer the salvific mysteries of his death and resurrection.

Indeed, "For as often as you eat this bread and drink the cup, you proclaim the death of the Lord until he comes" (1 Cor 11:26).

3. The Sacraments of Christian Initiation

By the phrase "Christian initiation" is meant introduction into the paschal mystery of Christ which, welcomed in faith through the Word, is penetrated by the intellect and by the heart through the catechesis, participated in through the paschal sacraments — Baptism, Confirmation, and the Eucharist, and experienced and lived in the experience of faith of the Christian community.

---

[24] *SC*, n. 7.

[25] Augustine, *In Evangelium Ioannis*, 80, 4 (*PL* 35, col. 1842).

[26] *LG*, n. 21; cf. also Second Ecumenical Vatican Council, Decree on the Ministry and Life of Priests *Presbyterorum Ordinis* (7 December 1965), n. 2.

As the term "initiation" indicates, this is a steady and gradual entrance of man into the mystery of Christ and the Church, starting with faith, which is born from the *"kerigma"* as the first proclaiming, and is then developed by the catechesis, as a penetration by the intellect and heart of the word of God, and by conversion, to achieve an increasingly full encounter with Christ in the Church.

In this way is outlined and created through the three Sacraments of Baptism, Confirmation, and the Eucharist, which are all intimately connected, a dynamic journey with three synergic stages of a single Christian maturation within the Christian community as a setting for a paschal experience that leads to the true and full maturity of Christ (cf. Eph 4:13).

The first stage is Baptism: the consecration of a person who through faith adheres to Christ, participates in the life of the Trinity, and comes to be a part of the people of the new Covenant.

The second stage of the journey of faith is Confirmation or Sacrament of the Spirit, which leads a person to a fuller configuration with Christ and a deeper participation in the life and the witness of the Church, in intimate connection with Baptism, which it completes and confirms.

The third stage is the Eucharist, which is the fullness of all this initiation, containing Christ who is total reality; it is maturation of the Christian life, as life; commitment and concrete witness to a "paschal" existence.

These three sacraments are in fact like a single sacrament of Christian maturity which is initiated by Baptism and accomplished in the Eucharist.

Tertullian described in summarizing fashion the rite of initiation that was used in the Church of his time:

> For example, the flesh is washed that the soul may be made spotless: the flesh is anointed that the soul may be consecrated: the flesh is signed with the cross that the soul too may be protected: the flesh is overshadowed by the imposition of the hand that the soul may be illumined by the Spirit: the flesh feeds on the Body and Blood of Christ so that the soul also may be replete with God.[27]

This is important testimony to a very old practice according to which you were introduced into the ecclesial community through a

[27] Tertullian, *De carnis resurrectione*, 8, 3 (*PL* 2, col. 806).

pathway of initiation which included three sacramental ritual acts — Baptism, Confirmation (expressed by baptismal washing, anointing, the Sign of the Cross, and the laying on of hands) and the Eucharist (food and nutriment for the soul).

From the first centuries of Christianity onwards, the Church organized a gradual and progressive journey of becoming a Christian which she called "Christian initiation" — initiation in the sense of living insertion into the paschal mystery of Christ and the life of the Church. In the discourse of Peter on the day of Pentecost we already find a summary of what would be the structure of Christian initiation: "Now when they heard this, they were cut to the heart, and they asked Peter and the other apostles, 'What are we to do, my brothers?' Peter (said) to them, 'Repent and be baptized, every one of you, in the name of Jesus Christ for the forgiveness of your sins; and you will receive the gift of the holy Spirit'" (Acts 2:37-38).

Those who have heard the proclaiming of the mystery of Christ (*kerygma*), with the grace of the Holy Spirit knowingly and willingly look for the living God and begin their journey of faith and conversion (catechumenate-catechesis). At a suitable time they will complete their journey of becoming Christians, receiving as a positive outcome the Sacraments of Christian initiation (Baptism, Confirmation, the Eucharist).

The two inseparable moments of this journey and celebration together form that unique program of becoming Christians called Christian initiation.

This program of initiation reached its greatest splendor in the golden age of the catechumenate (third to fifth centuries) only to then disappear.

The Second Vatican Council wanted the very ancient rite and practice of Christian initiation to be restored, revised and adapted.[28]

Today our ecclesial communities feel with greater intensity the need for pastoral activity that leads to a rediscovery or progressive and personal awareness of one's faith through an ongoing catechesis that gradually follows a Christian from infancy to the subsequent stages of life.

[28] Cf. *SC*, nn. 64-66; Second Ecumenical Vatican Council, Decree *Ad gentes*, n. 14; Second Ecumenical Vatican Council, Decree on the Pastoral Mission of Bishops in the Church *Christus Dominus* (28 October 1965), n. 14.

4. The Sacrament of Penance or Reconciliation

The reconciliation of God and man was accomplished by the Lord Jesus with the mystery of his death and resurrection (cf. Rom 5:10). He himself then entrusted the ministry of reconciliation to the Church in the persons of the Apostles (cf. 2 Cor 5:18) and the Church exercises it giving men the good news of salvation and baptizing them with water and in the Holy Spirit (cf. Mt 28:19).

It can indeed happen that because of human weakness Christians abandon initial charity (cf. Rev 2:4) through sin and break the friendship that unites them to God.

This is why in the sacramental economy, as well as the three sacraments of Christian initiation (Baptism, Confirmation, and the Eucharist), the Lord, "physician of the flesh and the spirit," also provided for two medicinal sacraments: one for the health of the soul (penance) and one for the health of the body (anointing of the sick).

He who removed the sins of the paralyzed man giving him health of the body as well (cf. Mk 2:1-12), making himself the physician of our souls and our bodies, wanted to continue through the Church his work of healing and salvation in the paschal gift of the Holy Spirit.

Specifically to remove sins committed after Baptism, the Lord instituted a special sacrament, the Sacrament of Penance (cf. Jn 20:21-23), which the Church down the centuries has faithfully proclaimed and celebrated. The mystery of reconciliation thus forms a part of both the history of salvation and the history of the Church.

Reconciliation in the history of salvation is God who calls men to enter into communion with Him. The answer to the call of God requires conversion and penance.

According to His design the Lord manifested His mercy reconciling the world to Him through Christ, restoring peace, with the blood of his cross, between the things of this world and the things of heaven (cf. 2 Cor 5:18; Eph 2:14).

This God, who revealed Himself to us to the point of sending to us in the fullness of time His Son, is a God who is immensely demanding and immensely merciful.

He is a demanding God because in assigning to us a goal above all human prediction and imagination, He is never satisfied with the state of holiness of His children, He always asks for more, He pursues and troubles their laziness, inviting them to raise their lives to new and always higher orbits.

But at the same time He is a God whose mercy "is greater than our heart" (1 Jn 3:20): He takes us as we are, patiently bears our waywardness, weakness and slowness, and where He finds guilt, even the gravest and the most ungrateful, He always manages to overcome it with love and transcend it with forgiveness.

Thus even the defeats and the despondency of those who are already "born of water and the Spirit" (Jn 3:5) and should by now be definitively living a new life, do not take the clemency of the Father by surprise. Specifically with the Sacrament of Penance, He always allows us to start afresh and recover each time the fresh innocence of Baptism.

4.1. *The Message of the Prophets*

The invitation to penance is also a pressing appeal of the prophets. With the Hebrew term *shûb* they pointed to the need to change direction, to return, to turn a journey around; to turn one's back on what is evil, to aim once again for God.

The Greek Bible, to express the total character of penance-conversion as an act of the entire man (thought and action), used more than one word. By *metànoia* it expressed inner repentance; by *epistrèphein* it expressed change in usual conduct.

Whereas in the ages of antiquity divine forgiveness was implored with fasting, almsgiving, supplication and expiatory rites (cf. Num 16:6-15), in what the prophets proclaimed emphasis was placed more on *conversion of the heart.*

Hosea, for example, stigmatized superficial conversions, inviting people to inner conversion inspired by love (*hesed)* and knowledge of God (Hos 6:1-6).

Worship on its own is worth nothing, says Isaiah (Is 1:11-15), without submission to God in the practice of justice, piety and sincerity (cf. Zep 3:12ff).

Notwithstanding the efficacy of the sacrifice of a contrite heart (Ps 51:18, the *Miserere* of David), conversion of the heart and forgiveness would be above all else a grace freely offered by God to the people of the new Covenant when He "will place my law within them, and write it upon their hearts" (Jer 31:33).

4.2. *Jesus: the Merciful Face of the Father*

The merciful work of the Father took practical shape in the paschal mystery of the Son. The Lord Jesus, the Son of God made man, lived amongst men to free them from the slavery of sin (Jn 8:34-36) and to call them from the shadows to his admirable light (1 Pet 2:9).

For this reason, Christ began his mission on earth by preaching repentance and saying: "Repent, and believe in the Gospel" (Mk 1:15). Jesus not only exhorted men to repentance so as to abandon sin and convert with all their hearts to God (Lk 15), he also welcomed sinners and reconciled them with the Father (Lk 5:20,27-32; 7:48).

Christ also healed the sick in order to provide a sign of his power to forgive sins (Mt 9:2,8). Lastly, he himself died for our sins and rose again for our justification (Rom 4:25).

For this reason, on the night he was betrayed he began his saving Passion and instituted the sacrifice of the new Covenant in his blood for the forgiveness of sins (Mt 26:28). After his resurrection he sent the Holy Spirit to his apostles so that they would have the power to forgive sins or retain them (Jn 20:19-23) and receive the mission to preach repentance and the forgiveness of sins in his name to all the nations (Lk 24:47).

In the formula of absolution we hear that the Lord Jesus "sent the Holy Spirit among us for the forgiveness of sins."

The Spirit brings the newness of the Covenant (2 Cor 3:6); he makes the law of the Spirit and of justice succeed the law of sin and the flesh (Rom 7:18,25; 8:2,4); and he transforms us from carnal beings into "spiritual men" (1 Cor 3:1).

4.3. *The Church: A Holy Place of Reconciliation*

Ever since the day of Pentecost the Church, through the mouth of Peter, has preached forgiveness of sins through Baptism: "Repent and be baptized, every one of you, in the name of Jesus Christ for the forgiveness of your sins" (Acts 2:38; cf. Acts 3:19,26; 17:30).

The Lord said to Peter: "I will give you the keys to the kingdom of heaven. Whatever you bind on earth shall be bound in heaven; and whatever you loose on earth shall be loosed in heaven" (*Mt* 16:19). Ever since its paschal origins, therefore, the Church has never omitted to call men of sin to conversion, and to manifest, through the celebration of penance, the victory of Christ over sin. The Church is holy but she needs purification. Christ "loved the church and handed himself over for her to sanctify her" (Eph 5:25-26) and united her with himself as his bride (Rev 19:7). And since she is his body and his fullness, Christ fills her with his divine gifts (Eph 1:22-23) so that she stretches out and receives all of the fullness of God (cf. Eph 3:19; *LG*, n. 7).

The members of the Church, however, are exposed to temptation and often fall miserably into sin. And thus whereas Christ "holy, innocent, undefiled" (Heb 7:26) did not know sin (2 Cor 5:21) and expiated the sins of the people (cf. Heb 2:17), the Church, which includes sinners within her, is holy but always needs purification: she never omits to engage in penance and to renew herself.

It is true that with Baptism we were washed, we were sanctified and we were justified in the name of the Lord Jesus Christ and in the Spirit of our God (1 Cor 6:11). But, as the apostle John says, "If we say, "We are without sin," we deceive ourselves, and the truth is not in us" (Jn 1:8).

Divine life is carried by us in "earthen vessels" (2 Cor 4:7) and this means that baptismal regeneration did not eliminate in us the frailty and the weakness of human nature, nor the inclination to sin that tradition calls concupiscence. Helped by the grace of Christ, we must join the good fight against the forces of evil and live in a state of permanent conversion with a view to holiness and the eternal life to which the Lord calls us.

4.4. *The Ecclesial* Topoi *of Forgiveness*

The victory of Christ over sin and the ministry of reconciliation exercised by the Church shine forth above all in three sacramental moments:

- In Baptism when the "old man" is crucified with Christ, so that the body of sin is destroyed and because we are no longer slaves of sin but, in rising again with Christ, we now live for God (cf. Rm 6:4-10). For this reason, the Church professes her faith "in one baptism for the forgiveness of sins."
- In the Eucharist, in which, as a sacrifice that makes the Passion of Christ present, his Body given for us and his Blood shed for us in forgiveness of sins are offered anew by the Church to God for the salvation of the whole world (Mt 26:28).

> In the Eucharist, indeed, Christ is present and offered as a "sacrifice of reconciliation" and so that his Holy Spirit "unites us in a single body." However, although recognizing that the Eucharist, because of its paschal and sacrificial nature, has the renewing grace of forgiveness, the constant tradition of the Church has pointed to sacramental penance as the ordinary way for the forgiveness of sins. Indeed, before presenting the first offering one should first be reconciled with one's brother (Mt 5:23-24); "A person should examine himself, and so eat the bread and drink the cup" (1 Cor 11:28) so as not to answer for the body and blood of the Lord (v. 27).
>
> — In penance, given that the Lord instituted this sacrament in his Church when he bestowed upon the apostles and their successors the power to forgive sins (Jn 20:22-23) and the power of the keys to fasten and to loose (Mt 16:19).

Saint Ambrose observed that in the Church "there are water and tears: the water of baptism and the tears of repentance."[29] After the first and fundamental conversion achieved in Baptism, the Lord makes us share again in his paschal victory over sin by admitting us to sacramental penance. For this reason, tradition has given penance the name "*Baptismus laboriosus*" because one returns to the new and complete life of the children of God, albeit not without tears and hard work. Just as Baptism is necessary for those who have still not been reborn to the divine life, so penance is necessary for those who weaken or lose that life because of their personal sins.

4.5. *The Confessional as a "Place of Faith," of the Transmission of Healthy Doctrine and Experience of Divine Mercy*

The Church, in making sound out in time the proclaiming of forgiveness and reconciliation proclaimed by Jesus, never ceases to invite the whole of humanity to convert and to believe in the Gospel:

> She makes her own the call of the Apostle Paul: "So we are ambassadors for Christ, as if God were appealing through us. We implore you on behalf of Christ, be reconciled to

[29] Ambrose, *Epistulae*, 41, 12 (*PL* 16, col. 1116).

> God" (2 Cor 5:20). Jesus, during his life, proclaimed and made present the mercy of the Father. He came not to condemn but to forgive and to save, to give hope in the deepest darkness of suffering and sin, and to give eternal life; thus in the sacrament of Penance, in the "medicine of confession," the experience of sin does not degenerate into despair but encounters the Love that forgives and transforms.[30]

As Pope Francis has observed in numerous speeches, God never tires of forgiving. It is we ourselves who at times tire of imploring His mercy:

> In the sacrament of penance the desire for salvation of man, awareness of and pain caused by the evil that has been committed, the need to be healed and the wish to live as a child encounter the healing action of God who "does not want the death of the sinner but wants him to convert and live." The Church, through her priests and in the name of Jesus Christ, grants to the faithful forgiveness of their sins, points out to the positive results of penance, prays for repentant sinners and does penance with them. "Thus the sinner is healed and re-established in ecclesial communion" (*CCC*, n. 1448). The Church is the place of encounter between the sinner and the Saviour, the human face of the mercy of the Father.
>
> God, "rich in mercy" (Eph 2:4), like the father in the Gospel parable (cf. Lk 15:11-32), does not close his heart to any of his children, but waits for them, looks for them, reaches them where their rejection of communion imprisons them in isolation and division, and calls them to gather around his table, in the joy of the feast of forgiveness and reconciliation ... He, in his great love, always and everywhere watches over our lives and awaits us so as to offer to every child that returns to him the gift of full reconciliation and joy.[31]

Drawing near to the Sacrament of Penance becomes for a member of the faithful an authentic personal encounter with Jesus, a favorable opportunity to allow oneself to be attracted by him, the

---

[30] Benedict XVI, Message for the World Day of the Sick, 20 November 2011, n. 2.

[31] Ibid., n. 2.

sole physician of souls and bodies. The confessional is a favorable place where a Christian concretely experiences the joy of the return to the Father. It is from the confessional that so many penitents have received the internal strength to "begin" a new life more in conformity with Christ.

> Let us recall that beautiful, beautiful parable of the son who left his home with the money of his inheritance. He wasted all the money and then, when he had nothing left, he decided to return home, not as a son but as a servant. His heart was filled with so much guilt and shame. The surprise came when he began to speak, to ask for forgiveness, his father did not let him speak, he embraced him, he kissed him, and he began to make merry. But I am telling you: each time we go to confession, God embraces us. God rejoices![32]

If we turn our gaze to him, if we take only a short step towards him, we discover that he was waiting for us with open arms and we see that our name was written in signs of fire on his hands which are wounded by love. As Pope Francis writes:

> Now is the time to say to Jesus: "Lord, I have let myself be deceived; in a thousand ways I have shunned your love, yet here I am once more, to renew my covenant with you. I need you. Save me once again, Lord, take me once more into your redeeming embrace." How good it feels to come back to him whenever we are lost! Let me say this once more: God never tires of forgiving us; we are the ones who tire of seeking his mercy. Christ, who told us to forgive one another "seventy times seven" (Mt 18:22) has given us his example: he has forgiven us seventy times seven. Time and time again he bears us on his shoulders. No one can strip us of the dignity bestowed upon us by this boundless and unfailing love. With a tenderness which never disappoints, but is always capable of restoring our joy, he makes it possible for us to lift up our heads and to start anew. Let us not flee from the resurrection of Jesus, let us never give up, come what will.[33]

[32] Pope Francis, General Audience, 19 February 2014.

[33] *EG*, n. 3.

Sacramental confession is the practice that more than any other enables us to experience the greatness, the beauty and the regenerating power of faith in Divine Mercy. When a penitent enters the confessional they truly draw near to the love of the Father, they enter the merciful heart of God who alone is able to heal the wounds of humanity, to remove the sin that impedes us from remaining in friendship with Him, to make new all things in a member of the faithful who with humility and sincere repentance implores forgiveness. The Sacrament of Penance is an effective instrument that regenerates man from within because it helps him to understand the truth of himself, that truth, that is to say, of being the chosen son of the Father who is always ready to give unconditionally His forgiveness and peace.

In this way the confessional also becomes a "theological space," a privileged place where it is possible to obtain the beneficial and redemptive effects of the resurrection of Jesus, who was the first to proclaim the great news of Divine Mercy and entrusted its ministry to the apostles: "Peace be with you. As the Father has sent me, so I send you ... Receive the holy Spirit. Whose sins you forgive are forgiven them, and whose sins you retain are retained" (Jn 20:21-23).

In administering the Sacrament of Reconciliation a valuable opportunity is offered for evangelization and proclaiming the good news. Indeed, it is in the confessional that every priest, absolving the penitent from the sin that has been committed, becomes a privileged communicator of Divine Mercy which penetrates into the innermost part of every conscience, to the point of provoking the conversion of the heart and the joy of rediscovered salvation. To evangelize is not only to bring a doctrine; it is not only proclaiming the truth. To evangelize is above all else to proclaim the good news of the gospel that is able to touch the hearts of men and to open them to welcoming the love of God:

> A priest who does not foster this aspect of his ministry, both in terms of the amount of time he dedicates to it and in terms of its spiritual quality, is like a shepherd who does not take care of lost sheep; he is like a father who forgets his lost son and neglects to wait for him. But mercy is the heart of the Gospel! Do not forget this: mercy is the heart of the Gospel![34]

[34] Pope Francis, Address to those Taking Part in the Course Organized by the Apostolic Penitentiary, 28 March 2014.

We should bear in mind that one of the most urgent cultural and pastoral challenges that the Church has to address today is to place the subject of conversion, the forgiveness of sins and reconciliation, at the center of every pastoral initiative and activity. We know that in relation to this aspect of Christian faith connected to the "forgiveness of sins," which is an immense gift of the Divine Mercy of the Father, there is present and continues a great difficulty because of a dominant and increasingly growing process of secularization that characterizes the "rich" world but also the poor world as well.

Modern man has great difficulty in listening to the Gospel of the forgiveness of sins. We encounter here a situation of profound crisis that affects both our civilization and our Church. This difficulty that modern man has of recognizing sin and forgiveness also explains, at their roots, the difficulties of the Christian practice of confession or reconciliation. I believe that the anthropological turning point that for years characterized theological thought, catechesis, pastoral care and ecclesial practice after the new Pentecost of the Second Vatican Council, strongly asks us and requires us to start from this observation.

On this point one should stress that it is necessary today, more than ever, for priests to receive a good formation and know at a deep level Church doctrine as it applies to the Sacrament of Reconciliation, as well as relevant canonical practice, so as to achieve the right and correct administration of that sacrament. Since good evangelization also starts from the confessional, we have to retrieve the correct habit of administering the Sacrament of Reconciliation in the confessional. "Let us not forget that the faithful often find it difficult to approach this Sacrament, both for practical reasons and for the natural reticence in confessing their sins to another man. For this reason, it is essential to prepare ourselves, our humanity, in order never to be an obstacle, but rather always to foster their drawing near to mercy and forgiveness."[35]

The Apostolic Penitentiary, because of its special mission of being the first of the Tribunals of the Roman Curia whose responsibilities relate to the sacramental and non-sacramental internal forum, has always been at the service of confessors and penitents. The purpose of the Apostolic Tribunal of mercy and compassion is the reconciliation of a sinner with God and thus it seeks to ensure that the Sacrament of Reconciliation is administered in the right way and is increasingly appreciated. As a part of this undertaking, for the last twenty-nine years the Apostolic Penitentiary has organized a

[35] Ibidem.

course on the internal forum for newly ordained priests and deacons who are about to be ordained so that they acquire a good formation and in-depth knowledge as regards doctrine and the Sacrament of Reconciliation, as well as in relation to canonical and pastoral practice, all with a view to a sound and correct administration of this sacrament. In addition, the Apostolic Penitentiary is always happy to act through its Superiors, Prelates and Officials with papers and talks on the subject of reconciliation at conferences and similar initiatives that are concerned with the Sacrament of Penance. Lastly, since 2008 the Apostolic Penitentiary has organized symposiums whose goal is historical analysis of the theology and pastoral practice of penance.

I have sought to present in summarizing form the theological framework of the salvific work of Christ in the Sacraments, as effective instruments of grace and sanctification in the Church and with the Church, which is their instrument. She is the mystical Body of Christ, also an assembly, which takes advantage of this gift in its individual members on a journey of "Christification" and achievement of their full maturity in Christ (cf. Eph 4:13).

We are aware that although our lives are continuously reached by, and enveloped in, the grace of God through the sacraments, we carry this treasure in "earthenware vessels" (2 Cor 4:7); for the whole of our earthly journeys this "life of grace" is exposed to tiredness, temptation, infidelity and sin. Thus, the Lord Jesus wanted to give to his Church the sacraments of healing that cure the wounds of our personal sins and reconcile us with God and with our brothers and sisters. If it is true that the Church exists to be a sacrament of salvation, and if it is true that her principal mission is to proclaim the Kingdom of God, then this glorious proclaiming produces and sets in motion, first and foremost, a process of healing. The Church is a healing community and is sent by her Lord to "heal the broken-hearted" (Is 61:1; cf. Lk 9:1-2; Mt 10:1,5-14; Mk 6:7-13). Just as a physician bends down to the wounds of the body and cures them, so Christ the Good Samaritan, through the ministry of the Church, bends down every day to the wounds of the soul and the heart and heals them. Precisely with this relationship of the physician and the sick person in mind, St. Augustine, when commenting on the words of the Psalm "God heals all your diseases" (Ps 102:3), explained: "Do not be afraid therefore: all of your infirmities will be healed ... You must only allow him to cure you and you must not reject his hands."[36]

[36] Augustine, *Enarrationes in Psalmos*, 102, 5 (*PL* 36, coll. 1319-1320).

It is equally useful to recall the interesting and stimulating thoughts of Benedict XVI expressed to those taking part in the twenty-second course on the internal forum organized by the Apostolic Penitentiary on the pedagogic value of sacramental confession. They help us to go more deeply into how Christ works in the Church through the sacraments, especially as regards confession:

> I would like to reflect with you on an aspect not sufficiently thought about but which is of great spiritual and pastoral importance: the pedagogical value of Sacramental Confession ... How does the sacrament of Penance educate? In what sense does its celebration have pedagogical value, especially for ministers? We may start by recognizing that the mission of priests is a unique and privileged observation point, from which it is daily granted to contemplate the splendour of divine Mercy. How often in celebrating the sacrament of Penance the priest witnesses real miracles of conversion which, in renewing "the encounter with an event, a person" (*Deus Caritas Est*, n. 1), reinforces his own faith! Basically, hearing confession means witnessing as many *professiones fidei* as there are penitents, and contemplating the merciful God's action in history, feeling tangibly the saving effects of the Cross and of the Resurrection of Christ, in every epoch and for every person ... If, on the one hand knowing and, in a certain way, visiting the depths of the human heart, even its darkest aspects, tests the humanity and the faith of the priest himself, on the other, it fosters within him the certainty that it is God who has the last word over human evil and history, it is his Mercy which can make all things new (cf. Rev 21:5) ... In our time, marked by noise, distraction and loneliness, the penitent's conversation with the confessor can be one of the few — if not the only — opportunities to be truly heard in depth. Dear priests, do not neglect to allow enough room for the exercise of the ministry of Penance in the confessional: to be welcomed and heard is also a human sign of God's welcoming kindness to his children ... Dear priests, our own prior experience of divine Mercy and of being humble instruments teaches us an ever more faithful celebration of

the Sacrament of Penance and profound gratitude to God who "gave us the ministry of reconciliation" (2 Cor 5:18).[37]

[37] Benedict XIV, Address to those Taking Part in the Course Organized by the Apostolic Penitentiary, 25 March 2011.

THE PRIEST WHO PROVIDES FORMATION: A SERVANT AND A WITNESS TO THE MERCIFUL FACE OF GOD

A beautiful and significant phrase of Henri De Lubac, which places our subject in a contemporary context, reads as follows: "Every time that the Church investigates faith, her thought and her theology, she returns to the Fathers."[1] We could, therefore, state that every time attention is paid to the manifestation of the merciful face of God in the lives and the works of the disciples of the Lord, we cannot but return to the founding experience of the Gospel in which the Incarnation appears in all its holiness and beauty, the "rendering visible" of the loving and merciful face of the Father — Jesus Christ.

From the evidence of the New Testament we know that Jesus was very great in words and deeds, and we know that he passed amongst men doing good and healing all of those who were under the power of the devil, because God was with him (cf. Acts 10:38). It is not my intention here to go through all the moments when the Lord Jesus expressed the healing and salvific mercy of the Father towards men. This would be impossible. However, somewhat by way of an introduction, I would like to dwell on two episodes in the gospels where Jesus, through the offering of forgiveness, reconciliation and peace, led men and woman back from spiritual death to new life in God, enabling them to savor how sweet the experience of mercy of God the Father was. In them we can detect, moreover, the Christological and pneumatological features of the being and acting of every Christian and in a special way of the priest who provides formation on the Sacrament of Reconciliation and thus the manifestation of the merciful face of Christ.

[1] H. De Lubac, "La costituzione Lumen gentium e i Padri della Chiesa," in *La teologia dopo il Vaticano II. Apporti dottrinali e prospettive per il futuro in una interpretazione ecumenica*, edited by J.M. Miller (Brescia, 1967), p. 228.

"Neither do I condemn you. Go, (and) from now on do not sin any more" (Jn 8:11). This sentence, I believe, deserves our attention because it represents a summary of the encounter of the infinite breadth of the mercy of God and the reality that Divine Mercy can bring copious fruits of grace and conversion in hearts. This sentence is a consequence of something that has happened that is beyond the conceivable. Jesus works justice but he goes beyond justice because he goes beyond the Law. This law had, in a certain sense, been superseded by the prophet Ezekiel in the advance of the revelation of God. Since Holy Scripture prophesises repentance, penance and conversion, expressing a wider and perfect vision of the heart of God, Jesus forgives the woman but he goes beyond forgiveness because he has re-established her before God and men and points out to her the way of the reconstruction of her authentic humanity.[2] For this reason, this lapidary sentence reminds us that the mercy of the Lord is always with a view to repentance and the conversion of hearts to the Gospel.

"Her many sins have been forgiven; hence, she has shown great love" (Lk 7:47). When reading carefully the passage in the gospel that contains this phrase of forgiveness and mercy of the Lord, we notice that this woman, who is aware of her own condition, goes infinitely beyond what it was fitting to do. She engages in a gesture of very great love for Jesus, a sign of a repentance that is overwhelming her life and projects her into the arms of the merciful love of God which does not delay in expressing itself. The words of forgiveness of Jesus, indeed, give to the life of the woman a new scent, which already began when she went to Jesus to ask for forgiveness, knowing who he was and what he could do for her. The words of the Teacher give redemption to the woman; her heart can now go in peace.

When we draw near to these two paradigmatic episodes of this expression of the mercy of the God who forgives, reconciles to Himself and saves, we encounter the whole of the Face of God which is perfectly present in the Face of Christ: that loving and merciful face that had already been proclaimed in the present-future people of God according to His promise. The promise that He Himself, as the Good Shepherd, would have looked after his flock (cf. Ez 34:11), and that through that unique, holy and perfect model, His Son, He would continue to be present and at work in human shepherds chosen and made according to His heart (cf. Jer 3,15). Here, therefore, is the

[2] Pope Francis, Morning Meditation in the Chapel of *Domus Sanctae Marthae*, 7 April 2014.

authentic image towards which every person who provides formation, especially if he is a priest, must turn and by which he must allow himself to be shaped: a provider of formation according to the heart of God at the service of his fellow men in order to enable them to engage in loving service to evangelical and credible Christian communities and institutions. For these reasons, I want to communicate through this work of a theological-pastoral approach how a priest who is a confessor and shapes consciences, in the light of the Word of God and the recent Magisterium of the Church, should live the ministry of mercy through the Sacrament of Reconciliation as a privileged experience of the merciful love of God, and, as a consequence, teach it as well.

1. At School on the Benches of the Synagogue of Nazareth

Let us imagine for a moment that we, as providers of formation, are attending a refresher course at the synagogue of Nazareth and listening — together with our classmates — to commentary on the passage from Isaiah that the Teacher would shortly address. Jesus had received the Holy Spirit in the waters of the River Jordan and had been consecrated the Messiah of God after expressing his total readiness to do only the will of the heavenly Father and to carry out the plan of salvation prepared since the beginning of time. He is now in Nazareth with the approval of the Father and the power of the Spirit after overcoming the temptations of reneging on what he had promised at the River Jordan. We are in the presence of one of the greatest manifestations of the Most Holy Trinity in the New Testament. When referring to the roll that has just been opened, Jesus declared: "The Spirit of the Lord is upon me, because he has anointed me to bring glad tidings to the poor. He has sent me to proclaim liberty to captives and recovery of sight to the blind, to let the oppressed go free, and to proclaim a year acceptable to the Lord" (Lk 4:18-19). We have gone to the benches of the synagogue to learn from his own voice who Jesus Christ is, what his relationship with the Father and the Holy Spirit is, what his mission of salvation is, and what should animate every process of formation that we intend to plan and carry out in every Church institution, above all in the case of those baptized who are journeying towards ministerial priesthood.

Jesus appears as consecrated through anointing, sent out to proclaim the happy message to the poor; the message that brings liberation from every kind of death to those who are prisoners; and to give light and truth to those blind to God, after freeing them from the oppression of evil and sin, inviting them to allow themselves to be reconciled in a definitive way with God. This is the Face of Christ on which the eyes of all providers of formation must fix their gaze because this is the face of the Messiah-Shepherd promised by God to His people and on which first the synodal Fathers, and then the Apostolic Exhortation of St. John Paul II *Pastores dabo vobis*, reflected to draw fundamental guidelines for the formation of priests in the contemporary world. *Pastores dabo vobis* states that an upright and in-depth knowledge of the nature and the mission of ministerial priesthood is possible only if one has an upright and in-depth knowledge of the priesthood of Jesus Christ himself. Such knowledge is required not only to leave behind the possible crises of identity of a priest which, both during the formation stage and during his activity involving pastoral care, can emerge with a certain regularity, but also to embody in a better way the unique model of priesthood, the only way to follow: the priesthood of Christ, a unique source and irreplaceable paradigm in which a priest takes part through the love of the Father and the power of the Spirit. This is the founding reality from which greater awareness is achieved of the ontological and specific tie that unites a priest to Christ, the High Priest and Good Shepherd.[3]

In essential terms, the reasons why we went to the school of the synagogue of Nazareth are: to understand the specific relationship of a priest with the Trinity, according to the model of Jesus Christ, and to learn from him the difficult art of educating ourselves and future priests about the exercise of charity according to the heart of God. But in particular to liberate people from sin and its sorrowful consequences and to build up an evangelically new life through the work of the Spirit, and this in a particular way in the Sacrament of Reconciliation from which is received the forgiveness of sins and new life in Jesus Christ.

[3] John Paul II, Post-Synodal Apostolic Exhortation *Pastores dabo vobis* (25 March 1992) (hereafter *PDV*), n. 11.

2. Loving, that is to Say Serving According to the Specific Nature of a Priest

We all know that loving in a Christian sense means serving God and our fellows. However, if we read the service of love, above all of a priest, in the light of the truth of love of the Christian God, God who is one and three divine Persons, we can receive a more intense light as regards the exercise of ministry as an expression of the loving mercy of God for people. Here I will attempt to explain, in terms of service, the analysis of the Trinity attempted in the previous part, bringing in what is expounded in the *Directory for the Ministry and the Life of Priests*:

> the priest, by virtue of the consecration received with the sacrament of Holy Orders, is placed in a particular and special relationship with the Father, with the Son and with the Holy Spirit. In fact, "our identity has its ultimate source in the charity of the Father. He sent the Son, High Priest and Good Shepherd, and we are united sacramentally with the ministerial priesthood through the action of the Holy Spirit. The life and ministry of the priest are a continuation of the life and action of the same Christ. This is our identity, our true dignity, the fountain of our joy, the certainty of our life."[4]

A priest who provides formation, specifically because he has a special relationship with each Person of the Trinity, should learn from them the uniqueness — albeit always in communion — of the love expressed by each individual divine Person, from which the priest who provides formation also learns the uniqueness of his way of loving.

During their years of formation, future priests must become increasingly aware of their future identity and their role as witnesses-mediators of the merciful love of God, in Christ in the Spirit, in which emerge the lineaments of the living Face of Christ, a face that attracts, raises up to God and transforms men of all ages.[5]

Indeed, the essence of the divine is characterized by the triple subsistence of the Persons of the Father, of the Son and of the Holy Spirit, in their distinction, through a triple and personal donation.

[4] Congregation for the Clergy, *Directory*, n. 3.

[5] Cf. Benedict XVI, Address at the Sanctuary of the Holy Face of Manoppello, 1 September 2006.

As we know from revelation and dogmatic theology, the divine life is personal-relational life: unique in nature, distinct in the divine Persons and therefore in ways of loving. The Father gives life eternally to the Son through generation: this is the truth of the love of the Father. The Son receives it eternally from the Father and gives it back, not only in eternity but also in time, when he came amongst us, entering history making himself real man with a perfect obedience to the will of the Father and reacquiring for the Father the whole of humanity. This is the truth of the love of the Son. The Holy Spirit is the communion of the truth of the Father, which is the eternal generation of the Son and of the truth of the Son, which is love generated and given to the Father. Starting from this mystery, the three divine Persons love man and each of them give to him the specific reality of their own personal truth.

In God, love is the gift of truth of the individual divine Person; the same law that is lived in God must be lived by every Christian and in a particular way by priests. Thus, the charity of mercy lived by a priest must be the outcome of the gift of the uniqueness of the truth of his person. In order to be able to manifest, according to truth, the merciful love of God, in Christ, in the Holy Spirit, a priest must every day immerse himself in his mysterious and personal being. As happens in God, every priest must live, and make others live, the merciful love of God, starting with the truth of his own person, remaining, indeed growing, in it. In essential terms, a priest can live mercy only as a priest. This is the reason why we went to the school of Nazareth: to know who Jesus Christ is, what the Holy Spirit made him, as well as the style and the ways by which he lived being the Messiah and the Good Shepherd.

3. The Priest who Provides Formation at the Service of the Sacrament of Reconciliation, an Instrument of the Merciful Love of God

Because of the fact that the totality of his person — in virtue of his ordination — is conformed to Jesus Christ, Head and Good Shepherd, the priest who provides formation by his nature is a minister of forgiveness and reconciliation. It is for this reason that he in a special way must make men experience the breadth, the height and the depth of the merciful love of God for them. At the school of Christ one learns and from the school of Christ one teaches in our institutions how to live, through the Sacrament of Reconciliation, the ministry of mercy and how to facilitate the privileged experience of the merciful love of God. I would now like to dwell specifically on this subject.

Man in his daily life is aware of his inability to free himself on his own from sin and obtain mercy and forgiveness. The limitation of our nature appears in all its dramatic character. The attitudes of Jesus the Good Shepherd whom we had an opportunity to listen to at the synagogue of Nazareth, and the examples of his behavior towards forgiven men and women sinners, encounter our experience of limitations and human caducity. Priests who provide formation have an insuperable example to imitate. For this to take place, I believe a choral commitment to formation is needed in order to foster a greater work of "consciousness-raising" about the importance of the ministry of reconciliation in the life of a priest. The formation team should do this during the years of formation of candidates for the priestly ministry. But this should also be done for priests who "navigate" in the ministry of pastoral care, giving value to courses or days dedicated to study or updating that involve subjects and issues inherent in the life and the mission of priests. We are well aware that the crisis that is afflicting the life and the celebration of the sacraments, and especially the Sacrament of Reconciliation, is the ruinous consequence of the crisis of faith that is traversing Christian communities, even though not always to the same extent. This crisis has generated the loss of a sense of God, of man, of his healthy reactions, and of sin itself.[6] Often one notices a watering down of consciousness of sin and its consequences, like the breaking of the Covenant of love with God, the difficulty of feeling and seeing ourselves as disciples and fathers, loved by God. We should not be scandalized if this, in the long term, should also take place in priestly life.

We heard in the synagogue that the Spirit of the Lord came down and remained with Christ; he consecrated him as the Messiah. With his strength, Christ proclaimed the good news of the reconciliation of the Father with humanity and then, in the Cenaculum, he bestowed upon the Apostles the power to forgive sins in his name with the same power of the Spirit. This should help us to penetrate the great mystery of God's merciful love for us, but also through us. The mystery, that is to say, of being and feeling ourselves reconciled before being

[6] Cf. *RP*, n. 18; Conferenza Episcopale Italiana, *Evangelizzazione e sacramenti della Penitenza e dell'Unzione degli infermi* (12 July 1974), nn. 13-14.

instruments of reconciliation and forgiveness; the experience of being loved before proclaiming the merciful love of God which goes well beyond our hearts. And what is the most beautiful and significant way of educating in this dynamism of love if not loving it personally as priests? The words of St. John Paul II, taken from the *Directory for the Ministry and Life of Priests,* are truly of contemporary relevance. He states that priests, ministers of the Sacrament of Penance, become themselves "witnesses of God's mercy toward sinners ... The priest's spiritual and pastoral life, like that of his brothers and sisters, lay and religious, depends, for its quality and fervor, on the frequent and conscientious personal practice of the Sacrament of Penance."[7] As a consequence, "If a priest were no longer to go to confession or properly confess his sins, his *priestly being* and his *priestly action* would feel its effects very soon and this would also be noticed by the community of which he was the pastor."[8] The ways by which a priest shows the beauty, as well as the holiness, of the ministry of reconciliation thus appear clear and feasible: his personal witness, which should precede the other faithful in experiencing the greatness of the forgiveness of God, is said to be also the first condition for a pastoral reassessment of the Sacrament of Reconciliation.[9]

For this reason, I would like to clarify certain points, in valuing which a priest who provides formation, in the celebration of the ministry of mercy, not only experiences the mercy of God but also becomes its valuable and important instrument.

3.1. *The Importance of the Formation of a Priest in the Sacrament of Penance*

I would like to take up the words of St. John Paul II who, in one of the very many messages that he addressed to the Apostolic Penitentiary, invited priests who hear confessions to return to the experience of the Cenaculum to rediscover the deep motivation behind their formation as ministers of the mercy of God and administrators of the Sacrament of Reconciliation. Theology highlights that a holy minister acts *in persona Christi*[10] and the experience of the outpouring of the Spirit in the Cenaculum, after the resurrection, took place beforehand

[7] *PDV*, n. 26.

[8] *RP*, n. 31.

[9] Cf. Congregation for the Clergy, *Directory*, n. 53.

[10] Cf. ibid., n. 10.

for the apostles specifically in relation to the ministry of the forgiveness of sins. Thus, this Pope and saint states: "We priests, in imparting to the faithful the grace and the forgiveness of the Sacrament of Penance, perform the highest act after the celebration of the Eucharist of our priesthood, and in it we accomplish, one may say, the purpose itself of the Incarnation."[11] Therefore, in absolving in what is the ministry of mercy to the utmost, the priest who provides formation goes beyond the forgiveness of sins, advancing to achieving almost a mystic identification with Jesus Christ. This is why St. John Paul II in his *Pastores dabo vobis* refers to the urgent need to rediscover in the spiritual formation of priests the beauty and the joy of the Sacrament of Reconciliation. Indeed, he asserts that there is an urgent need "to educate future priests to have the virtue of penance, which the Church wisely nourishes in her celebrations and in the seasons of the liturgical year, and which finds its fullness in the sacrament of reconciliation. From it flow a sense of asceticism and interior discipline, a spirit of sacrifice and self-denial, and an acceptance of hard work and of the cross."[12]

However, although, on the one hand, it is important or urgent to educate future priests in the beauty of penance, which finds its fullness in the Sacrament of Reconciliation, it is equally urgent to educate them in loving dedication to this sacrament, aware that this passion will be truly involving in line with how much Divine Mercy is personally experienced. As regards this last assertion, there comes to my mind the paradigmatic experience of Paul (cf. 1 Tm 1:12-16). The Apostle to the Gentiles knows that he has been a blasphemer because he dishonored the person of Christ, combatting his truth and his grace, his body — the Church. He knows that he has also been a persecutor of Christ, attacking the lives of his disciples. In him, there is a desire for truth, but not knowledge of truth; his conscience, and thus his knowledge, were deformed. But something special happens in his life that means that his story is transformed into a proclaiming of faith, into a profession of faith. Paul moves out of his situation of spiritual death, which generated other forms of death, through the grace of Christ and the mercy of God. If through his forgiveness and his mercy the Lord saved him, a sinner, this means that the Lord wants to save every sinner, without distinctions. Sinners are called to conversion and to salvation, on the condition that that they allow

[11] John Paul II, Address to the Penitentiaries of the Patriarchal Basilicas of Rome, 20 March 1989.

[12] *PDV*, n. 48.

themselves to be reconciled and saved by Him. Paul certainly does not speak about eschatological salvation: with reference to his experience he speaks about salvation already in time, as a passage from the shadows to light, from sin to grace. Hence his greater awareness of — and total involvement in — the mission entrusted to him by the Lord: that of being proclaimers of the Word of reconciliation and servants of the ministry of reconciliation (cf. 2 Cor 5:18-21).

This is the reason why the Magisterium emphasizes educating ourselves as priests and educating not only in theological-sacramental knowledge of the Sacrament of Reconciliation and its health-inducing effects but also through dedicating "time and energy to hearing the confessions of the faithful, who, as experience demonstrates, come freely to receive this sacrament as long as there are priests available."[13]

3.2. *The Art of Accompanying (Providing Formation to) Those Who Draw Near to the Sacrament of Forgiveness*

The other great aspect that I am keen to emphasize in relation to the priest who provides formation is the art of spiritually *accompanying* those who draw near to the sacrament of forgiveness. The relationship of nearness through the sign of pastoral accompanying is the challenge that makes the proclaiming of the mercy of Christ credible. I wish to dwell upon the mission of accompanying our fellow men pastorally as a singular expression of the ministry of mercy that concerns the priest who provides formation from close at hand in a particular way.

In *Evangelii gaudium* the word "accompany" often appears.[14] The message of Pope Francis is that the maternal mercy of the Church is not a "part" of evangelization. A mother halts what she is doing and turns from her worries to her child. In the same way the Church moves, together with the merciful Jesus, towards those who have been abandoned.[15] There must be a serious approach towards every person and their divinely given project; there must be no pastoral apathy, with its generation of not accompanying the poorest and those who seek reconciliation with the Church and with God. Pope Francis invokes the "art of accompanying." This means above

[13] Congregation for the Clergy, *Directory*, n. 52.

[14] Cf. *EG*, nn. 12, 25, 44, 46, 69-70, 76, 99, 103, 169-173, 199, 214, 241, 286.

[15] Cf. ibid., n. 46; Pope Francis, Encyclical Letter *Lumen fidei* (29 June 2013) (hereafter *LF*), n. 37.

all else respecting the holy ground of other people, adopting the health-giving effects of proximity, and with mercy and valuing the dignity of others attending to their needs when this is required.[16] With caring eyes fixed on his flock, the Holy Father refers to practical forms of accompanying. Mercy cannot be without preparation and vulnerable to being unhelpful. Being close to people, in the view of Pope Francis, has certain specific requisites: the pastor must be prudent, attentive in listening, and communicate the mystery of earthly existence.[17]

Since accompanying tells the truth about interpersonal relationships with the intent of *service* (another aspect of accompanying), the Supreme Pontiff refers to the example of the Good Shepherd in order to be a witness to the living experience of mercy in the encounter with Christ.

For this reason, the Pope invites priests, whether they are providers of formation or confessors, not to feel owners of the sacrament of forgiveness but to welcome the faithful like the father in the parable of the prodigal son. A father who waits, goes forward, clasps, forgives, forgets and re-establishes; a father who knows how to grasp, from one heart to another, the invocation of help and forgiveness.[18] Here the two episodes of the two sinful women who are forgiven, about which I spoke to begin with, are illuminating and significant.

The Church, and in her each one of us, in the spirit of *Evangelii gaudium* is called to be a setting for freely given mercy where everyone can feel welcomed, loved, forgiven and encouraged to live according to the good life of the gospel,[19] but also a place where every person and their processes of growth are taken seriously. She is the setting from which, and in which, the invitation to allow oneself to be reconciled with God (cf. 2 Cor 5:20) and abandon oneself to the arms of His mercy through the Sacrament of Reconciliation must continuously re-echo. This sacrament of healing — suitably prepared and celebrated — manifests through the mediation of the Church the tender face of the mercy of God, the compassion of the love of Christ in the Spirit. This is because it raises up from spiritual death, creates a new life, cures and relieves the wounds of a heart offended by sin, bandages it and stewards it through the mercy that has been

[16] Cf. *EG*, n. 169.

[17] Cf. ibid., nn. 171-172.

[18] Cf. ibid., n. 67.

[19] Cf. ibid., n. 114.

received.[20] The *Catechism of the Catholic Church*, quoting *Lumen Gentium* n. 11, states that "Those who approach the sacrament of Penance obtain pardon from God's mercy for the offence committed against him, and are, at the same time, reconciled with the Church which they have wounded by their sins and which by charity, by example, and by prayer labors for their conversion."[21] One draws near to this sacrament because, through grace, one becomes aware of one's own misery, one sees the days of humiliation and shame provoked by sin, and one perceives the wish to return to communion with the heavenly Father and a nostalgia to share in His merciful tenderness in His home.[22]

In engaging in this analysis, referring to the very high ministry of a priest who provides formation in a specific way as witness to, and educator in, the mercy of God through the Sacrament of Reconciliation, I have advanced with a special perspective: looking at the theological-sacramental truth of the priest who provides formation one can identify with greater precision the being and the forming style of the Lord Jesus who as the Good Shepherd and provider of formation to the apostles of all ages and places points out to us the art, the motivations and the talents/virtues that every priest who provides formation must possess. It is true that through grace the good Lord continues to give us "shepherds with His heart." However, it is also true that every priest who provides formation needs to enrich himself continuously in the specific training of being an educator because "seminary educators occupy the key position that determines the spirit and efficacy of the work of formation."[23] We have spoken about the need to become more aware of the truth of being priests and of the ministry that the Lord entrusts to us as providers of formation. For this reason, we went to the synagogue of Nazareth. But we have also spoken about the need to walk forward in the art of accompanying those whom the Church entrusts to us in the work of formation as regards the Sacrament of Reconciliation. The *Ratio* of 1985 itself stated that the mission of the providers of formation is the "art of arts."[24]

[20] Cf. *MV*, n. 15.

[21] *CCC*, n. 1422.

[22] Cf. *RP*, n. 5.

[23] Congregation for Catholic Education, *Directives on the Preparation of Seminary Educators* (4 November 1993), n. 1.

[24] EAD, *Ratio fundamentalis institutionis sacerdotalis* (19 March 1985), n. 30.

And yet I am convinced that there is no better lecture hall in which to learn, and as a consequence to teach, the beauty of the experience of Divine Mercy than knowledge of the things of God and personal experience. For the doctrinal, spiritual, pedagogic and pastoral training of a priest who provides formation to be truly effective, every priest must often go back to attending the school of the merciful love of Christ in the womb of Mother Church. It is no accident that at the outset we referred to some paradigmatic episodes in which was manifested the greatness of the forgiveness of God in Christ, he who in his own person experienced, and continues today through the activity of priestly ministry to make us experience, the deep mercy of the Father for us. I have presented the ministry of mercy through formation in, and experience of, the Sacrament of Reconciliation and this because in our lives as priests we always perceive the need to contemplate the mystery of mercy.[25] The "ministry and the mystery of mercy" is not a clever linguistic formula. It is a single reality of theology and formation by which, through continuous experience of welcoming and the exercise of the sacrament of forgiveness, our lives as providers of formation acquire the scent of that credibility and those responsibilities that we seek and desire in order to be increasingly pastors with the heart of Christ.

[25] Cf. *MV*, n. 2.

THE SACRAMENT OF PENANCE: AN APOSTOLATE OF MERCY. SOME GUIDELINES FOR CONFESSORS

As everybody knows, Pope Francis lays a great deal of emphasis on communicating that God is infinite mercy because he wants to generate in the hearts of men and women of good will the trust and the hope that in life changes are always possible. The Supreme Pontiff wanted to center his meditation of the General Audience of 19 February 2014 on the importance and the beauty of the Sacrament of Reconciliation, the Sacrament of Penance, which he defined as a "sacrament of healing" because, the Pope observed, "When I go to confession, it is in order to be healed, to heal my soul, to heal my heart and to be healed of some wrongdoing." Indeed, he emphasized that:

> celebrating the Sacrament of Reconciliation means being enfolded in a warm embrace: it is the embrace of the Father's infinite mercy. Let us recall that beautiful, beautiful parable of the son who left his home with the money of his inheritance. He wasted all the money and then, when he had nothing left, he decided to return home, not as a son but as a servant. His heart was filled with so much guilt and shame. The surprise came when he began to speak, to ask for forgiveness, his father did not let him speak, he embraced him, he kissed him, and he began to make merry. But I am telling you: each time we go to confession, God embraces us. God rejoices![1]

How can we not also remember St. John Paul II who in indicating authoritatively the priorities of the Church on her journey towards the third millennium exhorted us to engage in a rediscovery and celebration of the Sacrament of Penance in its most authentic

[1] Pope Francis, General Audience, 19 February 2014.

meaning: "The call to conversion as the indispensable condition of Christian love is particularly important in contemporary society, where the very foundations of an ethically correct vision of human existence often seem to have been lost."[2]

Current and future pastors of souls cannot but share this concern: let us think of the very many members of the faithful who encounter a great deal of difficulty in understanding and living the sacrament of conversion.

Every priest, every pastor of souls, must be intimately convinced that the rediscovery and the full valuing of the Sacrament of Penance also depends to a great extent on priests and their awareness that they are the custodians of a valuable and irreplaceable ministry.

As St. John Paul II declared: "We priests in imparting to the faithful the grace and the forgiveness of the Sacrament of Penance perform the highest act, after the celebration of the Eucharist, of our priesthood. I want therefore to affectionately exhort all priests ... to attribute in the hierarchy of their tasks a privileged role to the silent and not always gratifying service of confession."[3]

It is absolutely necessary, to exercise well and faithfully his ministry, for every confessor, with assiduous study, under the guidance of the Magisterium of the Church and above all with prayer, to obtain the learning and the prudence needed for this task.

On this point, Benedict XVI, in his address to the course on the internal forum organized by the Apostolic Penitentiary in 2010, exhorted priests "to dedicate themselves generously to hearing sacramental confessions; to guide the flock courageously so that it does not conform to the mindset of this world (cf. Rom 12:2) but may even be able to make decisions that run counter to the tide, avoiding adjustments and compromises. For this reason it is important that priests have a constant aspiration to ascetism, nourished by communion with God, and that they tirelessly dedicate themselves to keeping up to date in the study of moral theology and the human sciences."[4]

There is an abundant literature on penance as a sacrament. No sacrament has had such a long and complex development as the Sacrament of Penance. The Church, during her history of many centuries,

[2] John Paul II, Apostolic Letter *Tertio millennio adveniente* (10 November 1994), n. 50.

[3] John Paul II, Address to the Penitentiaries of the Patriarchal Basilicas of Rome, 20 March 1989.

[4] Benedict XIV, Address to those Taking Part in the Course Organized by the Apostolic Penitentiary, 11 March 2010.

has always been aware that only God can forgive sins (cf. Mk 2:7). However, one had to wait until the Council of Trent for a clear and overall formulation by the Magisterium of the Catholic Church on the Sacrament of Penance. It is certainly the case that at that moment the concern was to respond to Protestant doctrine on the subject, but it would be wrong to read the teaching of the Council of Trent solely in these terms. The teaching that comes to us from that council, beyond the response to the Protestants, remains a point of reference because of its doctrinal authoritativeness.

On the basis of the Council of Trent and after the Second Vatican Council, the liturgical and disciplinary rules of the Sacrament of Penance were reformulated in the *Ordo Paenitentiae* of 1974, in the *Code of Canon Law* (can. 959 for the question of absolution, cann. 961-963), in the *Code of Eastern Churches* (cann. 718-736), as well as in the post-synodal Apostolic Exhortation *Reconciliatio et Paenitentia* (nn. 28-34). All of these texts subsequent to the Second Vatican Council involve liturgical, disciplinary and pastoral applications. As regards the doctrine of the faith and this sacrament, the doctrine and the canons of the Council of Trent have remained the relevant normative foundations.

Special attention is paid to the priest who is the minister of reconciliation, that is to say the person who offers the possibility of the mercy of the Lord, even if he cannot always perform this mandate. A bishop can reserve to himself certain cases of absolution. As regards censures and the so-named "reservation," there are a significant number of people, including priests, who believe that the canon law that disciplines this reservation is too restrictive; that it has, that is to say, a somewhat bureaucratic character. Whereas we know well that the reservation has above all a pedagogic function: it teaches a member of the faithful the gravity of sins, also through the obligation to address those in the Church who have a higher authority as regards the absolution of certain sins.

In the context of the challenges that the Sacrament of Penance poses, the priestly ministry of confession is a demanding service, one that is difficult but also exalting. It makes visible the merciful love of God the Father in the confessional and is one of the most gripping aspects of the priestly ministry, although it is also a responsibility that requires — above all today — an in-depth knowledge of what the doctrine of the Church teaches. Indeed, in the confessional special cases can present themselves that require, for example, a suitable knowledge of bioethics, and a priest, therefore, can find himself in difficulty. In such cases, he can request a little time before expressing a view on the question and consult the Apostolic Penitentiary which enters the picture in situations where the priest does not have the faculty to absolve and in cases where he may not be sufficiently informed and is ill at ease. The training in doctrine of the confessor should be such as to allow him at least to perceive the possible existence of a problem. In this case, pastoral prudence, united to humility, taking account of the urgency of the matter or otherwise and of the worry or otherwise of the penitent, will lead him to decide whether to send the penitent to another confessor or fix an appointment for a new meeting and, in the meantime, inform himself on the question. Always engaging in absolute respect for the sacramental seal, it is advised that in the meantime he has recourse to priests who have more experience and in particular to the Apostolic Penitentiary, which is always ready to offer for concrete and thus individual cases its service of consultation — a service which has authoritative value.

In the exercise of the ministry of reconciliation, priests must seek to carry out their mission of being fathers, advisers, "judges" and animators, in harmony with the doctrine of the Magisterium of the Church, obtaining the necessary learning for this purpose and proceeding with prudence, discretion, discernment and goodness. What must be avoided is creating "anxiety" as regards the sin or a "guilt complex" in the penitent who, in opposite fashion, needs to be encouraged to place all of their trust in the infinite mercy of God. A confession of sins that is authentically Christian, precisely because it restores or intensifies participation in the life of the Trinity, must break forth into a joyous song of praise and gratitude for the Father who "first loved us" (1 Jn 4:19).

In a priest greatness and poverty live together in an ongoing way; at times greatness and abject realities also live together.

Greatness ... because of the powers that God has given to him; poverty or some grave abject realities because of his limitations as a man or a frail being.

The human dimension of the priest, with his good aspects and his defects, has a notable influence in the confessional, indeed more than in any other sacrament.

Every priest who has received this faculty from the Church can validly absolve a sinner who, being repentant, confesses their sins to him. However, often penitents do not only need forgiveness. They may also need light to illuminate certain "dark areas" of their conscience; they may need strong stimuli or an authentic shake-up so as not to go on being rooted in sin; they may need some words of encouragement which give them peace of mind and help them to believe that with the help of God they can get through and change their lives; they may need some words of comfort at a moment of pain or a friendly presence that gives them a sense of security and comfort at a moment of hopelessness ... And a confessor can transmit all of this only if he has achieved his own human maturity, good moral and Christian formation, and if he cultivates a healthy spiritual and priestly life. The personal character of the man who is this priest cannot enter, for good or evil, his relationship with the penitent.

The same may be said about his sensitivity and spirituality as a Christian. As a sinner, who needs, like other people, the forgiveness of God, how does he see, how does he feel, and how does he experience his own confession? If he experiences it as a regeneration and restoration of his soul, then he is able to understand what treasure the Lord has placed in his hands for his brothers and sisters.

And as a priest what spiritual, cultural and pastoral formation has he received? If Christ and the good of his brothers and sisters (above all their spiritual and eternal good) are his constant concern, then there are the requisites for that priest to be a good confessor as well.

1. Being Ministers of Reconciliation is not an Easy Task

Exercising the ministry of confessions — as has already been observed — is one of the most difficult and tiring tasks of a priest because, albeit with all the influences that come from his history and from his contemporary situation, he has to relate to people whom most of the time he does not know and who are different from each other. In addition, frequently he only has a little time to deal with complex situations and the penitents themselves often do very little to help him to understand the truth of their situations.

He has to be equipped with sensitive antennae to detect situations of frailty, anxiety and pain, or situations of superficiality, arrogance or pride that often a penitent does not make known.

In addition, with every person whose confession he is hearing the priest must know how to cast off his personal state of mind, or that of the person who had confessed a short time previously, so as to enter as much as is possible into empathy with the penitent who is there at that moment.

This continuous emptying and filling of himself, this moving from one state of mind to another, requires a human and psychological elasticity that nobody is endowed with as a gift of nature and which easily generates an interior tiredness.

Those priests who regularly and for hours face up to the "hard work" of the confessional thus deserve our great admiration and gratitude.

Understanding is also required for those priests who on occasions, without wanting it, allow the penitent to detect some sign of tiredness or tension from their words or their tone of voice. In this case, it is not so much readiness to help or generosity that are absent in the priest — perhaps it is just a matter of "run-down batteries," namely tiredness and nothing else.

But in some priests there are attitudes that do not come from a particular state of mind or from a state of tension and which are therefore much more troubling.

2. The Negative Attitudes of Some Confessors

Hurry — In order "not to lose too much time" some confessors deal with their penitents as hurriedly as they can, at times even preventing them from ending an account of their sins, or anyway without dedicating to those sins the attention and the time that are necessary.

Those who wish to confess experience the hurry of the priest with suffering and are disappointed by him, and this is even more the case if in addition to confessing their sins they wanted to present some problem to the priest.

Certain other penitents, on the other hand, are very happy to deal with things hurriedly because in his way they can get through things without too much trouble, without being invited to look inside themselves and above all else without any commitment to conversion.

However, both the first, who are disappointed, and the second, who are satisfied, remain gravely damaged by this behavior of the priest. The first because they leave the confessional without that light of truth or without those words of comfort that they hoped to find; the second because they go on living in their sins with peace of mind, not in the least disturbed by that very light of truth that they desired … not to receive.

Boredom — Some confessors can give penitents the impression of being absent. In this case, the person engaging in confession senses a detachment, almost indifference, on the part of the priest; they feel that they are treated more as a "number" than as a person and this certainly does not facilitate openness.

Not being very available — The Christian community needs to know when, how and where to find a priest for confessions but there are rather few parishes who provide precise indications as to place and time so that the faithful can go knowing that they will find a confessor.

Thus members of the faithful who need and wish to "unload" their burden continue with their "raft" and their interior suffering for who knows how long.

Excessive harshness — Believing that they are serving the truth and doing good to souls, it may be the case that some confessors use severe language without justification, forgetting that confession is essentially the sacrament of mercy. A certain harshness is useful and necessary with the falsely repentant, with those who more than converting would like to "convert" the priest and convince him that their vices … are not vices but virtues. Such a situation is experienced ever more frequently today in the confessional.

Yet with those who sin because of weakness, recognize they own sin and have a wish to free themselves of it, all the goodness, understanding and encouragement possible is needed.

Do-goodery — Often the confessor displays an exaggerated sensitivity. This is not an example of authentic goodness that derives from a wish to communicate mercy but an approach that is produced by apprehension about being truthful and direct with the penitent. Balm is thus given in cases where forceful phrases are needed. An appropriate evaluation of the state of the soul is put to one side and an exaggerated and erroneous emphasis is placed on the benevolence of the Lord. When a confessor does this, he does not benefit the penitent spiritually. Quite the opposite — a disfigurement of the conscience is generated.

In the confessional dressed in civilian clothes? — The Church rightly wants the priest to be always clearly recognizable, in his way of dressing as well, and to this end has established precise rules.

When a priest is engaged in liturgical activity, the Church obliges him, even more firmly, to wear holy vestments, that is to say clothes that help the faithful to perceive more easily the sacredness of the activity they are about to engage in.

Moreover, the vestments wanted by the Church help to reduce the human personhood of the priest, almost to the point of him disappearing as a person, so that the majesty of he who the minister represents appears to greater effect — Jesus Christ, our Lord and Savior.

When a priest hears confession, it is Jesus who acts in him; it is Jesus who listens to the humble expression of the penitent of his sins and it is always Jesus who absolves.

The Church imposes on a priest who hears confession the wearing of vestments (not a dog collar and even less any kind of clothes) and on these vestments also a stole. Except when there are urgent cases, which can occur in unforeseen circumstances, any variant on what the Church wants is an arbitrary act that is completely unjustified, a choice that does not help but, instead, obstructs the recourse of the faithful to the sacrament of confession.

How can a priest educate penitents in obedience to God (because although it does not do only this, confession aims at this as well), if he sets a bad example of disobedience to the rules and the laws of the Church?

3. The Graver Sins

The uselessness of confession — It is not unusual to hear someone say: "I went to confess and the priest, seeing that I had not committed any sin, a little discontented said to me: don't come to confession for these trifles!"

To ask for and receive forgiveness, are a few venial sins not sufficient? Does one perhaps have to commit grave and mortal sins to draw near to the Sacrament of Reconciliation?

According to these "not very prudent" pastors, confession would not have any meaning or any usefulness for those who have not committed grave sins.

As regards "old ladies" or children, for some priests confession would be practically useless: for children because "they are not yet able to commit mortal sins" and for "old ladies" because "they are no longer able to commit them."

What would these "wise" pastors of souls say if in their homes their maids did the most demanding cleaning and did not dust the furniture? Would they be happy? And would they be prepared to pay her?

There is a great deal of talk about hygiene of the body, but some pastors do not even know what hygiene of the soul is!

And they do not realize that with these methods they make the faithful lose the sense of sin and they distance them even more from the sacrament of forgiveness, so that gradually they no longer go to confession, with the consequence that:

a) Those who are in a state of moral sin remain so, perhaps for many years or until the end of their lives, with what could follow for eternity.

b) Those who have only committed venial sins are denied the most valuable help there is to correct their less good inclinations as well as the increase in grace that they could obtain through confession.

No penance — A number of people at times ask what they should do if the priest who has heard their confession does not assign them a penance. It is advisable to remember that a priest has no right to omit the penance — it is not an optional but an integral part of the Sacrament of Confession.

Nobody authorizes the priest to commit this grave omission, this out-of-place discount. He must always remember that he cannot behave as a master of the sacrament: he is its servant.

4. Absolution Guaranteed!

At times some confessors ask how they should behave in cases where the penitent says that they have no intention of changing their behavior in very grave cases. There are some priests who argue that "one should not deny absolution to anybody. We are ministers of mercy, not of severity. If someone comes to confess this means that after a certain fashion they have repented!"

When we think of the words of Jesus "Whose sins you forgive are forgiven them, and whose sins you retain are retained" (Jn 20:23), this is not the way things are. Indeed, Jesus posited the refusal of forgiveness, not thinking of some possible whim of a confessor but because he knew, better than us, that there can be grave and objective reasons for denying absolution.

We are ministers of mercy! This is certainly true. But is mercy deceiving a sinner and making them believe that they have set themselves right with the Lord even if they continue to sin as before? And are we not also, and above all else, ministers of truth and not ministers of lies?

Invalid absolutions — At times there is a confessor who uses words for an absolution that are different from those laid down by the Church, for example "In His great love God forgives you your sins, go in peace," not making any reference to the three persons of the Most Holy Trinity, to the Father, the Son and the Holy Spirit.

The Baptism given by Protestants is valid because it is administered "in the name of the Father, the Son and the Holy Spirit" (according to the formula established by Jesus). The baptism of Jehovah's Witnesses is not valid because it is imparted in the name of "Jehovah" (God) without any reference to the Divine Persons. An absolution imparted in the name of a vague and "ecumenical" God, who is certainly not the God of Jesus Christ, is invalid.

The Gospel distorted and betrayed —The greatest distortion and damage takes place when a priest, a confessor, reassures the penitent in a misleading way, not speaking to them, that is to say, about the goodness of God: "Bear up, the Lord forgives you. You say that you are worried, what you told me you did is not a sin." And thus, thanks to an imprudent confessor who from being a "bearer of salvation" is transformed into a "corruptor of consciences," in some confessionals sexual relations before marriage, contraception, adultery, a new cohabitation after divorce, homosexual relations, and very many other miseries of the human heart, are "baptized" as licit.

It may occur that penitents return to confess their mortal sins again, being disappointed at the fact that another priest had not seen them as such. Although, on the one hand, the sensitivity of the consciences of these people (who for that matter were not obliged to confess anew) is moving, on the other thinking about the responsibility of those priests who are not truthful, are enemies of God and traitors to the Gospel, is deeply troubling.

5. The Principal Characteristics of a Good Confessor

The priest who is a confessor must also try to be what Jesus was for the sinners that he encountered on his journey. The penitent has the right to see in him not only the powers but also the Heart of Jesus.

As regards the characteristics of a good confessor, how can we not remember that great "saint and confessor" Alphonsus Maria Liguori who in his *Moral Works* describes the "tasks of a confessor": a *father* who welcomes, a *physician* who cures, a *teacher* (or doctor) who educates, a *judge* who uses mercy.[5]

A father — The confessor must have a great capacity for welcome and fatherly love towards every penitent and above all else towards "lost" sons who return from very far away. The father of the "prodigal son" is a lesson here.

He is a true father because he regenerates and increases in the soul of the penitent the life of grace. This paternity of his, which is like a shadow of the paternity of God, must emerge clearly from his way of doing things.

The confessor is fully a "father" if he regenerates the repentant members of the faithful not only with the grace that comes from on high but also through his contribution of being a good example, prayer and expiation.

A judge — The confessor must not be like the judges of this world, who ascertain whether in the accused there is guilt to be punished by a sentence. He must be a judge who discerns if in a soul there are the conditions to receive the forgiveness of the Lord; a judge who works according to the justice of God by applying mercy. Pope Francis observes:

> The ministers of the Church must be merciful, take responsibility for people, accompanying them like the Good Samaritan who washes, cleans and raises up his neighbor. This is pure Gospel. God is greater than sin. Organizational and structural reforms are secondary, that is to say they come afterwards. The first reform must be that of the approach. The ministers of the Gospel must be people who are capable of warming the hearts of people, to walk in the night with them, to know how to engage in dialogue and also to descend into their nights, into their darkness without getting lost. The people of God want pastors and not state functionaries or clerics.[6]

[5] A.M. Liguori, *Practice of the Confessor to Exercise well his Ministry.*

[6] "Intervista a Papa Francesco," p. 462.

A physician — "Those who are well do not need a physician, but the sick do" (Mt 9:12). Man is sick in the depths of his being and the effects are often seen in how he behaves.

The authentic physician is Jesus. The priest is a physician as well, but only by his delegation, with his powers and his therapies. Or, to put it another way, Jesus is the consultant and the priest is his assistant. Thus only in this way, as a good physician, can he heal "the maladies of the soul" of those penitents who draw near to the Sacrament of Reconciliation with the desire to be freed from the sin that worries them and afflicts them.

A teacher — "make disciples of all nations ... teaching them to observe all that I have commanded you" (Mt 28:19-20). Thus a priest is and must be a teacher of virtue in the confessional as well, a teacher who proposes anew the teaching of Jesus about what is good and what is bad, without any power of interpreting gospel truth according to his own way of seeing things.

In addition to these principal requirements, I would like to point out others that are no less important, like being an educator of the conscience and a brother on the journey of conversion.

An educator of consciences — In administrating the Sacrament of Penance, the confessor performs the delicate task of forming and illuminating the conscience of the penitent. There come to mind those intense words that St. Pope John Paul II used in his Apostolic Exhortation *Reconciliatio et Paenitentia* to emphasize the human and spiritual qualities of a confessor who is always also an educator of consciences:

> the confessor must necessarily have human qualities of prudence, discretion, discernment and a firmness tempered by gentleness and kindness. He must likewise have a serious and careful preparation, not fragmentary but complete and harmonious, in the different branches of theology, pedagogy and psychology, in the methodology of dialogue and above all in a living and communicable knowledge of the word of God. But it is even more necessary that he should live an intense and genuine spiritual life. In order to lead others along the path of Christian perfection the minister of penance himself must first travel this path. More by actions than by long speeches he must give proof of real experience of lived prayer, the practice of the theological and moral

> virtues of the Gospel, faithful obedience to the will of God, love of the church and docility to her magisterium.[7]

A brother — "If your brother sins ... tell him his fault" (Mt 18:15). Thus no one is more your brother than he who admonishes you, reproves you and corrects you in order to free you from sin which is the worst of evils. One should always see a priest in this light, but above all when he is in the confessional.

The history of the Church shines with the light of very many saints who were saints and spent their lives in the confessional. I am thinking of St. John Vianney, St. Joseph Cafasso, St. Leopold Mandić, St. Pio of Pietrelcina and very many others whom only the Lord knew. Did they waste their time? The answer comes to us from the flow of people whom they moved and brought back to the arms of the Father.

It is there in the penumbra of the confessional that they reignited a wish for God in so many souls and reawakened so many hibernating Christians to the divine life. It is there that they obtained amazing conversions and shaped other saints.

On this point I would like recall that during the thirteenth ordinary general assembly of the Synod of Bishops (2012) it was emphasized that the confessional is a privileged place for evangelization and the transmission of the faith and healthy doctrine. Here I would like to remember resolution n. 33 of the list of final resolutions of the general assembly of that Synod of Bishops:

> The Sacrament of Penance and Reconciliation is the privileged place to receive God's mercy and forgiveness. It is a place for both personal and communal healing. In this sacrament, all the baptized have a new and personal encounter with Jesus Christ, as well as a new encounter with the Church, facilitating a full reconciliation through the forgiveness of sins. Here the penitent encounters Jesus, and at the same time he or she experiences a deeper appreciation of himself and herself. The Synod Fathers ask that this sacrament be put again at the centre of the pastoral activity of the Church.[8]

When speaking about the principal characteristics of a good confessor, how can we not remember here the important words that

[7] *RP*, n. 29.

[8] Synod of Bishops, *XIII Ordinary General Assembly. Final List of Resolutions*, n. 33.

Pope Francis pronounced during his meeting with the parish priests and the priests of the clergy of Rome of 6 March 2014? The Holy Father, in addition to remembering the perception of St. John Paul II that for the whole of the Church "this was the time of mercy" emphasized that:

> The priest reveals a heart especially in administering the Sacrament of Reconciliation; he reveals it by his whole attitude, by the manner in which he welcomes, listens, counsels and absolves... But this comes from how he experiences the Sacrament firsthand, from how he allows himself to be embraced by God the Father in Confession and remains in this embrace.... If one experiences this in one's own regard, in his own heart, he can also give it to others in his ministry... The priest is called to learn this, to have a heart that is moved... Neither the laxist nor the rigorist bears witness to Jesus Christ, for neither the one nor the other takes care of the person he encounters. The rigorist washes his hands of them: in fact, he nails the person to the law, understood in a cold and rigid way; and the laxist also washes his hands of them: he is only apparently merciful, but in reality he does not take seriously the problems of that conscience, by minimizing the sin. True mercy *takes the person into one's care*, listens to him attentively, approaches the situation with respect and truth, and accompanies him on the journey of reconciliation.[9]

I will end this section with the words of the Holy Father Francis at the press conference on the return flight from the World Youth Day (28 July 2013): "I believe that this is the season of mercy ... The Church is a mother: she has to go out to heal those who are hurting, with mercy. If the Lord never tires of forgiving, we have no other choice than this: first of all, to care for those who are hurting. The Church is a mother, and she must travel this path of mercy. And find a form of mercy for all."[10]

---

[9] Pope Francis, Address to the Parish Priests of Rome, 6 March 2014.

[10] Pope Francis, Press Conference on the Return Flight from Brazil, 28 July 2013.

THE SACRAMENTAL SEAL IN CANON LAW

The Church has always attributed a special relevance to confidentiality in the encounter between a member of the faithful and the priest in the administration of the Sacrament of Penance. The defence of what would be called "the sacramental secrecy" of confession is bound up with the historical development of the form of this sacrament. With the progressive disappearance of public penance, the introduction of the privately heard confession, which was already general practice at the end of the twelfth century, in the form that we know today, acquired particular relevance, as did the development of canonical discipline of confession in its specifically juridical — and not only theological and moral — forms. The history of the sacramental seal goes back to as early as the ancient Church and Ambrose, Augustine, Aphrahat and Origen all spoke about it. During the high Middle Ages, Hincmar of Reims, and Lanfranc, the Archbishop of Canterbury, who himself wrote a work entitled *De celanda confessione*, did the same. But it was with the Fourth Lateran Council (1215) that we find a canon that lays down for the first time that there is a moral and juridical obligation to respect the sacramental seal as a universal law of the Church, with grave penalties for priests that break it. Indeed, canon 21 *Omnis utriusque sexus*, already famous in the history of canon law for requiring confession at least once a year, observed:

> *Caveat autem omnino ne verbo vel signo vel alio quovis modo prodat aliquatenus peccatorem … quoniam qui peccatum in poenitentiali iudicio sibi detectum praesumpserit revelare, non solum a sacerdotali officio deponendum decernimus, verum etiam ad agendam perpetuam poenitentiam in arctum monasterium detrudendum.*[1]

[1] *Conciliorum Oecumenicorum Decreta. Edizione bilingue*, p. 245.

The discipline of the Church *in subiecta materia* has always remained substantially the same with the exception of where special cases have been specified such as the absolution of the accomplice, which goes far back, or, more recently, the expansion of the violation of the sacramental seal using technological instruments. Naturally, my analysis seeks to have an approach that is first and foremost related to canon law, that is to say seeing the violation of the sacramental seal as a delict. Therefore, it will center essentially on this rather than on tangential questions such as, perhaps, the *sollicitatio ad turpia*, the absolution of the accomplice, or an invalid attempt at, and the simulation of, confession. However, before beginning this analysis it seems to me to be advisable to offer some Biblical-theological references in order to understand in a better way the reasons why the Church attributes this special importance to the absolute inviolability of the sacramental seal of confession.

1. The Concept of Seal and Secrecy in "Biblical-Theological Understanding"

The Second Vatican Council observes in number 24 of the Constitution *Dei Verbum* "*Ideoque Sacrae Scripturae studium sit veluti anima Sacrae Theologiae*" and it is in this sense that we will analyze the semantic and theological-spiritual importance of the concepts of seal and secrecy in the Bible.[2]

In the background of the Bible the terminology of seal and secrecy refer to the dimension of the reality of *mysterion*,[3] which, remains and must remain, closed in its essence and truth. Only God can open and reveal the secret that the seal closes and bears with it in its essence. On this point, it is important to remember how in the Book of the Apocalypse it is God who, through the Victorious Lamb, opens the seals of life (cf. Rev 6:1-17) to the point of opening the seventh seal (cf. Rev 8:1), where it is emphasized that when this was opened "there was silence in heaven for about half an hour" (Rev 8:1). Man, therefore, absolutely cannot open, or go against the closed character, of the seal, whose origins and foundations are located in the truth and transcendence of God.

[2] Cf. G. Fitzer, "Sfraghis," in *Grande Lessico del Nuovo Testamento*, XII, coll. 378-418; A. Oepke, "Kryptô," in *Grande Lessico del Nuovo Testamento*, V, coll. 1161-1169.
[3] Cf. G. Bornkmamm, "Mystérion," in *Grande Lessico del Nuovo Testamento*, VII (Brescia, 1971), coll. 643-715.

As regards the logic of the seal (of the *sfraghìs*), we certainly cannot forget to what this term refers in the context of the theology of the Apostle Paul where this noun is necessarily associated with the spirit, of which we have received an instalment: "But the one who gives us security with you in Christ and who anointed us is God; he has also put his seal upon us and given the Spirit in our hearts as a first instalment" (2 Cor 1:21-22).

The dimension of the secret refers, in the Biblical spiritual understanding as well, to the dimension of the intimacy of the relationship that links the relational You of God with the relational you of man, who is made in his image and likeness (cf. Gen 1:26-28 and Psalm 8). This relationship becomes the *maqôm qadosh*, the holy place of this communication of love and friendship in which the Father and the Son in the communion-based force of the Holy Spirit can dwell and remain: "Whoever loves me will keep my word, and my Father will love him, and we will come to him and make our dwelling with him" (Jn 14:23).

In this light, the invitation of Jesus in the "Sermon on the Mount" in the Gospel of Matthew to the believer to accept and adopt the practical logic of secrecy becomes evident and completely clear. In verses 1-18 of chapter 6 of this gospel, the formula with the adjective made a noun *en tô krypyô* refers to the need to be secret in prayer experienced in the dimension that Catherine of Sienna called the "interior cell,"[4] secret in almsgiving, and secret in fasting, as a move from the law of the Pharisees of what was due to the fullness of the law of the freely-given Love and Grace of God.[5]

From a theological point of view, there are two essential and fundamental reasons for the absolute inviolability of the sacramental seal and secrecy without any exceptions (as is observed in canons 983-984 of the *CIC*). The first belongs fundamentally to natural law where it is clear and evident that penitents, who confess their sins and their guilt, approve and sign a sort of agreement-contract in which it is guaranteed that their confession will remain a secret and will never be disclosed for any reason. The second belongs to, and remains in, the sphere of divine law which is located in the very essence of the Sacrament of Penance.

---

[4] Caterina da Siena, *Lettere*, edited by G. Di Ciaccia, I, (Bologna, 1996), n. 37, pp. 145-149.

[5] Cf. G. Barbaglio, *Il pensare dell'apostolo Paolo* (Bologna, 2004), pp. 105-112.

The confessor, when listening to the confessions of sins, does not live this ministry in his own name but, rather, substantially and exclusively, he does so in the name and in the place of God. Penitents, in opening their hearts, therefore confess their sins to God Himself, and only God, through the ministry of the priest, absolves sins. On this point, the *Catechism of the Catholic Church* observes that "what the penitent has made known to the priest remains "sealed" by the sacrament."[6] We should therefore remember and emphasize with great force and intensity that the confessional seal is protected by natural law, by divine law and by Church law.

2. The Sacramental Seal from a Canonical Perspective

After offering some observations on the seal and the secrecy of confession from a Biblical-theological point of view, we will now move to addressing this subject from a primarily canonical point of view, where the violation of the confessional seal is a delict.

2.1. *The Discipline in Force: Objective Cases*

The confessional seal is certainly a defining chapter of the Sacrament of Penance because it clearly demonstrates the divine character of the sacrament and why it is "privately heard" and not public. The obligation of the sacramental seal has always been a very grave matter and very much alive in the Church. The precept of the fourth Lateran Council is the distant source of canon 983 §1 of the current *Code of Canon Law* which observes: "The sacramental seal is inviolable. Accordingly, it is absolutely wrong for a confessor in any way to betray the penitent, for any reason whatsoever, whether by word or in any other fashion."[7]

For that matter, canon 889 of the *Code of Canon Law* of 1917 says the same thing. Canon 983 §1 of the *CIC* refers directly to canon 1388 which I will quote in its entirety:

> §1 A confessor who directly violates the sacramental seal, incurs a *latae sententiae* excommunication reserved to the Apostolic See; he who does so only indirectly is to be punished according to the gravity of the offence.

[6] *CCC*, n. 1467.

[7] *CIC*, can. 983 §1: "*Sacramentale sigillum inviolabile est; quare nefas est confessario verbis vel alio quovis modo et quavis de causa aliquatenus prodere poenitentem.*"

> §2 Interpreters and the others mentioned in Canon 983 §2, who violate the secret, are to be punished with a just penalty, not excluding excommunication.[8]

From what these two canons both say derive two forms of violation of the sacramental seal — one of which is direct and one of which is indirect — punished by different penalties, both of which are reserved to the Congregation for the Doctrine of the Faith in the external forum and to the Apostolic Penitentiary in the internal forum.[9] In the first case, for the delict to have taken place the disclosure of the sin and of the sinner is required; in the second (indirect violation) it is enough for one of these two to be disclosed, and that as a result the danger of the disclosure of the other exists. In other terms, if one can go back to the penitent or suspect that someone has committed a sin.

There is a violation of the seal even if the person listening does not know that the confessor has received that knowledge when hearing a confession. However, this receives the application of canon 1330 which lays down that "An offence which consists in a declaration or in some other manifestation of doctrine or knowledge, is not to be regarded or effected if no one actually perceives the declaration or manifestation."[10]

In both cases for there to be a violation of sacramental secrecy there has to be dissemination or disclosure of the subject matter of the sacrament. Subject matter under this secrecy is in general all sins, or any element connected to them, learned about in confession, knowledge of which enables one to go back to the sinner.

All grave sins, and each grave sin, fall under the sacramental seal, as do lesser sins or venial sins, but only if disclosed individually or in a specific way. To disclose that a person has committed lesser sins is a violation of secrecy but not of the seal because all of us commit

[8] *CIC*, can. 1388: "§1. *Confessarius, qui sacramentale sigillum directe violat, in excommunicationem latae sententiae Sedi Apostolicae reservatam incurrit; qui vero indirecte tantum, pro delicti gravitate puniatur.* §2. *Interpres aliique, de quibus in can.* 983, §2, *qui secretum violant, iusta poena puniantur, non exclusa excommunicatione.*" Can. 983 §2: "*Obligatione secretum servandi tenetur quoque interpres, si detur, necnon omnes alii ad quos ex confessione notitia peccatorum quoquo modo pervenerit.*"

[9] Cf. *PB*, articles. 52 and 118; *Regolamento generale della Curia Romana* (1 July 1999), art. 128, §2; Congregation for the Doctrine of the Faith, *Rescriptum ex audientia SS.mi* of 7 February 2003.

[10] *CIC*, can. 1330: "*Delictum quod in declaratione consistat vel in alia voluntatis vel doctrinae vel scientiae manifestatione, tamquam non consummatum censendum est, se nemo eam declarationem vel manifestationem percipiat.*"

at least some lesser sins. However, it remains an illicit act because in behaving with this lack of seriousness the confessor violates a secret learned in confession and in this way undermines the trust of the faithful in the confidentiality of the penitential conversation. It should be observed that a sin, and that includes a lesser sin, known about by the community but anyway learned about in confession is subject to the seal, and in the same way a confessor who knew about the sin before and outside the confession, and discloses that he heard it in confession, violates this seal.

Equally, the circumstances of sin declared in confession fall under the sacramental seal, as do the occasion, the purpose, the place, the time, the forms and the circumstances of the confession itself, the gravity or otherwise of the penance imposed or the denial of absolution. Obviously, the same applies to the name and the sin of the accomplice.

It should also be stressed that no violation at all has occurred if the interlocutor of the confessor is the penitent who has confessed. The question has in some of its aspects been discussed in the literature in the field but beyond the obvious inadvisability of returning to the penitential conversation outside confession, one cannot see how in this case there can occur that "*prodere poenitentem*" (betrayal of the penitent) required by canon 983 §1.

Vice versa, it is not sufficient for the penitent to have exonerated the confessor from the sacramental seal since this is not protected by the penitent — it is protected by the sacrament itself. On the other hand, if the seal were a matter of private responsibility, the penitent could be subjected to pressure that could in fact be equivalent to the cancellation of the real protection of the sacramental seal.[11]

2.2. *The Discipline in Force: The Case of the Subject*

If we take the canons already referred to, we can deduce that the subject of the sacramental seal is the confessor alone and thus the priest or the bishop who heard the confession, even if he did not impart absolution, or did not have the faculty to hear it, or even if he had been excommunicated.[12]

[11] According to G.P. Montini, "La tutela penale del Sacramento della Penitenza. I delitti nella celebrazione del Sacramento (cann. 1378; 1387; 1388)," in *Le sanzioni nella Chiesa. XXIII Incontro di Studio, 1 luglio–5 luglio 1996*, edited by the Gruppo Italiano Docenti di Diritto Canonico (Milan, 1997), pp. 226-227.

[12] Cf. A. Calabrese, *Diritto penale canonico* (Vatican City, 2006, third edition), p. 307.

From the lexicon of canon 983, §2 one deduces that an interpreter and others to whom knowledge of sins has arrived are certainly subject to the obligation not to disclose, but this is not specifically a matter of the sacramental seal. Indeed, "*ubi lex voluit, dixit, ubi noluit, tacuit.*"

Although this is after a certain fashion self-evident, it is advisable to refer to the fact that in this area as well the general principles of canon law are in force. This is true above all else as regards malice, as laid down by canon 1321, §2:

> A person who deliberately violated a law or precept is bound by the penalty prescribed in that law or precept. If, however, the violation was due to the omission of due diligence, the person is not punished unless the law or precept provides otherwise.[13]

The fault is precisely the omission of due diligence, as we all know. Only he who is fully conscious of the violation, is about to disclose a confessional secret, who realizes this and intends to do it, is thus subject to excommunication: "not when the confessor believes that he is disclosing subject matter acquired *aliunde*; or discloses inadvertently or because of superficiality what he has learnt in a confession."[14] In this sense, it is helpful to remember that on the occasion of the plenary assembly of the *Pontificia Commissio Codici Iuris Canonici Recognoscendo* (today the Pontifical Council for Legislative Texts) held in October 1981, one father proposed the addition to the canon in question of the phrase "*plene conscious*" in order to avoid scruples of conscience on the part of confessors. The response of the secretariat was that this addition was not necessary because the requirement of the presence of malice was understood on the basis of reference to the current canon 1321, §2.[15]

As we have observed, the penalty envisaged for a direct violation of the sacramental seal is excommunication *latae sententiae* reserved to the Apostolic See. On the other hand, the inviolability of the seal does not impede the application of exemptions and mitigating circumstances specific to general canon penal law.

[13] *CIC*, can. 1321 §2: "*Poena lege vel praecepto statutis tenetur, qui legem vel praeceptum deliberate violavit; qui vero id egit ex omissione debitae diligentiae, non punitur, nisi lex vel praeceptum aliter caveat.*"

[14] According to Montini, *La tutela penale del Sacramento della Penitenza*, p. 227.

[15] Cf. ibidem. In support of this thesis the author observed that the omission in the canon of the phrase "*caveat diligenter*" of can. 889, §1 of the Code of 1917 in favor of the locution "*nefas*" present in the current can. 983, §1 means that the explicit reference to mere fault has been lost.

In addition, in conformity with more general provisions the confessor is not liable to the canonical penalty when he is unaware of the existence of the penal sanction (cf. can. 1323, 2), or when he was in one of the conditions described in canons 1322, 1323 and 1324, §1 which relate to individuals liable to penalty.[16] In the case of a solely indirect violation of confessional secrecy, as we have already seen, the penalty is *ferendae sententiae*. This is obligatory but not specified.

2.3. *Further Prohibitions (Canon 984)*

In order to protect in a more effective way the secrecy of confession, the Church has established other rules, in addition to the above-mentioned penalties.

1. The confessor is absolutely forbidden to use in any way knowledge acquired from a confession to the detriment of the penitent ("*cum paenitentis gravamina*"), even when any danger of disclosure is excluded (§1). The *gravamen* could also be of other people, to whom such a "use" would render the Sacrament of Penance not attractive.
2. A person who is in authority may not in any way for the purpose of external governance use knowledge about sins which has come to him at any time from the hearing of confession (§2).
3. Canon 1550, §2, 2 excludes priests, who are deemed incapable of doing so, from providing testimony at a trial in relation to everything that has become known to them in sacramental confession, even in a case where it was the penitent who asked for such testimony. Indeed, everything that is heard from anyone and in any way in confession cannot be accepted even as an indication of the truth.

3. Civil Legislation Regarding the Sacramental Seal

Civil legislation itself recognizes the sacramental seal as a part of professional confidentiality, attributing to it special protection. I will cite here two fundamental texts that form a part of Italian legislation:

---

[16] He we clearly follow the analysis already cited of Montini, *op. cit.*, p. 228.

— *New Code of Penal Procedure* (entered in force on 24 October 1989), art. 200, first comma: "The following cannot be obliged to testify about what they have learnt because of their ministry, office or profession … a) ministers of religious confessions, whose statutes are not in contrast with the Italian law."[17]

— *New Agreement between the Holy See and the Republic of Italy*, 18 February 1984, art. 4, n. 4: "Ecclesiastics are not obliged to provide to magistrates or other authorities information about people or matters they have come to learn about because of their ministry."

4. The Recording of Confessions

As regards this subject, we should remember the special severity that the Church adopts for those who violate the secrecy of confession by recording with a technological device or divulging through the means of social communication what is said by the confessor or by the penitent in confession. Those who commit this delict are punished according to the gravity of the offence, not excluding dismissal or deposition if the person involved is a cleric (cf. *SST*, art. 4, §2).

This is a recent rule. The first intervention of the Church in this area took place on 23 March 1973 when it was widely indicated that a scandalous book would be published that reported transcriptions from some — real or simulated — sacramental confessions recorded in an underhand way.

By a Declaration of the Congregation for the Doctrine of the Faith, the penalty of excommunication *latae sententiae* was applied to the authors or publishers of the text and to anybody who had formally cooperated in such an initiative. However, this was a single intervention relating to a specific situation.[18]

The same Congregation on 23 September 1988 issued a decree that in the future extended this sanction to all similar cases. The aim of this decree was to "protect the sanctity of the sacrament of Penance and … defend the rights of ministers and Christian faithful."[19]

---

[17] Cf. also art. 249 of the *Codice di Procedura Civile.*

[18] Cf. *AAS* 65 (1973), p. 678.

[19] *AAS* 80 (1988), p. 1367.

The text of this decree, by which was applied the excommunication *latae sententiae*, in order to protect the secrecy of the Sacrament of Penance, to anyone who records with technological devices or divulges through the means of social communication what is said by the confessor or the penitent, reads as follows:

> The Congregation for the Doctrine of the Faith, in order to protect the sanctity of the sacrament of Penance and in order to defend the rights of ministers and Christian faithful within the same sacrament regarding the sacramental seal and secrecy connected to Confession, in virtue of the special faculty conferred by the Supreme Apostolic Authority of the Church (can. 30), has determined that: Without prejudice to the prescription of can. 1388, anyone who by means of any technical device makes a recording of what the priest or the penitent says in a Sacramental Confession (either real or simulated) by oneself or by another person, or who divulges it through the means of social communication, incurs excommunication *latae sententiae*.

In the light of what has been observed, it is helpful to emphasize that the confessional seal does not only bind the confessor. It also binds any possible interpreter and all those who in any way, even by chance, came to know about the sins confessed.

The confessional seal, as I have sought to demonstrate, constitutes a substantial, qualifying and diriment element of the Sacrament of Penance because it reveals and substantially shapes the divine character of this sacrament which is the essential reason why this is and must be always rigorously "privately heard." The Church is so jealous of the sanctity of the sacramental seal and so respectful of the secrecy of penitents that in canon 1550, §2, 2 she excludes priests from providing testimony at a trial in relation to anything that has become known to them in an individual sacramental confession, even in a case where it is the penitent who asked for such testimony. Not even the death of a penitent can release the confessor from this obligation. The law of the sacramental seal does not allow of any exceptions. No confessor can be dispensed from it, even if in wanting to disclose the contents of a confession he intended to avoid a grave and imminent evil.

In the new Code the sacramental seal is mentioned only in reference to the confessor while for the other figures reference is made to secrecy. Obviously, this secrecy is also in a certain sense profoundly and radically sacramental even though it is not called a seal. Therefore, the protection of the sanctity of the Sacrament of Penance is a primary task for everyone and cannot be left or relegated solely to ordained ministers.

In canon law relating to the sacramental seal, the Church, on the one hand, seeks to transmit the pedagogy of the love of the Father of mercy, and, on the other, she wishes to direct her ministers to experience and live the gift of ministerial and spiritual fatherhood, which enables them, in every experience of this seal/secrecy of the privately-heard dialogue of confession, to be privileged witnesses to the sanctity of this sacrament, following the example of St. John of Nepomuk (1349-1393).[20] This saint went as far as martyrdom of the blood to guard the absolute importance of the value of the inviolability of the sacramental seal. The sacramental seal understood in this way also becomes a guarantee of the *mirabilia Dei* in the heart of each individual penitent who gives himself or herself over to the hearts of pastors. These hearts reverberate, in the existential here and now of each pastor, with the beauty of the merciful and transfiguring Love of the Father given by the redemptive sacrifice of Christ.

---

[20] John was the son of Velflin, a citizen of Nepomuk, a town thirty kilometers from Pilsen in Bohemia, and studied theology and law at the University of Prague. In 1373 he took Holy Orders and became a notary at the episcopal chancellery. In 1374 he was appointed a proto-notary of Archbishop John of Jenštejn, before becoming his secretary. To begin with, he was the canon of the cathedral of the Church of St. Aegidius in Prague and in 1389 he became the parish priest of the Church of St. Gallen and canon of the cathedral of Vyšehrad. In 1390 he left the parish of St. Gallen to become the archdeacon of Žatec (Saaz) and at the same time canon of the cathedral of St. Vitus without, however, receiving the ecclesiastical benefits that fell to the canons of the cathedral. Shortly afterwards the Archbishop of Prague appointed him the president of the ecclesiastical tribunal and in 1393 he made him his vicar general. King Wenceslaus IV of Bohemia and Emperor of the Holy Roman Empire wanted to found a new diocese for one of his favorites and ordered that on the death of Abbot Racek of the Monastery of Kladruby no new abbot should be elected and that the church of the abbey should be transformed into an episcopal see. The vicar general of the Archbishop energetically opposed this order which violated canon law. When Abbot Racek died in 1393 the monks of Kladruby immediately held an election. Their choice fell on the monk Olenus and John as vicar general readily confirmed this election without taking into account the wishes of the monarch. In this atmosphere of open and evident hostility between King Wenceslaus and John of Nepomuk, the chronicles report that the king, having doubts about the faithfulness of his wife, Queen Jane of Bavaria, who had John as her confessor, repeatedly and persistently asked John to reveal to him what the queen had said in confession. John never agreed to violate the secrecy of the confessions of the queen and thus on 6 May 1393 he was thrown into the River Moldova on the orders of the king and drowned. The next morning the body was found on the bank of the river surrounded by a special and intense light.

PART TWO

THE SACRAMENT OF PENANCE AND RECONCILIATION: THEOLOGICAL-EDUCATIONAL ASPECTS

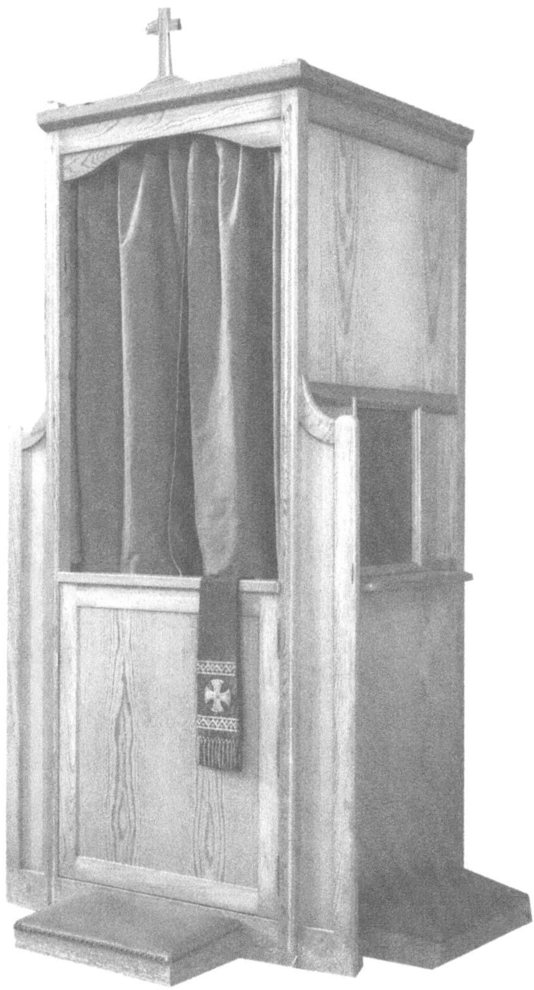

MISERICORDIAE VULTUS: THE MAGISTERIUM OF POPE FRANCIS

"This should be a *kairós*, our epoch is a *kairós* of mercy, a truly favorable time:"[1] a time when the Church takes the initiative to go towards people, looks for, gathers and cares for the wounded of life, making them feel loved.[2] Hence the importance of living the experience of the extraordinary Holy Year of Mercy, the importance for believers of passing by way of the Holy Door of mercy. Pope Francis has reflected on all of this since the beginning of his experience as a priest and has affirmed, following in the footsteps of his recent predecessors, that "mercy" is the most marvellous attribute of the creator and redeemer — the very name of God.[3] As mercy — in the view of the Holy Father — is the approach of the divine that embraces, the self-giving of God who welcomes, who bends down to forgive,[4] we understand that this is what the children of the Church must be convinced of at a deep level, what they must choose every day: the Church must "learn to choose only 'what pleases God most' ... Forgiving his children."[5]

The subject of mercy, therefore, is the cardinal motif of the magisterium of Pope Francis and for this reason I feel the need to approach it with respect and healthy trepidation. One can understand the complexity of the subject starting with another phrase of the Holy Father: "Mercy is something that is difficult to understand. It does not cancel sins, but it is the way by which God the Father forgives."[6] Nonetheless, I will seek to grasp the principal aspects of the merciful

[1] Papa Francesco, *Il nome di Dio è misericordia. Una conversazione con Andrea Tornielli* (Vatican City/Milan, 2016), p. 22.

[2] Cf. ibidem.

[3] Cf. ibid., p. 23.

[4] Cf. ibid., p. 24.

[5] Pope Francis, General Audience, 9 December 2015.

[6] Papa Francesco, *Il nome di Dio è misericordia*, p. 12; Pope Francis, Morning Meditation in the Chapel of *Domus Sanctae Marthae*, 7 April 2014.

Face of God described in the phrases of Pope Francis, in line with a very precise itinerary. To use an image of the production of a painting, *Misericordiae vultus* is the background on which the face of the mercy of God is painted, whereas the encyclical *Lumen fidei* and the exhortation *Evangelii gaudium* are the brushstrokes that, in turn, fill in, and give substance to, the painting. Lastly, some addresses and homilies of the Supreme Pontiff involve finishing touches that bestow upon the painting that element of preciousness that a painting by a special painter deserves. All of this can certainly not depart from some references to the papal magisterium of the recent past and to the *Catechism of the Catholic Church* as a completion of the overall pictorial structure.

1. Jesus Christ is the Face of the Mercy of the Father (*MV*, n. 1)

In this first section I will seek to dwell — with a brief analysis — on the mysterious manifestation of the merciful face of God in Jesus Christ, according to the spirit of *Misericordiae vultus*, in order to offer some points of meditation that will certainly help us to live anew and with greater impetus the mystery of the thrice holy God made visible in humility and poverty in the human face of His only begotten Son. The Apostle Paul states that when in the fullness of time the Word, who was in the beginning God Himself, became flesh, he came to dwell amongst his own. Thus the greatest wish that characterizes and gives force to the hope of those who believe through the gift of mercy found fulfillment and completion in history. Thus it was that the face of God was revealed in Christ: the vision of that glory which led the heart of the Prophet Moses to burn,[7] and the hearts of others after him, was now beheld, admired and made accessible to everyone. Jesus Christ is the image of the invisible God (cf. Col 1:15), the Son who comes from the breast of the Father; thus he who alone is capable of revealing the Father, showing Him and making Him palpable.[8] In the face of so much greatness, evidently not understood, one understands the perplexity of the Apostle Philip when he perceives, in the words of the Teacher, the possibility, which is so near and "easily" reachable, of already listening to and seeing the face of God: to see Christ, indeed,

[7] Cf. *MV*, n. 1.

[8] Cf. ibidem.

is to see the Father.[9] The response to Jesus was overwhelming, albeit in all its simplicity: Philip and the others found themselves faced with a singular event that is inconceivable at a human level. Christ, indeed, satisfied the unsatisfied wish of entire generations of the Jewish people, and in substantial terms of every individual, because the face of Jesus is the human face of God that not only breaks the dark loneliness of man but also allows him to rediscover himself. Every man can be reflected in Christ; in him, Christ, the face of every man, is not opaque — it can no longer be such.

In the light of all of this, it seems to be licit to ask what the manifested aspects of the Face of God, its "characteristic" traits, really are. Amongst its many features that stand out, that of mercy is especially evident. Saint Thomas Aquinas in his *Summa Theologiae* states that it is specific to God to use His mercy because in it is expressed His omnipotence.[10] By this, however, Aquinas does not express only an exterior approach of God which, furthermore, is said to coincide paradoxically with a feature that expresses weakness. He goes well beyond this because he does not make this divine attribute coincide with its manifestation, even though it is the greatest one, but makes it correspond to the revelation of His name, of His being: God manifests and uses mercy because He is mercy!

It seems to me to be interesting to emphasize that Pope Francis in *Lumen fidei* stresses that believers manage to experience the merciful love of God, in Jesus Christ, when they gradually and really enter a loving and wise knowledge of God, in that intertwining of two willed and looked for acts: seeing and hearing.[11] Thus the features of the human face of God, that Face that embodies and personifies the mercy of the Father,[12] shines forth with truth, goodness and beauty.[13] This four-pointed diadem is the first Christological level of the face of the incarnate Word.

The merciful face by which God, our Father, wants to attract us to Him with ties of love and life,[14] is the face of the "fairest of the sons of men; grace is poured upon your lips," as the psalmist sings (Ps 44:2); the merciful face of a total and complete beauty that goes beyond somatic features alone. We well know that the New Testament

[9] Cf. *LF*, n. 30.
[10] Cf. T. Aquinas, *Summa Theologiae*, II, II, q. 30, a. 4c.
[11] Cf. *LF*, nn. 30-31.
[12] Cf. *DM*, n. 2.
[13] Cf. *EG*, n. 167.
[14] Cf. ibidem.

never describes the physical lineaments of Jesus. However, it is not difficult to affirm that the merciful beauty of the Lord is animated by meekness, tenderness and holiness — the absolute beauty of God that fascinates and attracts.

In another context of Holy Scripture, on the other hand, the merciful face of the fairest of the sons of man appears in all its dramatic character. The dismay of the Prophet Isaiah before he who "had no form or comeliness that we should look at him, and no beauty that we should desire him," a face "from whom men hide their faces" (Is 53:2-3), does not in the least cause us to wonder.

The paradox is, therefore, that we have, on the one hand, an extreme, total, involving beauty that translates in a prophetic way the relationship of Christ with the Church, but, on the other, a disfigured image, a reverse beauty.[15] It is clear that we are in the presence of the superimposition of the changed likenesses of the single face of Christ, in which his mercy is traversed at times by beauty and at times by unspeakable suffering, and thus by great goodness.

Goodness is specifically another feature of the human face of the mercy of God. In the Gospel of John, Jesus the Lord is defined by, and recognized in, the image of the Good Shepherd (Jn 10:11), who, with his human and divine harmony at one and the same time, attracts and asks questions,[16] sacrifices himself and gives his life for his sheep. It is interesting to read anew, as Pope Francis observes, the image of the Good Shepherd in the light of his passion, death and resurrection, because only in this way does the adjective "good" appear in all its luminosity.[17] In essential terms, Jesus Christ displays a beautiful and good face, but also one that is suffering and crucified which, when "lifted up from the earth, will draw all men to myself" (Jn 12:32) and continues to call on man and the Church, making them move out of themselves,[18] as took place with the centurion in front of the cross. Saint Augustine conjoins in an admirable way the raising up of Christ on the cross with the image of a grain of wheat that dies in order to bear fruit according to its mission. The beauty of Christ, raised up on the scandalous throne of the cross, will attract everyone, specifically when his not being presentable in the eyes of the world appears most strongly.

---

[15] Cf. P. Rattin, "Non ha apparenza né bellezza. Il rovescio della bellezza," *Parola Spirito e Vita*, 2 (2001), pp. 67-77, see p. 68.

[16] Cf. *EG*, n. 35.

[17] Cf. Pope Francis, Address before the *Regina Coeli*, 26 April 2015.

[18] Cf. *EG*, n. 24.

One thus understands that the disfigured, crucified and raised-up face of Christ revealed the depth — which is not easily imaginable — of the mercy of Christ, a masterpiece of charity that has the tones of enchantment.[19] Christ is the most eloquent declaration of how the beauty of his mercy is the last word of history. It is in this intertwining of beauty, goodness and mercy that in a special way all Christians are called to place themselves to achieve their true identity as disciples of Jesus and authentic children of God, with and for other people.

As *Misericordiae vultus* observes, in fixing our gaze on the merciful face of Jesus we discover the multiple relationships of the people that met him, the signs of goodness and mercy that he worked as a manifestation of that kingdom of love that he came to establish. Here it would not be suitable to list gospel episodes, which are many in number and important, where the power of the mercy of the Lord is highlighted. However, I do wish to point in a special way to the icons of the Good Samaritan and the widow of Nain where the mercy that is exercised is clothed in all of its compassionate tenderness,[20] which, indeed, only the paternal-maternal heart of God is able to express. Obviously, we will do this without diverting our gaze from all the other signs of the merciful presence of Jesus who in the words of the Beatitudes and in meetings with tax-collectors, prostitutes, blind people, the lame and the excluded, demonstrated to everyone, and invited everyone to, citizenship of the kingdom of God.

2. The Church has the Mission to Proclaim and Live the Mercy of God amongst Men (*MV*, n. 12)

The by-now universally known fundamental ideas of Pope Francis, that is to say seeing our community as an "outward going Church"[21] and a "field hospital,"[22] find their source or foundation in the intimate relationship of the Church with Jesus Christ which is seen as an itinerant intimacy defined as "missionary communion."[23] According to this model, which is that of the Teacher, the Church is invited to move

[19] Cf. *Dio Padre di misericordia*, published by the *Commissione Teologico-Storica del Grande Giubileo dell'Anno Duemila* (Milan, 1998), p. 49.

[20] Cf. Papa Francesco, *Il nome di Dio è misericordia*, p. 101.

[21] *EG*, n. 24.

[22] Pope Francis, Morning Meditation in the Chapel of the *Domus Santae Marthae*, 1 April 2015.

[23] *EG*, n. 23.

out of her traditional settings to proclaim and manifest the gospel of mercy to everyone, everywhere that man lives his daily life. A Church that can proclaim the mercy of the Father, in Christ in the Spirit, and take that initiative that becomes involvement and accompanying in human affairs, not because she trusts automatically in a force that is her own but because this force comes to her from her Spouse. The holiness of Jesus gives to the Church the missionary impetus to reach even the last sinner in the most forsaken place in the world because this holiness — while it moves the Church towards those who are distant as well as those who are nearby — has already preceded her in love: Jesus Christ is already present and at work in the hearts and places to which the Church goes to proclaim the gift of mercy.[24]

In these phrases, the reference of Pope Francis to the illuminated insight of his predecessor St. John XXIII is evident. We all remember the fine and surprising words of that Pope's address at the opening of the Second Vatican Council: "Nowadays, however, the Spouse of Christ prefers to make use of the medicine of mercy rather than that of severity."[25] These terms indicate a choice and a shift of attitudes first, and of behavior thereafter, that are seen as necessary; in addition, they highlight an increased consciousness of the idea of the Church as a "mother." It is specifically the Church, Pope Francis affirms, that "must be a place of mercy freely given, where everyone can feel welcomed, loved, forgiven and encouraged to live the good life of the Gospel."[26]

Because she is the Mother, the Church, following the example of Jesus, proclaims and lives mercy, and this image is perceived more strongly the more pockets of human poverty expand. Despite the fact that this is a reality that is already consolidated and on a large scale, the maternal dimension of the Church is not confined to some charitable actions alone — it needs education in, and the teaching of, mercy, which is expressed above all in a totalizing promotion of humanity. A profound revision of ecclesial practice is thus required, aiming, as Pope Francis observed, at pastoral conversion,[27] in which is outlined a mature awareness of the motherhood of the Church, a

---

[24] Cf. ibid., n. 24.

[25] John XXIII, Address before the Opening of the Second Ecumenical Vatican Council (11 October 1962).

[26] *EG*, n. 114.

[27] Cf. ibid., nn. 25, 30.

Mother who always has an open heart.[28] According to this approach, we can say that the ecclesial community is called to recognize the signs of the action of the Spirit in the current socio-cultural panorama and at the same time to respond to challenges as new opportunities to form relationships of full mercy and not as elements that only "restrain or weaken the impulse of missionary renewal in the Church."[29]

I have referred to interpersonal relationships which are the new "settings," existential spaces that by now have become points of no return, in which the transmission of faith and the experience of fraternal mercy take place. These are precisely the places in which the Church must live in order to bring the announcement of mercy that offers answers, gives hope, infuses courage and renews the vigour of the Christian journey of faith.[30] I would like here to refer in this context to the first encyclical of Pope Francis which asserts that the human person is not an isolated being, a contemplator of himself or herself, but a being who is always in relationships: "We come from others, we belong to others, and our lives are enlarged by our encounter with others. Even our own knowledge and self-awareness are relational; they are linked to others who have gone before us."[31] This explicit reference to interpersonal relationships does not divert our gaze from the maternal dimension of the Church; indeed, it sharpens it. To encounter the other, to be with the other with an approach of nearness, through the courageous sign of pastoral accompanying, is the challenge that makes credible the proclaiming of the mercy of the Church. I would like to dwell upon the mission of accompanying our brothers and sisters in a pastoral sense as a singular expression of the merciful Church, something that the Holy Father has greatly recommended.

As I have already observed, "accompany" is a word that stands out in *Evangelii gaudium*.[32] The mercy of a mother is an integral part of the pastoral care provided by the Church. Motherly love should be imitated in what pastors do, in the accompanying that they provide. Seeing others as children of God and approaching them with all due reverence, both for what they are and for God's design for them, the communicators of God's mercy should reach out to those who are

---

[28] Cf. ibid., nn. 46, 139.

[29] Ibid., n. 51.

[30] Cf. ibid., n. 114.

[31] *LF*, n. 38.

[32] Cf. *EG*, nn. 12, 25, 44, 46, 69, 70, 76, 99, 103, 169, 170-173, 199, 214, 241, 286.

in any kind of difficulty, above all as regards relationships.[33] In doing this, pastors must be imbued with suitable training and the relevant virtues, following those pathways of the art of accompanying that the Holy Father points to as being most suitable.[34]

The purpose of the art of accompanying is clear from the outset: to proclaim and live mercy with those (and they are very many in number) who think that they have been abandoned by God or are distant from His merciful love. Since accompanying tells the truth about interpersonal relationships under the heading of service (another aspect of accompanying), the Supreme Pontiff himself as a "good shepherd" and witness to mercy walks ahead setting an example. In his high magisterium and in daily life, the poor and the excluded of every latitude have heard and seen that the God of Jesus Christ is not a pitiless judge or a Lord unable to understand the limits and the sufferings of living, hardness of hearts and the difficulties of human relationships. But as is said in another context, as a merciful and compassionate Samaritan Christ through His Church comes near to every man bent in body and spirit and pours on his wounds the oil of comfort and the wine of hope.[35]

How often have we seen this behavior in Pope Francis! In the incipit of his speech to those being helped in the center for rehabilitation of Palmasola (Bolivia), one can already see his message of mercy: "I could not leave Bolivia without seeing you, without sharing that faith and hope which are the fruit of the love revealed on the cross of Christ."[36] On that occasion he did not hesitate to invite those brothers and sisters who were in need of forgiveness and mercy to turn their gaze to the crucified Christ — mercy of the Father. I want here to cite another moment, that of his meeting with poor people and prisoners in the city of Cagliari in Sardinia when the Holy Father encouraged those brothers and sisters to undertake the journey of faith and hope on the Way that is Jesus Christ, in a constant effort to cooperate, to understand each other and to forgive each other, each recognizing their own limitations and mistakes because the work of mercy has to be performed according to the "rules" of mercy.[37]

---

[33] Cf. *EG*, n. 70.

[34] Cf. ibid., nn. 171-172.

[35] Cf. *Roman Missal,* Common Preface VIII.

[36] Pope Francis, Address to those Helped in the Centre for Re-education of Santa Cruz di Palmasola, 10 July 2015.

[37] Cf. Pope Francis, Address to the Poor and the Prisoners of the City of Cagliari, 22 September 2013.

3. The Sacrament of Reconciliation is the Rediscovery of the Merciful Face of the Father (*MV*, n. 17)

In my view, a decisive point in *Misericordiae Vultus* seems to be n. 17. We encounter here a positive tension that exists between the essence and the fruits of the Sacrament of Reconciliation and the ministry of this sacrament. The exhortation of the Holy Father leaves no room for doubt: confessors must always be a sign of the mercy of the Father. Specifically in this context, he takes up the famous observation of the *Apologeticum* of Tertullian and applies it to confessors: one does not improvise being a confessor, one becomes such.[38] By this, he intends to highlight how a good confessor can truly show himself such if he is the first to have adopted in his own life, and constantly renews, the experience of forgiveness and mercy through reconciliation.[39] By now we are learning the style of Pope Francis and it will certainly not escape us that what he emphasized in n. 17 he clearly explained when referring to himself at the prison of Palmasola in Bolivia, where he presented himself to those in this rehabilitation center with the following words:

> The man standing before you is a man who has experienced forgiveness. A man who was, and is, saved from his many sins. That is who I am. I don't have much more to give you or to offer you, but I want to share with you what I do have and what I love. It is Jesus Christ, the mercy of the Father.[40]

Again connecting to n. 17 of *Misericordiae vultus*, the Pope has invited confessors not to feel that they are the owners of the sacrament of forgiveness but, rather, to welcome the faithful like the father of the parable of the prodigal son. A father who waits, who goes out, clasps, forgives, forgets and re-establishes; a father who knows how to detect and accept the invocation of help and forgiveness from the heart of the other.[41]

The Church, in the spirit of *Evangelii gaudium*, is called to be a setting of freely given mercy, where everyone can feel welcomed, loved, forgiven and encouraged to live according to the good life of

---

[38] Cf. *MV*, n. 17.

[39] Cf. Papa Francesco, *Il nome di Dio è misericordia*, p. 43.

[40] Pope Francis, Address to those Helped in the Centre for Re-education of Santa Cruz di Palmasola, 10 July 2015.

[41] Cf. Papa Francesco, *Il nome di Dio è misericordia*, p. 67.

the gospel,[42] but also a place where every person, their processes of growth and the design that God has for them, is taken seriously.[43] She is the place from which, and in which, echoes the invitation to allow oneself to be reconciled with God (cf. 2 Cor 5:20) and to abandon oneself to the arms of His mercy through the Sacrament of Penance and Reconciliation.

Thus it is that the Church, by her vocation and mission, emerges ever more as a concerned Mother who welcomes, cares for and watches over,[44] but also a place where internally she serves and fosters the coming of the Kingdom of God and encounter-communion with God and his fatherly and merciful face. The Church as a minister of the Gospel and the forgiveness of God displays the traits of a reassuring face, we could say a face of the maternal tenderness of God that encourages and goes beyond asking for the performance of simple scrupulous precepts. Love and mercy, made into a concrete act of welcome, forgiveness, sharing and shared journeying, attract and convince the men and women of our epoch that the Church is an experience and life of charity in truth that is able and always ready to open "our hearts to those living on the outermost fringes of society ... so they can feel the warmth of our presence, our friendship, and our fraternity!"[45] This makes the merciful face of Jesus Christ, his Gospel, his forgiveness and his grace, credible and loveable.

Eloquent indeed is the invitation of Francis to priests to ensure that reconciliation is not a moment of torture and notable embarrassment for penitents who want to receive the mercy of God but, rather, a favorable space in which the confessor:

> receives penitents not with the attitude of a judge, nor with that of a simple friend, but with the charity of God, with the love of a father who sees his son returning and goes out to meet him, of the shepherd who has found his lost sheep ... If it is true that Tradition points us to the dual role of physician and judge for confessors, let us never forget how the physician is called to heal and how the judge is called to absolve.[46]

---

[42] Cf. *EG*, n. 114.

[43] Cf. ibid., n. 160.

[44] Cf. ibid., n. 46.

[45] *MV*, n. 5.

[46] Pope Francis, Address to those Taking Part in the Course Organized by the Apostolic Penitentiary, 28 March 2014.

The experience of forgiveness and mercy received from God, through the mediation of the Church, must help the believer or the indifferent to rediscover and explore the transcendent dimension of life, the meaning of Faith in God, through Christ, in the Holy Spirit, and the meaning of belonging first and foremost to the human family and thus to the ecclesial community. In front of a man gravely wounded and bent in his soul and body, it is useless to ask whether the chemical examination of his blood is normal.[47] One has to lead him back to the essential, to a perception of God, to the observance of the Commandments, and to gradual love of Christ, with words and by example.

4. Received and Lived Mercy: a Criterion to Live Truly as Children of God (*MV*, n. 8)

As baptized men and women we are called, because we are loved, to live according to our new natures, reborn by the water of the Spirit, and to transform the mercy of God received into mercy lived as true disciples, according to the healthy rhythms of nearness.[48] In his first encyclical Pope Francis observes that experience of the merciful love of God is not a gift that can be kept to oneself; the true disciple of Jesus cannot allow this to happen. Rather, it is a gift that should be shared with one's brothers and sisters of faith and of one's journey, a gift that opens up the heart in words and works to profession of faith in the God of mercies, thereby being transformed into a proclaiming of salvation.[49] Thus daily life, with its troubles and hopes, constitutes that "field" in which our spiritual "hospital" of witness and fraternal charity should be built and made to live. The gospel images that refer to this reality are very many in number. Amongst many, there are the works of mercy (cf. Mt 25) which are in essential terms the manifestation of a human and Christian face renewed by forgiveness and the love that has been received, works that go beyond individualistic, indifferent and selfish mentalities that have nothing to do with a gospel style based on love.[50] Pope Francis invites all of us to

[47] Cf. A. Spadaro (ed.), "Intervista a Papa Francesco," *La Civiltà Cattolica*, 3918 (2013/III) p. 461.

[48] Cf. *EG*, n. 169.

[49] Cf. *LF*, n. 37.

[50] Cf. *EG*, n. 208.

take care of each other, like brothers and sisters, above all those who find themselves in particular situations of frailty and poverty, and to recognize in them the face of poor and needy Christ.[51] This is because the experience of being forgiven and saved must lead us to love him ever more with words and concrete and small actions.[52] Such as, for example, works of mercy: concrete and small actions, ones that are an expression of fraternal mercy not on a grand scale but on a small scale, and, specifically for this reason, ones that are practicable.

Once again we return to the important and fundamental need to have an assiduous and personal relationship with Jesus, the outcome of an authentic encounter with his gospel which generates and leads to the maturation of faith[53] and makes every relationship between peers a true one, without closing one's eyes to the needs of mercy that knock at the doors of our lives.[54] Giving food and drink, clothing and visiting, proclaiming the gospel of mercy and teaching, accompanying and advising, must make up that movement of *primerear* that involves us for, and with, the lives of other people.[55] This was the approach, in essential terms, of the Virgin Mary at the home of Elizabeth and at the marriage feast of Cana; the approach of the divine Teacher who did not come to be served but to serve; the approach of the Father, lastly, who did not hesitate to send His only Son when we were still sinners and distant from Him. "By this all men will know that you are my disciples, if you have love for one another" (Jn 13:35). It is incontestable that a life lived according to the Gospel in mercy is the distinctive and original feature of true children of God, who are loved, forgiven and saved. And since the essential thing, according to the gospel, is mercy, then everyone must feel the "obligation of charity" to give of their own, what is due, without expecting anything in exchange.[56] It is certainly the case that being merciful like the Father — the theme of the Jubilee of Mercy — makes us reflect and at the same time makes us vulnerable. The first thing to strike the mind and the heart is how is it possible that God, in Jesus Christ, invites us to live this "perfection"? However, we must remember that it is characteristic of the justice and love of God not to ask of man what he cannot do or bear.

---

[51] Cf. ibid., n 209.

[52] Cf. ibid., nn. 264-265.

[53] Cf. *LF*, n. 51.

[54] Cf. *EG*, n. 211.

[55] Cf. ibid., n. 24.

[56] Pope Francis, General Audience, 10 September 2014.

Consequently, each person, according to charity, can and must give what they have received as a gift of mercy, and since mercy has been abundantly poured into our lives it appears clear that we, before others, must feel the zeal of charity so as to share it with the *living flesh* of the other.[57]

5. Forgiveness and the Consequences Achieved by the Infinite Mercy of God. The Gift of Indulgences (*MV*, n. 22)

The Letter by which Pope Francis granted the indulgence on the occasion of the Extraordinary Jubilee of Mercy states in a clear way that the practice of indulgences of the Church is closely united to the Sacrament of Reconciliation and the celebration of the holy Eucharist.[58] As we know, sin is disobedience to the loving and salvific will of God which can lead to corruption,[59] fracture with His charity, and a distancing and the autonomy of our lives in relation to His life. Although sin, as a free and personal act, provokes its first and most important sorrowful consequences in the sinner himself or herself, it also "causes a perturbation in the universal order established by God in His ineffable wisdom and infinite charity, and the destruction of immense values with respect to the sinner himself and to the human community."[60] Disobedient to God, because of the sin that has been committed, "man almost inevitably causes damage to the fabric of his relationship with others and with the created world. This is an objective law and an objective reality, verified in so many ways in the human psyche and in the spiritual life as well as in society, where it is easy to see the signs and effects of internal disorder."[61] Specifically because of the *mysterium pietatis* that Christ himself is, and thanks to the mediating action of the Church, the Sacrament of Reconciliation

[57] Cf. *EG*, n. 88.

[58] Cf. *CCC*, n. 1471.

[59] Pope Francis in his book/interview with Andrea Tornielli is keen to emphasize that to be a sinner is one thing, to be corrupt is another. A sinner is someone who recognizes that they are a sinner, repents and asks forgiveness for their weakness. A corrupt person does not feel humility and without repenting elevates their sin to a system, to a mental *habitus*, making it become a way of life: Papa Francesco, *Il nome di Dio è misericordia*, pp. 92-93.

[60] Paul VI, Apostolic Constitution *Indulgentiarum doctrina* (1 January 1967) (hereafter *ID*), n. 2.

[61] *RP*, n. 15.

returns us to the grace of God, embracing Him in an intimate and great friendship,[62] also restoring reconciliation with the Church, our brothers and sisters and the whole of creation.

We can certainly not fail to notice the great sensitivity of the Pope to the daily difficulties of people or the problems of life, in particular unborn life. For this reason, he did not hesitate to extend to all priests the faculty to absolve the sin of abortion. One is not in the least dealing with endorsing the superficiality of an approach/behavior in the face of the enormously grave drama of abortion. But it is rightly emphasized that nobody can be excluded from mercy. The forgiveness of God cannot be denied to anyone who has repented and through this sacrament wants reconciliation with the Father, their own life and the lives of their brothers and sisters.

Just as the Church administers the Sacrament of Reconciliation so that the reconciliation of sinners with God and with their brothers and sisters is re-established, so she provides indulgences with an "educational" aim: "The aim pursued by ecclesiastical authority in granting indulgences is not only that of helping the faithful to expiate the punishment due sin but also that of urging them to perform works of piety, penitence and charity — particularly those which lead to growth in faith and which favor the common good."[63] Truly the mystery of compassion, which is expressed above all in penance and indulgences, represents the greatest expression of the merciful tenderness of our God. The Extraordinary Jubilee of Mercy represented a "considerable time to prepare themselves properly for acquisition of a plenary indulgence,"[64] not only to take advantage of, and appreciate personally, the abundance of the mercy of God and experience its salutary benefits, but also to become educated in and live the communal and charitable positive outcome of this indulgence.

Specifically for this reason, the Holy Father saw in this jubilee a unique opportunity to have a living experience of nearness to the Father, to touch His tenderness with one's hand, because through this genuine experience of mercy that completely forgets the sin that has been committed the faith of every believer is strengthened and testimony to it becomes increasingly effective:[65]

---

[62] Cf. *Letter of His Holiness Pope Francis According to which an Indulgence is Granted to the Faithful on the Occasion of the Extraordinary Jubilee of Mercy* (1 September 2015); *CCC*, n. 1468.

[63] Ibid., n. 8.

[64] Ibid., n. 12.

[65] Cf. *Letter of His Holiness Pope Francis According to which an Indulgence is Granted to*

> Indeed the faithful when they acquire indulgences understand that by their own powers they could not remedy the harm they have done to themselves and to the entire community by their sin, and they are therefore stirred to a salutary humility. Furthermore, the use of indulgences shows us how closely we are united to each other in Christ, and how the supernatural life of each can benefit others so that these also may be more easily and more closely united with the Father. Therefore the use of indulgences effectively influences charity in us and demonstrates that charity in an outstanding manner when we offer indulgences as assistance to our brothers who rest in Christ.[66]

In order to be able to help each other in the exchange of spiritual goods, through prayer and penitential expiation, every member of the faithful must allow himself to be educated firmly in the fact that his life as a child of God and member of the Church is not only a singular particularity — it also, and even more, involves him being "joined by a wonderful link to the life of all his other Christian brothers in the supernatural unity of the Mystical Body of Christ till, as it were, a single mystical person is formed."[67] This is the reason why Pope Francis exhorted Christians to allow themselves to be fully reconciled with God and to draw near to the mercy of the Father with the certainty that His forgiveness extends in a full way to the life of a believer for the benefit of all their brothers and sisters: "Let us live this Jubilee intensely, begging the Father to forgive our sins and to bathe us in his merciful 'indulgence.'"[68]

6. With our Gaze Fixed on the Virgin Mary, the Mother of Mercy (*MV*, n. 24)

There are some key words in the magisterium of Pope Francis that invoke an unequivocal Christian style of life and translate profound attitudes that refer to the experience of a very precise maternal face of mercy — that of the Virgin Mary. Terms such as "journeying,"

---

the Faithful on the Occasion of the Extraordinary Jubilee of Mercy (1 September 2015).

66 Ibid., n. 9.

67 Ibid., n. 5.

68 *MV*, n. 22.

"accompanying," "nearness" and "caring for" are not only elements that must exclusively mark the rhythm of our jubilee epoch: they must also be a *habitus* to be learned and internalized from she who lived her own life as mercy and in Divine Mercy and to whom the Holy Father entrusted the accompanying of the Holy Year.[69]

The relevant pontifical documents offer us in summarizing form the most significant moments in the life of the Virgin Mary as regards Christ and the Church. We have before us an existential itinerary, if we can use this image, to be followed with her from Nazareth, through Cana, until reaching Jerusalem, where the bitter experience of the shared cross and the maternity that accompanied the first ecclesial community become for us the poles that direct out spiritual journey. "Her entire life was patterned after the presence of mercy made flesh. The Mother of the Crucified and Risen One has entered the sanctuary of divine mercy because she participated intimately in the mystery of His love."[70]

She is the door of this sanctuary[71] and as regards the mystery that crucified her soul she is the privileged witness to supreme forgiveness and mercy that knows no limits because it reaches everyone without excluding anyone.

As priests and confessors we must increasingly perceive the need, following the example of our heavenly Mother, to turn our gaze of mercy to our fellow men, make ourselves responsible for other people and implement new possibilities of life. The life of mercy — as we observe every day — matures in us according to certain previous conditions, such as awareness of our limitations, experience of forgiveness and mercy experienced personally, the magnanimity of the heart of God towards everyone (sinners and the righteous), and so forth. In us, mercy develops, as Pope Francis often observes, in the awareness that to begin with we need the forgiveness and mercy of God. This means that our human and fraternal tie with the other is expressed in taking on, at one and the same time, our own poverty and that of other people. Hence one understands another very fine phrase of the Pope, to the effect that Jesus, specifically at the foot of the cross, left us his Mother as our Mother, because he did not want his disciples to journey without the guidance, the support and the example of a mother.[72]

---

[69] Cf. ibid., n. 24.

[70] Ibidem.

[71] Cf. *Litanie lauretane.*

[72] Cf. *EG*, n. 285.

I would like to end these thoughts of mine by fixing the gaze of my heart on an approach of Mary present in the family icon of Bethlehem. As Pope Francis observes:

> Mary was able to turn a stable into a home for Jesus, with poor swaddling clothes and an abundance of love … She is the missionary who draws near to us and accompanies us throughout life … she walks at our side, she shares our struggles and she constantly surrounds us with God's love."[73]

I believe that these words from certain points of view translate the devotion and the entrusting of Pope Francis to the Holy Virgin who is offered as a sign of hope who welcomes, accompanies and journeys with her children, teaching them to practice the pathways of forgiveness and mercy, so as to contemplate and at the same time reflect the face of merciful God. We must absolutely be witnesses to these riches and this is especially true of confessors such as ourselves.

---

[73] Ibid., n. 286.

THE FAITH OF THE CHURCH IN DIVINE MERCY

I believe that it is extremely important to locate the subject of this analysis, which is so evocative and provocative, in the field of Biblical, theological and pastoral thought, not least with reference to the topic of the remission of sins. We know that today a great difficulty is present and continues specifically in relation to this aspect of Christian faith of the remission of sins as an immense gift of the Divine Mercy of the Father. Modern man, to whom is addressed the Gospel of the remission of sins, encounters great difficulty in listening to this Gospel.

I believe that to begin from this observation is strongly required by the anthropological turning point that for years characterized theological thought, catechesis, pastoral care and ecclesial practice after the new Pentecost of the Second Vatican Council. Modern man encounters difficulty in accepting the Christian discourse of the remission of sins and therefore the Divine Mercy of the Father because the idea of sin appears to him to impose the right of another, the right of God, over his own conscience, and the idea of forgiveness seems to keep him in a position of dependence and not of autonomy. Modern man does not recognize subordination: this is the cultural root that makes it difficult to recognize what grace and sin are.

This sensibility is the outcome of the whole of modern history which is characterized by the search for autonomy: from the scientific revolution that started in the seventeenth century, which defined man as belonging to the universe, the cosmos and its rules (Galileo) and to the world of living beings (Darwin); to claiming his adulthood and reasoning on his own (Kant and the Enlightenment of the eighteenth century); to the liberation from religious tutelage that was regarded with suspicion (Marx, Nietzsche and Freud in the nineteenth century); and on to the terrible experience of the twentieth century in which the vision of unimaginable violence and slaughter made the idea of an order established by God collapse and generated the problem of the existence of evil (Camus).

This is the cultural climate in which Christians today have to speak about sin and the remission of sins in the light of Divine Mercy. With sin, indeed, we are at the center of the religious question of our time, of the interpretation of Christianity after the era of secularization and secularism.

This is a situation of profound crisis that concerns, at one and the same time, our civilization and our Church. It is this difficulty that modern man encounters in recognizing sin and forgiveness that also explains, at its roots, the difficulties of the Christian practice of confession or reconciliation. It is no accident that Benedict XVI, when describing the modern epoch, defined it as an epoch of "spiritual desertification." At first sight, this phrase could seem pessimistic because it sadly highlights what are the great contradictions of our epoch which, indeed, is going through an evident spiritual emptiness, as though God did not exist (*etsi Deus non daretur*). However, when exploring this image in the teaching of Benedict XVI one sees that it is not at all pessimistic. In Benedict XVI there is, rather, a healthy realism that leads him to look with confidence at this emergency, which is spiritual, moral and educational in character, because "it is in starting from the experience of this desert, from this void, that we can again discover the joy of believing." Indeed, in the desert, as Benedict XVI himself points out, "we rediscover the value of what is essential for living; thus in today's world there are innumerable signs, often expressed implicitly or negatively, of the thirst for God, for the ultimate meaning of life. And in the desert people of faith are needed who, with their own lives, point out the way to the Promised Land and keep hope alive."[1]

Deserts thus become a propitious opportunity for purification, for spiritual growth: an obligatory passage, we might say, to becoming aware of reality with all of its limits. Deserts are, therefore, also expectations that often remain implicit and require deciphering to be transformed into opportunities. Behind the emptiness of our time, behind the gravest problems that we observe in the practice of pastoral care, are quite often concealed deep needs of the heart, aspirations and hopes for a more sensible and human life. The deserts of our time also reveal a great thirst for truth and good.

[1] Benedict XVI, Homily during the Holy Mass Opening the Year of Faith, 11 October 2012.

We may ask ourselves: why have we reached this state of "spiritual desertification"? What is it that the modern conscience rejects? The burden of a sense of guilt that subjects man to the dominion and fear of God and impedes him from being his own master and master of his world. Modern man instinctively feels an opposition between religious claims and the defense of the dignity of man. But is this a Christian idea? Is it not rather an ancestral religious approach?

The current idea of sin is often linked to a primitive religious sense of the sacred and the divine. It translates an awareness of violating the order and the prohibitions established by the gods over nature and living things. As long as divinity is felt as being connected to the forces of nature, man is continuously exposed to the danger of invading the "field" of the gods, of breaking their laws, of offending their honor; he lives with the fear of always living in a situation of transgression, of disobedience, of debt towards the gods. He carries inside himself a feeling of anxiety and guilt, of fear of malediction and condemnation.

This idea of sin clearly channels the image of a dominating, angry, vengeful God who is concerned above else with ensuring respect for the order that he has put in everything, jealous of the fact that man enters his field. He is a God conceived in the image of a despotic father of a family that is typical of patriarchal societies.

The mentality of today's Christians — also of our Catholicism, the inheritor of a traditional religiosity — is profoundly marked by this archaic religious background which is mixed in a confused way with "modern" culture.

It is important to discern these elements of the conscience and that includes the Christian conscience. Above all, there is an urgent need to retrieve, in our discourse on sin and forgiveness, the logic and the dynamic of Christian revelation in order to penetrate the core of the faith of the Church in Divine Mercy.

1. Divine Mercy and the Remission of Sins in the Dynamic of Revelation

Biblical man is not immune to this archaic religiosity. However, it was reworked within the development of the worship of Jehovah of Moses which introduced, and led to, faith in a single God and Creator.

The revelation of God has its own history and Holy Scripture contains the revelation of the face of God and His relations with man, in which is necessarily included the reality of sin and forgiveness.

Everything that the Bible takes on from archaic religiosity is reinterpreted and relocated in the framework of a "Law" and a Covenant, the *berît*, which at a deep level transforms the meaning of sin and more in general of the relations between God and man.

The Law, the *Torah*, which God gives to man outlines and defines sin through precise prohibitions whose nature and gravity are demonstrated and which are accompanied by proportionate punishments. Sin is freed from the confusion of a shapeless sacredness and is referred to the responsibility of individual acts. In addition, side by side with the many proscriptions of a cultural and religious character there are — having a central importance — the moral commandments on fundamental relationships between people (do not kill, do not commit adultery, do not steal ...), while subsequent re-readings increasingly stressed the rights of the other and above all of the weakest, respect for the person as such and the responsibility of every individual.

Within the framework of the Law and in interpersonal relationships, sin is seen in this way against the background of the Covenant and is located in the transcendent order of the relations of man with God. Sin constitutes a fracture of the communion of life between God and His people that was established by the Covenant. The sinner becomes increasingly aware of the moral character of sin (as rejection of fraternity and justice) and its theological character at one and the same time: as lack of faithfulness to God, as rejection of His covenant and His promise, as ingratitude towards His grace and towards the way He proposes to us and offers us for our freedom. The Law no longer embodies the image of a God who dominates but has the people of Israel enter a process of liberation and gratitude. In this way, Israel is introduced to the experience of new relations with its God: a prevenient God who leads His people to freedom, a merciful and compassionate God who is slow to anger and is rich in grace (Ex 34:6). And even if the people of Israel always feel threatened by divine vengeance, that people discovers that forgiveness will always prevail over anger in God. In the logic of the Covenant, a new image of God comes to the fore in the alternating experience of sin and forgiveness.

The Apostle Paul compared the condition of man under the Law to that of a child taken care of who awaits his emancipation to enter the condition of being a son (Gal 4:1-3). It is true that the people of

Israel during their long history of political and military disasters continually had the feeling that they were being punished because of their lack of faithfulness to the Covenant. But, instructed by the prophets, they understood that these scourges were not due to the anger and the vengeance of God but to the goodness of a Father who corrects His sons. And repenting of the errors of youth, they felt comforted by the superabundant love of their God: "Thou hast chastened me, and I was chastened like an untrained calf," the Lord is told. And the Lord answers: "Is Ephraim my dear son? Is he my darling child? For as often as I speak against him, I do remember him still. Therefore my heart yearns for him; I will surely have mercy upon him" (Jer 31:18-20). Lived in this way, the experience of sin, repentance and forgiveness become a school of freedom and man learns in it to discover, a little at a time, the figure of the Father whom God reveals in Jesus. Man accedes to his deepest humanity and true freedom by accepting the revelation of God who is love and grace.

2. Jesus: the Completion of the Revelation of the Divine Mercy of the Father

The divine pedagogy of Divine Mercy towards man the sinner and the true meaning of sin are revealed fully in Jesus.

2.1. *Jesus Amongst the Sinners*

On coming down from the mountain with the two tablets of the Law in his hand, Moses found his people dancing around the golden calf. Full of holy fury he broke the tablets and called "those on the side of the Lord" to uphold His honor. Thus it was that the sons of Levy massacred 3,000 men and were rewarded for this by being made priests (cf. Ex 32:15-29). During his first appearance in public Jesus went into the waters of the River Jordan and mixed with the sinners who had come to ask for Baptism by John and confess their sins. God's pleasure was expressed in the following way: "Thou art my beloved Son; with thee I am well pleased" and the Spirit descended upon him (Mk 1:9-12). This inaugural scene of the mission of Jesus reveals the true meaning of the history of salvation, which is a divine economy of forgiveness, and at the same time manifests the radical change that was produced on the stage of the religious history of humanity. The essential innovation was that the envoy of God, the

"Holy One of God," placed himself at the level of sinners, lowered himself to their condition to represent them in front of God, and God "raised" him up by recognizing him as His Son.

In this light one understands profoundly and intensely the importance of that feature of the behavior of Jesus that causes scandal: on many occasions in his public life Jesus was surprised in the company of sinners, with whom the zealous Jews of the "holiness" of God had to avoid contact. He came not to call the righteous but to call sinners (cf. Mt 9:10-13). God did not send His Son to condemn the world but so that the world could be saved through him (cf. Jn 3:17). Jesus does not think that his mission is first of all to hunt for sin, threatening sinners with divine punishments. Instead, refusing to identify a man with his sin he shows that God searches for sinners, ready to give all of himself to bring them into His house and restore to them the honor of being sons (cf. Lk 15:22-23).

Sin is not so much an offence against God as a wound that man inflicts on himself that disfigures his humanity. This is why Jesus had to face up to his passion: "he has borne our griefs and carries our sorrow" (Is 53:4). This choice of Jesus led him to be listed amongst the malefactors, to be "cursed" (Gal 3:13). He did not withdraw from death because of "blasphemy" and from defamatory death on the Cross. And God, resurrecting him and enthroning him on his right side, made the Cross the setting for the revelation of His glory, His "justice" and His love. Paul, reflecting on this mystery of abasement and elevation (cf. Phil 2; 5-11), understands that the history of salvation reached its completion in the event of the death and the resurrection of Jesus: "God was in Christ reconciling the world to himself" (2 Cor 5:19). When God raised from the dead he who had given his life to Him and the heavens opened to welcome as the Son of God he who had been cursed in the name of the Law, it became manifest that "we were reconciled to God by the death of his Son" (Rom 5:10), that "Christ redeemed us from the curse of the law, having become a curse for us" (Gal 3:13), and that God accepted his death as putting away "sin by the sacrifice of himself" (Heb 9:26).

All sins were thus forgiven "once" (Heb 9:28) for men of all epochs and all situations in the sense that God abstains from punishing sin and makes known to those who see Him as an irritated and pitiless master that He will never persecute sinners with His anger but will besiege them with His love. He does this so that anyone who welcomes this love, this merciful face of God, is purified of their sins, conforms to His Son and passes with him from death to life. An event of universal importance was produced in the religious history of humanity and this is called "redemption," "remission of sins" and "reconciliation with God." The Cross in this way definitively eliminated the values of that ancestral religion, that religion that men constructed on a logic of exchange with God. The veil of the temple was broken, revealing the emptiness of the sanctuary and the uselessness of sacrifices; the Law that condemned to death the Righteous One manifested its powerlessness. God decreed the end of the sacrificial era, "Where there is forgiveness of these, there is no longer any offering for sin" (Heb 10:18), and opened up the way of trust which takes the place of fear because "There is no fear in love (1 Jn 4:18) now that it was revealed that nothing "will be able to separate us from the love of God in Christ Jesus our Lord" (Rom 8:39)

2.2. *Reconciled With Each Other*

The event of the Cross did not only transform the relationship of God with the world — it also transformed the relationship of people with each other. If the Law is the only way of salvation, the other peoples of the world are excluded from salvation unless they join the people of Israel through circumcision. This privilege led Israel to become excessively proud of its descendants in the flesh and to despise pagan nations. At the same time, it led these nations to jealousy of the chosen people and to revolt against God who had not chosen them: the Law seemed to generate hatred. But now it was dethroned by the Cross because this was the way of salvation: on the Cross Christ revealed himself and "is our peace, he who made both one and broke down the dividing wall of enmity, through his flesh, abolishing the law with its commandments and legal claims, that he ... might reconcile both with God, in one body, through the cross, putting that enmity to death by it" (Eph 2:14-16). It was thus that God, disarming religious enmities — the symbol of all other enmities — placed in Jesus the principle of the reconciliation of peoples with each other, "making peace by the blood of his cross" (Col 1:20).

The remission of sins achieved on the Cross went beyond the strictly religious framework and was extended to the whole world, becoming a source of real unity of mankind and, at the same time, it gave birth to a new humanity reconciled with itself and with God: "So whoever is in Christ is a new creation: the old things have passed away; behold, new things have come. And all this is from God, who has reconciled us to himself through Christ and given us the ministry of reconciliation" (2 Cor 5:17-18). In the eyes of Paul this is the "mystery of salvation," the "hope of the glory of God" with the pagans, the proclaiming of which constitutes the essential aspect of his personal mission and the mission of Christ (Col 1:25-27). This is a religious revolution where love of neighbor is identified with love of God. Love of God, which led Jesus to give his life for us, calls us to love each other so as to remain in His love. The Cross, by dethroning the Law to the advantage of faith, made people attain a new understanding of sin and salvation.

Sin was no longer only an offence against the honor of God, with a transgression of the religious law — it was also, and more radically, an offence against His love for men through contempt for them. God is offended in man every time that the transcendence with which man is clothed by the love by which God leads us to Him is not respected. In this way, sin took on a definitively ethical character that was not absent in the ancient Law but which was veiled by its location in a code that was first and foremost religious in character. As a consequence, salvation was not simply entering a sacred order that regulated relations with God and predisposed men to enter divine beatitude. It called them to banish selfishness, pride, the hatred that destroys the human order willed by God, the order of justice and fraternal love, and thus called them to enter the way of reconciled humanity that God wanted to transfer "to the kingdom of his beloved Son" (Col 1,13). The search for salvation, far from separating men from history and the construction of a human world, is a constituent part of a true "humanism" that meets the aspiration of the modern conscience, albeit infinitely going beyond its expectations and contesting its closures.

2.3. *The Gift and the Promise*

The Christian recognition of the new order of salvation revealed by the death and resurrection of Jesus was immediately expressed in the practice of Baptism. John already practiced a "baptism of repentance for the forgiveness of sins." This Baptism had an eminently eschatological character, it expressed, that is, the imminent expectation of the end of the world, of the coming of the "day of the Lord," of the judgment of the world by God and the establishment of His Kingdom.

The Baptism of Jesus is different from that of John, as we know, because it infuses the Holy Spirit as a gift of the love of God, of His forgiveness and His peace, of His life and His Holiness. On the day of Pentecost Peter invited those who repented to "be baptized, every one of you, in the name of Jesus Christ for the forgiveness of your sins; and you will receive the gift of the holy Spirit" (Acts 2:38). This gift is identified with the forgiveness of sins obtained by Baptism, according to the power conferred on the Apostles by the risen Jesus: "Receive the holy Spirit. Whose sins you forgive are forgiven them, and whose sins you retain are retained" (Jn 20:22-23).

Christian Baptism is thus experienced as participation in the death and the resurrection of Jesus Christ (cf. Rom 6:3-4). A contemporary gift, Baptism conserves, however, its character of being a eschatological promise. Indeed, if we can say that God "raised us up with him, and seated us with him in the heavens in Christ Jesus" (Eph 2:6), it is clear that we can only enjoy eternal life after our deaths, with the hope that "the one who raised Christ from the dead will give life to your mortal bodies also, through his Spirit that dwells in you" (Rom 8:11). The forgiveness of sins is directed to the future in another sense as well: the baptized, who live new lives, nonetheless constantly have the experience of frailty that continuously threatens to make them lose the grace that they have received. On the other hand, they remain linked to the whole creation which is "groaning in labor pains even until now" (Rom 8:22-23), to the history of men and to the "political" aspect of the remission of sins which commits them to working for a future of solidarity and fraternity.

3. The Remission of Sins at the Time of the First Christians as Experience of Divine Mercy

If what I have expounded in summarizing fashion hitherto is an understanding of the "remission of sins" in the light of Divine Mercy, which is offered to us by Biblical revelation, we must now ask ourselves how this is expressed in the faith of Christians. What place does it have in the *Creed* of Christians?

The *Symbol of the Apostles*, whose first formulation appeared at the end of the second century but took on its definitive form much later, revolved around two axes:

— Starting with the baptismal profession of faith, through the subsequent invocation of three divine names in the form of questions (Do you believe in God the Father? Do you believe in Jesus Christ? Do you believe in the Holy Spirit?), each of which corresponds to the immersion of the catechumen in the water of the pool.

— Starting with the *Rule of truth* that at the outset envisaged only two terms, by which the common belief in "God Father Almighty" was specified as Christian with the addition of faith "in Jesus Christ, his Son, our Lord."

Subsequently, the reference to Christ would be expanded to affirm his true humanity, identified with his historical journey from birth to death. A third article was added of baptismal provenance. One can therefore engage in two readings of the *Symbol of the Apostles*: as a doctrinal summary and as a profession of faith. Read as a doctrinal summary, the third article of the *Creed* is connected to the proclaiming of the "day of the Lord" (which until the end of the second century Christians believed was near to hand) and to the glorious manifestation of Christ who "will come to judge the living and the dead." This article proclaims the future realities awaited by Christians: the full gift of the Holy Spirit, awaited by the creation for its redemption, and the descent of the celestial Jerusalem of all the chosen with their resurrected bodies for eternal life.

From this point of view, the "remission of sins" is identified with the definitive redemption of our bodies, liberated for always from concupiscence and death, and in this way faith in the forgiveness of sins is the cry of a Christian who aspires to the "revelation of the children of God," to entering "the glorious freedom of the children of God" (Rom 8:19-21). The article as a whole is a proclamation of Christian hope about the end of the world, future salvation, the wish and hope for which is given to us by the Spirit (Rom 8:24-27). Read in the context of the baptismal profession of faith, this article, without losing its eschatological character, emphasizes goods currently received from God, through the mediation of Christ, in the act itself of Baptism, and thus the goods that are a pledge of those we hope for.

The first of these goods is the Holy Spirit: the primordial gift, the source of all other spiritual goods; then comes the Church, in which Christians are regenerated and adopted as children; followed by the communion of saints, whom the Spirit brings together to make them the dwelling of God and unified in a single body, the body of Christ; then the resurrection of bodies through the Spirit who dwells in them; and lastly eternal life of which the Spirit is the spring of living water. The forgiveness of sins, in this list, means the effect immediately produced by Baptism in its two aspects, negative and positive, and in its two moments, immersion in water and coming out of water: the purification of sins and the sanctification of the soul reconciled with God thanks to the gift of the Holy Spirit. A Christian thus comes out of the baptismal immersion ready to sit at the banquet of the wedding of the Lamb. But at this point, and at this moment, the test of time comes into play. Indeed, it is one thing to receive the gift, quite another to keep it until the end. What happens when a Christian falls back into sin and loses the grace of forgiveness?

For the early Christians the answer appeared obvious: just as the remission of sins took place "once" on the cross, so it was received "once and for ever" in Baptism, as, indeed, the Letter to the Hebrews says expressly:

> For it is impossible in the case of those who have once been enlightened and tasted the heavenly gift and shared in the holy Spirit and tasted the good word of God and the powers of the age to come, and then have fallen away, to bring them to repentance again, since they are recrucifying the Son of God for themselves and holding him up to contempt (Heb 6:4-6).

For those who awaited the imminent coming of Christ, it was as though time was suspended, already dissolved, and sin no longer had a place. Unfortunately, however, many Christians, immediately tired of waiting for the return of the Lord, stopped "frequenting the saints," returned to the things of the pagan world, gave way to seductions, to their previous sins, even sacrificed to idols because of fear of persecution, and abandoned the Christian life. When they returned to the Church and implored the remission of their sins, they heard that they had received it once and for ever. This was the vexation of Christians who lived in pagan contexts.

When reflecting on the parables of Jesus and considering the mission that he had entrusted to the apostles, the Church became aware that she had received the power to forgive sins in an unlimited way and introduced a practice that invited those who had left to return, to engage in penance and to receive a "second remission of sins" in order to be able to experience the permanent gift, linked to the here and now of every believer, of the experience of the return to the house of the Father and an embrace with Divine Mercy in the logic of the parable of Luke of the merciful Father (Lk 15:11-32) through the act of the remission of sins in every sacramental confession.

4. The Thought and the Original Contribution of Saint Faustina Kowalska

On our pilgrimage in the faith of the Church through the pathways of Divine Mercy, I believe it is incumbent upon me, and right, to halt now at a significant *kairòs* deposited in the spiritual experience of St. Faustina Kowalska (1905-1938), on which we should reflect, albeit briefly, to understand how this theological and pastoral subject entered the Church of the Second Vatican Council and went on to the special and original experience of St. John Paul II who, pervaded by the strong feeling of "Jesus I trust in you" given to St. Faustina, established on the second Sunday of Easter the liturgical feast day of Divine Mercy. The life of Sister Faustina, sorely tested by very severe difficulties and unprecedented graces, possesses the great meaning of bearing witness to total and impassioned abandonment and to the ineffable tenderness of the merciful love of God, transmitting new forms of worship of Divine Mercy and promoting a great movement of people devoted to Divine Mercy and apostles of Divine Mercy.

"My daughter, say that I am Love and Mercy in person,"[2] Jesus commanded Sister Faustina, having her experience all of his sweetness. "O inconceivable and unfathomable Mercy of God, who can worship and exalt You in a worthy way? O greatest attribute of Almighty God, You are the sweet hope of sinners."[3]

With the canonization of Sister Faustina, which took place on 30 April 2000, St. John Paul II, when consecrating the whole world to Divine Mercy, transmitted a message about it to the new millennium:

> I intend today to pass this message on to the new millennium. I pass it on to all people, so that they will learn to know ever better the true face of God and the true face of their brethren ... What will man's future on earth be like?

[2] M.F. Kowalska, *Diario. La misericordia divina nella mia anima*, n. 374.

[3] Ibidem, n. 951.

> We are not given to know. However, it is certain that in addition to new progress there will unfortunately be no lack of painful experiences. But the light of divine mercy, which the Lord in a way wished to return to the world through Sr. Faustina's charism, will illumine the way for the men and women of the third millennium … How many souls have been consoled by the prayer "*Jesus, I trust in you,*" which Providence intimated through Sr. Faustina! This simple act of abandonment to Jesus dispels the thickest clouds and lets a ray of light penetrate every life."[4]

I believe that it is right and incumbent upon me to observe that the deep contact with this spiritual sensibility of this Polish saint was certainly the inspiration for Pope Wojtyla in publishing on 30 November 1980 his wonderful and important encyclical *Dives in misericordia*. This encyclical ends with these significant and evocative words:

> The Church proclaims the truth of God's mercy revealed in the crucified and risen Christ, and she professes it in various ways. Furthermore, she seeks to practice mercy towards people through people, and she sees in this an indispensable condition for solicitude for a better and "more human" world, today and tomorrow. However, at no time and in no historical period-especially at a moment as critical as our own-can the Church forget the prayer that is a cry for the mercy of God amid the many forms of evil which weigh upon humanity and threaten it. Precisely this is the fundamental right and duty of the Church in Christ Jesus, her right and duty towards God and towards humanity. The more the human conscience succumbs to secularization, loses its sense of the very meaning of the word "mercy," moves away from God and distances itself from the mystery of mercy, the more the Church has the right and the duty to appeal to the God of mercy "with loud cries." These "loud cries" should be the mark of the Church of our times, cries uttered to God to implore His mercy, the certain manifestation of which she professes and proclaims as having already come in Jesus crucified and risen, that is, in the Paschal

[4] John Paul II, Homily during the Holy Mass for the Canonization of the Blessed *Maria Faustina Kowalska*, 30 April 2000.

> Mystery. It is this mystery which bears within itself the most complete revelation of mercy, that is, of that love which is more powerful than death, more powerful than sin and every evil, the love which lifts man up when he falls into the abyss and frees him from the greatest threats.[5]

5. The Confessional as a Setting of Faith, Education of the Conscience and Experience of Divine Mercy

Sacramental confession is the practice that more than any other enables us to experience the greatness, the beauty and the regenerating power of Divine Mercy. When a penitent enters the confessional, they really draw near to the love of the Father; they enter the merciful love of God who alone is able to heal the wounds of the soul, to remove the sin that impedes us from remaining in friendship with Him, to make all things new in a member of the faithful who, with humility and sincere repentance, implores forgiveness. The Sacrament of Penance is an effective instrument that regenerates man from within because it helps him to understand the truth of himself, that truth, that is to say, of being a chosen son of the Father who is rich in mercy and always ready to give him His forgiveness and peace unconditionally.

On a number of occasions in his speeches and public activity, Pope Francis has invited us not to be afraid of asking for the forgiveness of God because He is happy when He gives us His mercy. Indeed, when meeting the minor penitentiaries of the Basilica of St. Mary Major the day after his election as Pope he said to them: "Mercy, mercy, mercy. You are confessors, therefore you should be merciful towards souls."

Pope Francis has laid a great deal of emphasis on communicating that God is infinite mercy because he wants to generate in the hearts of men of good will the trust and the hope that in life changes are always possible. Our time is always a time for conversion and salvation. He wants the Church to show herself to the world as the Mother and Teacher of mercy, as "a house for everyone, where all can be renewed, transformed, sanctified by his love, the strongest and the weakest, sinners, the indifferent, those who feel discouraged or lost."[6] At the general audience of 20 November 2013 Pope Francis stressed once again that:

---

[5] *DM*, n. 15.

[6] Pope Francis, General Audience, 2 October 2013.

> God forgives every man in his sovereign mercy, but he himself willed that those who belong to Christ and to the Church receive forgiveness by means of the ministers of the community. Through the apostolic ministry the mercy of God reaches me, my faults are forgiven and joy is bestowed on me. In this way Jesus calls us to live out reconciliation in the ecclesial, the community, dimension as well. And this is very beautiful. The Church, who is holy and at the same time in need of penitence, accompanies us on the journey of conversion throughout our life. The Church is not mistress of the power of the keys, but a servant of the ministry of mercy and rejoices every time she can offer this divine gift.[7]

The positive consequences of these exhortations of the Holy Father are truly innumerable and affect various parts of the world, from which indeed we receive information, through the media as well, about a notable reawakening of people, of our faithful who draw near with greater trust and a sincere spirit of repentance to the sacrament of confession.

In this way, the confessional becomes a "theological setting," a privileged place to obtain the beneficial and redemptive effects of the resurrection of Christ who was the first to proclaim the great news of Divine Mercy and entrusted its ministry to the apostles: "Peace be with you. As the Father has sent me, so I send you … Receive the Holy Spirit. Whose sins you forgive are forgiven them, and whose sins you retain are retained" (Jn 20:21-23).

When administering the Sacrament of Reconciliation, the priest has a valuable opportunity to evangelize, to proclaim the good news and to educate morally the conscience of every member of the faithful who turns to him. We have an exemplary model of this in St. Pio of Pietrelcina who wrote in a letter: "It seems that Jesus has no other care for his hands than that of sanctifying your soul."[8] As a good confessor, Padre Pio's concern was to ensure that people reconciled themselves with God, that they were able to experience His mercy and, when renewed inwardly in their consciences, that they rediscovered the beauty and the joy of being Christians, of living in conformity with Christ, of loving the Church and of putting the Gospel into practice in their daily lives. Indeed, it is in the confessional that every

---

[7] Pope Francis, General Audience, 20 November 2013.

[8] Pio da Pietrelcina, *Epistolario*, II (San Giovanni Rotondo, 1987), p. 155.

priest, when absolving the penitent of a sin that has been committed, becomes a privileged communicator of Divine Mercy that penetrates the innermost part of every conscience to the point of bringing about the conversion of the heart and joy because of salvation that has been found again. To evangelize is not only to bring a doctrine, to proclaim truths. To evangelize is above all else to proclaim the good news of the gospel which is able to touch the hearts of men and to open them to welcoming the love of God. As Pope Francis observed: "*the priest is the instrument for the forgiveness of sins* ... he too is a man, who, like us in need of mercy, truly becomes the instrument of mercy, bestowing on us the boundless love of God the Father."[9]

There come to mind those intense words that St. John Paul II used in his apostolic exhortation *Reconciliatio et Paenitentia* to emphasize the human and spiritual qualities of a confessor who is also always an educator of consciences:

> the confessor must necessarily have human qualities of prudence, discretion, discernment and a firmness tempered by gentleness and kindness. He must likewise have a serious and careful preparation, not fragmentary but complete and harmonious, in the different branches of theology, pedagogy and psychology, in the methodology of dialogue and above all in a living and communicable knowledge of the word of God. But it is even more necessary that he should live an intense and genuine spiritual life. In order to lead others along the path of Christian perfection the minister of penance himself must first travel this path. More by actions than by long speeches he must give proof of real experience of lived prayer, the practice of the theological and moral virtues of the Gospel, faithful obedience to the will of God, love of the Church and docility to her magisterium.[10]

One thus understands that in the context of confession, as well, formation — as Romano Guardini suggests — is first of all a question of "self-formation,"[11] in the sense that a good confessor is called to "take care of himself," to promote the maturation of his own conscience, to exercise his relationship with God through the exercise of thinking in order to be aware of himself and of good, in the eyes of God.

---

[9] Pope Francis, General Audience, 20 November 2013.

[10] *RP*, n. 29.

[11] Cf. R. Guardini, *Lettere sull'autoformazione* (Brescia, 1994).

Indeed, just as faith is transmitted through the faith of those who bear witness to it, so is the conscience formed through the conscience of those who live habitually in the dynamic of discernment, carried out with the Lord and with the help of grace, in understanding truth and good, in assessing and deciding about reality and situations. Wise pastoral activity should be guided by this awareness. For the formation of consciences, in the sacramental context as well, the theological life is of central importance for those who have the task of educating.

A personal friendship with Jesus, prayer, spiritual discernment applied to one's own interior world and to relationships and experiences, emerge in an inevitable way in the person of the confessor. The experience of free giving and nearness to God in this way animate the ministry of the priest, especially when he welcomes the penitent in the confessional. Specifically because he has met the Lord and has experienced His love, he can be a father who welcomes, a physician who cures, a teacher (or doctor) who educates, and a judge who applies mercy.[12]

From this point of view, without doubt one of the pastoral priorities, especially for priests who care for souls, is to spend much time in the confessional. This is because through the administration of this sacrament there are very many opportunities to form the consciences of believers in an upright way, helping them to welcome Christ into their hearts and to open themselves to his presence, a presence that is always able to transform, to convert and to make all things new. All pastoral activity must know how to direct people to the confessional, in which, before and better than every human action, the power of grace acts: freeing us from all evil, it always restores us again to the dignity of being children of God and members of the Church. This is why during the deliberations of the thirteenth Ordinary General Assembly of the Synod of Bishops in 2012 there emerged a highly significant proposal to relaunch the importance and the centrality of the Sacrament of Reconciliation in the life of every parish and diocesan community:

> In every diocese, at least one place should be especially dedicated in a permanent way for the celebration of this sacrament, where priests are always present, allowing God's mercy to be experienced by all the faithful. The sacrament should be especially available, even on a daily basis, at places

[12] Cf. A.M. De' Liguori, *Pratica del confessore per ben esercitare il suo ministero.*

> of pilgrimage and specially designated churches. Fidelity to the specific norms which rule the administration of this sacrament is necessary. Every priest should consider the Sacrament of Penance an essential part of his ministry and of the New Evangelization, and in every parish community a suitable time should be set apart for hearing confessions.[13]

The rediscovery and valuing of the Sacrament of Penance depends to a great extent on us priests and our being aware that we are the custodians of a valuable and irreplaceable ministry, as Pope Benedict emphasized to the Apostolic Penitentiary during the audience he granted to those taking part in the course on the internal forum held in 2012:

> Dear priests and dear deacons who are preparing for the priesthood, in the administration of this sacrament you are given, or you will be given, the possibility of being instruments of an ever renewed meeting of people with God. All who turn to you, precisely because of their condition as sinners, will experience within them a profound desire: the desire for change, the desire for mercy and, ultimately, the desire for the encounter with Christ and for him to embrace them once again. You will therefore be collaborators and protagonists of a great many possible "new beginnings."[14]

This brief analysis of mine has sought to emphasize some substantial elements from a Biblical, theological, moral and pastoral point of view, with a more specific final reference to the spiritual experience of Saint Kowalska. I believe that one cannot address this subject in a fertile and meaningful way unless one enters a climate of deep and contemplative prayer, remembering the famous motto of Evragius Ponticus: "If you are a theologian, you will really pray, and if you really pray you are a theologian" (*De oratione*, n. 60).

[13] Synod of Bishops, XIII General Assembly, final list of propositions, n. 33.

[14] Benedict XVI, Address to those Taking Part in the Course on the Internal Forum Organized by the Apostolic Penitentiary, 9 March 2012.

THE JUBILEE OF MERCY: THE TENDERNESS OF GOD

The recent celebration of the great event of the Jubilee places us in front of thinking about and contemplating the mystery of the mercy of God, defined according to the category of "tenderness" which is so dear to the Holy Father Francis:

> I have often thought of how the Church may render more clear her mission to be a witness to mercy; and we have to make this journey. It is a journey which begins with spiritual conversion. Therefore, I have decided to announce an *Extraordinary Jubilee* which has at its centre the mercy of God. It will be a *Holy Year of Mercy*. We want to live in the light of the word of the Lord: "Be merciful, even as your Father is merciful" (cf. Lk 6:36).[1]

With these words the Holy Father Francis notified the whole of the Catholic world of his decision to hold an Extraordinary Jubilee which he defined as the Holy Year of Mercy. It would have at its center contemplation of the mercy of the Father manifested in the merciful face of Jesus Christ. The evocative context in which the Pope gave his address, namely the celebration of the penitential liturgy, was the place and the favorable moment for such an announcement to be heard by the whole world in all its meaning and efficacy.

This was followed some months later by the gift of the Bull of Indiction of the Extraordinary Jubilee with a title that contained a program, *Misericordiae vultus*, which all of us welcomed, read with particular attention, and thought about. The structure of the text and its theological-pastoral riches direct the journey of every believer and help every man and woman of good will to encounter that transcendent

[1] Pope Francis, Homily during the Penitential Liturgy and the Rite of Reconciliation, 13 March 2015.

God, the Father of everyone, who strongly wishes to grant His merciful love to all those who turn to Him with a sincere heart.

When analyzing the text of this Bull I was able to discern certain key insights. We have before us, it seems to me, a simple and linear architecture yet at the same time one that is rich in contents and images. We have an itinerary where Pope Francis, page after page, accompanies us so that the various moments and celebrations — as well as time passed — in daily life become the *existential space* in which we allow ourselves to encounter and reconcile ourselves with the merciful love of God, in Jesus Christ, in the Holy Spirit, in order to be, in our turn, "living" instruments of this kind and divine tenderness. Numbers 1 and 25 of the text, the first and the last of the Bull, constitute great inclusion because they contain in two similar phrases an explicit reference to who, alone, can manifest and offer the mercy of the father: "Jesus Christ is the face of the Father's mercy … contemplating the face of Christ … From the heart of the Trinity, from the depths of the mystery of God, the great river of mercy wells up and overflows unceasingly."[2] Therefore, "With our eyes fixed on Jesus and his merciful gaze, we experience the love of the Most Holy Trinity,"[3] not only to obtain from it a model useful for the Christian life and the Church, but also to see oneself, discover oneself and understand oneself in its light. Here we have the great protagonist of the Jubilee of Mercy, the Face of Christ, and when we gaze upon it we rediscover the Christian meaning of life, the transcendent dimension and the vocation to the blessed eternity of human existence. Thus the Extraordinary Jubilee of Mercy was an opportunity to rediscover that every day our earthly journey is an always new gift of God's merciful love for us[4] and that when we welcome it we allow ourselves to be enveloped by the cloak of divine tenderness, with which we see God and our brothers and sisters with the light of the face of Christ. In it, we live as merciful people — merciful as our heavenly Father is.

---

[2] *MV*, nn. 1, 25.

[3] Ibid., n. 8.

[4] Cf. *Roman Missal*, Preface of the Sundays of Ordinary Time VI.

1. The Face of the Merciful Tenderness of God in the Old Testament

After this short introduction, in which I have tried to discern some theological-pastoral principles of the meaning of the Extraordinary Jubilee of Mercy in the light of the Bull of Indiction, I would now like to dwell upon the tenderness of God as the essence of His nature, the force of His salvific action, and a relevant dimension of the event of the Jubilee. I make no attempt at an exhaustive analysis nor do I have the presumption of advancing exegetic hypotheses. I will seek in a certain way to highlight how the people of the new and the old Covenant experience the tenderness of God and how these events are for us a memory and a reality that we should look at. They do not belong to the past or just one people. They are useful not only to know and learn about the infinite and tender love of the Father — they also, and above all else, go into the depths of it and allow ourselves to conquered by it. At the end of the Jubilee event, but also of every experience of our lives, to paraphrase what the Apostle John writes in the incipit of his First Letter, we can proclaim to the world how great and sublime are the mercy and tenderness of God. We have seen, heard and touched them in Christ His Son and we have allowed ourselves to be enveloped and shaken by them. We have done this to go to our brothers and sisters, whoever they may be, so that they can take part in the proclaiming and the event of mercy that we have experienced, as Pope Francis himself requested.[5]

The terms "mercy" and "tenderness" when applied to God are, after a certain fashion, always present in the teachings of Pope Francis; they constitute the pillars on which the architrave of his magisterium are based. He has invoked them ever since his first homily as the Bishop of Rome when, at the Holy Mass of the beginning of his pontificate, in front of the great and the powerful of the world, he stated: "We must not be afraid of goodness, of tenderness! We must not be afraid of goodness, of tenderness!"[6] The foundations in Holy Scripture of his statements are evident in the same way as references

---

[5] "How much I desire that the year to come will be steeped in mercy, so that we can go out to every man and woman, bringing the goodness and tenderness of God!" (*MV*, n. 5).

[6] Pope Francis, Homily for the Petrine Ministry of the Bishop of Rome, 19 March 2013.

to the lives of saints of all epochs are evident. Specifically in the light of the fundamental stages of the history of salvation, narrated by Holy Scripture, I would like to read some moments that manifest attitudes and expressions of the mercy and tenderness of God as a unique intimate and profound movement of His love towards man, albeit with different declinations and shadings. I could begin, for example, with the greatest wish of man in relation to God and demonstrate His "maternal" nuances.

To encounter the face of God has been, and still is, the deepest aspiration of man. The unceasing prayer of the pious Israelite highlights this: "Thy face, Lord, do I seek. Hide not thy face from me" (Ps 27:8-9) and the prayers of the people who are suffering and troubled because of the fall of the city of Samaria because of the Assyrians express this yearning, united to the hope that salvation will show itself specifically through the splendor of the face of the Most High (cf. Ps 79:8,20). Undoubtedly, when an Israelite believer asked the Lord to gain access, after a certain fashion, to His face, he did not intend to ask for the gift of intimate and visual knowledge of God — he wanted, rather, the gift of benevolence and mercy.[7] Thus it is that terms such as "benevolence," "magnanimity," "compassion" and "mercy" in the Hebrew tradition translate the term "*hesed*"[8] with various shadings and nuances. The word "*hesed*," indeed, is employed with a certain fluidity and despite this expresses various aspects of the merciful approach with which God bends down to real man, His people, in order to express nearness, closeness, protection and salvation.

In recent Italian translations of Holy Scripture, and in particular of the Old Testament, it is evident that the terms "mercy" and "tenderness" appear as synonyms, and the merciful love of God is presented with maternal shadings. According to some recent studies, on the other hand, the term "*rāham*"[9] is very distinct from "*hesed*" and refers to a deeper feeling/impulse of a person, something that is felt in the innermost part of an individual, the seat of their most tender sensibilities and affections — *rahămîm* (the plural of intensity) which evokes the tender love of the *human womb* (*rehem*).[10] This is a

[7] Cf. E. Tiedtke, "Volto," in *Dizionario dei concetti biblici del Nuovo Testamento*, p. 2013.

[8] Cf. H.J. Stoebe, "Hesed," in *Dizionario Teologico dell'Antico Testamento*, I, coll. 520-539.

[9] Cf. H.J. Stoebe, "Rḥm," in *Dizionario Teologico dell'Antico Testamento*, II, coll. 685-692.

[10] Cf. A. Serra, "Tenerezza: tema biblico orchestrato a più voci," *Servitium*, 183 (2009/III), p. 39.

love of great intensity, of total involvement and commitment in providing help, with compassion, a love given freely and in one direction (from God to man), a unique and tender love which daily experience identifies in a special way in the bond between a father or a mother and their child. For these reasons, some scholars are inclined to make a net distinction between the term *hesed* (mercy through empathy) and *rahămîm* (the tenderness of moved and involving love), which is not always so marked. It is said that this distinction helps the drawing up and the existence of a theology of tenderness in addition to the theology of mercy, which is by now widespread.[11]

After this brief clarification, I intend to proceed with a presentation, as has already been indicated, of some significant episodes where the tenderness of God towards His people, the people of the Covenant as the firstborn, is most emphasized (cf. Ex 4:22). How can we not remember the famous and touching phrases of the prophets Isaiah, Hosea and Jeremiah? "But Zion said, "The Lord has forsaken me; my Lord has forgotten me." Can a mother forget her infant, be without tenderness for the child of her womb? Even should she forget, I will never forget you (Is 49:14-15). "How could I give you up, O Ephraim, or deliver you up, O Israel? How could I treat you as Admah, or make you like Zeboiim? My heart is overwhelmed, my pity is stirred" (Hos 11:8). "Is Ephraim not my favored son, the child in whom I delight? Often as I threaten him, I still remember him with favor; My heart stirs for him, I must show him mercy, says the Lord" (Jer 31:20). As one can see, God involves Himself tenderly and totally in our history, which is, and remains, a history of falls and denials, with few lights and weak impetus towards the heart of God. We should remember the merciful and tender love of God for us; it is incumbent upon us to lead our minds and hearts to contemplating how much He has done and does for us — the benefits granted by the Lord.

But what is wonderful in what Holy Scripture reveals is that sense of loss and perdition that then opens up to trust when a man who has betrayed the love of God seeks His loving and compassionate face, confessing His greatness: "I will sing of thy steadfast love, O Lord, for ever; with my mouth I will proclaim thy faithfulness to all generations. For thy steadfast love was established for ever, thy faithfulness is firm as the heavens" (Ps 89:2). This song of trust in

[11] Cf. C. Roccetta and R. Manes, *La tenerezza grembo di Dio amore. Saggio di teologia biblica* (Bologna, 2015), pp. 12-13.

God who is faithful to His promises opens the heart of man to the hope of forgiveness and reconciliation, giving him greater strength to contemplate the face of God, the face of that Father who is naturally, highly and totally Other, but at the same time is so close, near, a father and mother.[12] In the Biblical images that we have considered, and in many others, the loving and merciful God appears as essential otherness and, through His face, as ineffable nearness.[13] At one and the same time, God is other and neighbor. The point of intersection is specifically the manifestation of His loving and merciful face which is the expression through which one manages to say, to perceive, something that is Other and Beyond in relation to us, and which truly in His face is made tangible, palpable, almost in a corporeal sense. Thus God makes Himself present, living and at work, as He who takes care of us, as a father and a mother for a child that is the fruit of their love.

On this point, I would like to share another two episodes of the Old Testament that highlight in an effective way the extraordinary nearness and loving care of God towards His people. The first comes from the Book of Exodus where the particularly strong experience of slavery of the Israelites does not only reveal an aspect of the mystery of the iniquity present in humanity but also, and above all, demonstrates the mercy and the compassion of God who does not remain indifferent and impassive before the drama and the affliction of His people:

> But the Lord said, "I have witnessed the affliction of my people in Egypt and have heard their cry of complaint against their slave drivers, so I know well what they are suffering. Therefore I have come down to rescue them from the hands of the Egyptians and lead them out of that land into a good and spacious land, a land flowing with milk and honey, the country of the Canaanites, Hittites, Amorites, Perizzites, Hivites and Jebusites. So indeed the cry of the Israelites has reached me, and I have truly noted that the Egyptians are oppressing them. Come, now! I will send you to Pharaoh to lead my people, the Israelites, out of Egypt" (Ex 3:7-10).

---

[12] Cf. A. Amato, "Paternità-maternità di Dio. Problemi e prospettive," in A. Amato, *Trinità in contesto* (Rome, 1994), pp. 273-296; M. Cimosa, "Il linguaggio biblico (ebraico, greco e latino) dell'amore e della misericordia divina," in M. Marin and M. Mantovani (eds.), *Eleos: "L'affanno della ragione" fra compassione e misericordia* (Rome, 2002), pp. 197-213.

[13] Cf. P. Coda, "Il volto come metafora," *Nuova Umanità*, 149 (2003), pp. 509-518.

The words of the prophet Hosea are even more touching. They are words that express the relationship of God with His firstborn people as two sides of the same coin: the continual rejection of the love of God through transgression of the words of the Covenant by the people, and the continual manifestation of the loving and merciful fatherhood of God which, as we have seen above, touches chords of extraordinary tenderness: "Yet it was I who taught Ephraim to walk, who took them in my arms; I drew them with human cords, with bands of love; I fostered them like one who raises an infant to his cheeks; Yet, though I stooped to feed my child, they did not know that I was their healer" (Hos 11:3-4).

However, good and evil, faithfulness and transgression, are not the same thing in front of the Face of God. There is an undeniable connection, a certain relationship, between the manifestation of the mercy and tenderness of God and the need for conversion and faithfulness to the Covenant of the firstborn people of the Lord. Although, on the one hand, it is true that the Lord is merciful and compassionate, slow to anger and great in love, it is equally true that He is especially tender, like a father towards his children, towards those who fear Him (cf. Ps 103:8,13), towards those who worship Him and acknowledge that He is the Father, Lord and God in faithfulness to His Commandments. In addition, one cannot fail to notice that Ephraim, before God manifested to him His feelings and His great love, acknowledged his sin and professed his repentance to the God of the Covenant: "I turn in repentance; I have come to myself, I strike my breast; I blush with shame, I bear the disgrace of my youth I turn in repentance; I have come to myself, I strike my breast; I blush with shame, I bear the disgrace of my youth" (Jer 31:19).

Let us end this section by referring to the paradox of the love of God who punishes His chosen people with mercy in the same way as a father corrects his children for a greater good but does not do this in the case of unrepentant idolaters (cf. Wis 11:9-10). Mercy is the sign that God believes in man, believes that with His help he can convert to His words and live as His true son.[14] The tenderness and forgiveness of God towards a son who when growing emancipated himself from Him, forgetting about the tender and merciful love with which he had been enveloped ever since his childhood and for all of his adulthood (cf. Ez 16:6-22), has something truly incredible about

[14] Cf. R. Virgil, "Misericordia di Dio e conversione nella tradizione profetica," *Credere Oggi*, 34 (2014/4) 202, pp. 17-28, see p. 24.

it. The forgiveness and mercy of God always constitute a further opportunity, a time of grace, a new gift for a new life, and find in the womb of the tenderness of God their fundamental wellspring. After all, the experience of the Jubilee leads the faithful to live the essential elements of the dynamic of the love of the Father for His children: an invitation, repentance, forgiveness and then a new life.

2. Jesus: the Human and Tender Face of the Mercy of God

Although the Old Testament contains numerous images of the merciful tenderness of God through intense metaphors and a multiform language, the New Testament does this to an even greater extent from its very first pages — albeit perhaps with a less "charged" language. Pope Francis, in his *Evangelii gaudium*, when returning to the metaphor of the face of man, the epiphany of his mystery of life, joy and suffering, in encountering which everyone is called upon by the charity of God, declares that we should rediscover and be involved in the revolution of the tenderness initiated by the incarnation of the Son of God in order to adopt the approach/behavior of touching, and being reconciled with, the flesh of the other.[15] The mysterious tenderness of God, in the incarnation of His Son, truly produced a "revolution" of love because it provoked a great change, a kind of mutation in the very nature of God, as in the nature of man. What took place in the womb of the Virgin Mary, and then in a visible way in Bethlehem, manifests the omnipotence of the tenderness of God who made Himself littleness and poverty in the weakness of a baby. This is the scandal of the tenderness of the Man-God, in front of which the history of every man cannot remain impassive or extraneous: God is not sitting with indifference in His heaven. He is a Father who, in Jesus Christ, takes care of His own children, takes on the human condition except for sin, to the point of sharing in its events. It is precisely Jesus who is the visible expression of the memory of the mercy of God towards His people (Lk 1:54); he is that sun that rises on the shadows of a humanity wounded and exhausted by multiple transgressions of the love of God, the sun in relation to which — and from which — humanity expects divine love and mercy (cf. Lk 1:78-79).

[15] Cf. *EG*, n. 88.

2.1. *A Terminological Clarification*

In the previous section I emphasized the meaning of the terms *hesed* and *raham*. The Greek term *éleos*,[16] which expresses a feeling of mercy and compassion when faced with the miserable condition of the other, corresponds to the love of mercy, goodness and benevolence (*hesed*). This term is employed by the evangelist Luke in particular in contexts where the Old Testament is cited. *Éleos* requires a response in terms of solidarity — concrete actions for the poor and the unfortunate that manifest a certain conversion of the heart. The corresponding Greek term for the Hebrew *raham*, on the other hand, is the verb *splagchnízomai*, the plural noun of which is *splágchna* which refers to innards.[17] It comes to express, as with the term *raham*, the seat of the deepest sensibilities and feelings, and expresses "visceral compassion,"[18] we could say the "tender compassion" of a parent (father-mother) for their own child. A third Greek term refers to the mercy and compassion of God and, as a consequence, of man for his fellows. This is the noun *oiktirmós* which Luke uses only once in his gospel, specifically in the key quotation adopted by Pope Francis as the motto for the Extraordinary Jubilee of Mercy: "Be merciful (*oiktirmones*) as your Father is merciful (*oiktirmōn*)." Obviously, in the gospel of Luke the mercy referred to is first and foremost the mercy of God. In the first chapter of his gospel, the evangelist explicitly refers to it as many as five times. In the *Magnificat* of the Virgin Mary, in the *Benedictus* of Zaccaria, the real presence of the mercy of God during the course of the history of salvation is confessed. In addition, the wondrous maternity itself of Elizabeth is seen as a manifestation of the great mercy of the Lord. In all these instances, the evangelist always uses the noun *éleos*.[19]

2.2. *Luke and the Gospel of the Merciful Tenderness of Christ*

We cannot omit to analyze in a brief way some passages from the Gospel of Luke in which the merciful tenderness of God, in Jesus

[16] Cf. R. Bultmann, "Éleos," in *Grande Lessico del Nuovo Testamento*, III, coll. 399-424.

[17] Cf. K. Köster, "Splágchnon," in *Grande Lessico del Nuovo Testamento*, XII, coll. 903-934.

[18] *MV*, n. 6.

[19] Cf. E.M. Palma, "La misericordia: sigillo del vero uomo e del cristiano autentico," in *La misericordia e le sue opere. Atti del Convegno, a cura dell'Arcidiocesi Metropolitana di Catanzaro-Squillace* (Catanzaro, 2013), pp. 29-41, see pp. 29-30.

Christ, in the Spirit, appears in all its beauty and greatness in the use of the verb *splagchnízomai* (compassionate tenderness). Amongst the most famous passages we remember that of the parable of the merciful Father (cf. Lk 15:11-32).

After the presentation of the principal figures of the story ("A man had two sons," v. 11) and the description of the sad experience of the youngest son who had gone to a distant country (vv. 12-16), the deep feelings of the father when seeing him return home are revealed (v. 20). He sees him, runs out to meet him, clasps him and kisses him (v. 20). Furthermore, he orders his servants to bring the best robe, to put a ring on his son's hand and to place shoes on his feet. He also ordered them to bring the fatted calf and kill it in order to eat it and celebrate with a great celebration (vv. 22-24). In this way, that son who was lost, who had lost his identity as a son and who wanted to be treated by his father as the last of his servants so as to be with him again (v. 19), instead rediscovers his lost truth. And this thanks to the great mercy of the father who made him rediscover that truth, who gave it back to him. As has already been observed, the verb used in this case by the evangelist (*splagchnízomai*) is very significant and refers to the innards, becoming one of the strongest expressions of affective emotion and indicating, first of all, the fullness of the mercy with which God calls on man in His work of salvation. Thus, in the case of the parable, the use of this verb (v. 20) manifests the "visceral compassion" with which the father goes to meet his son who "was lost, and is found" (vv. 24:32).[20]

Another important icon is that of the Good Samaritan (cf. Lk 10:25-37), the account of whom presents the story of a man who when going down from Jerusalem to Jericho fell into the hands of a band of robbers (v. 30). Bleeding from being beaten, robbed and left half dead, the wretched man was in a situation of impelling need — it was a matter of life or death. In addition to the behavior of the priest and the Levite who passed by on the other side, what strikes one is the attitude of the Samaritan, seen by the Jews as an enemy, an outcast, somebody to avoid, who feels in his innermost self a visceral compassion or a tender compassion (*esplagchnisthē*). As in the case of the parable of the merciful Father, this tender compassion also flows into the concrete work of "taking care of him"; it becomes in practical terms immediate action. It is known that at the level of

---

[20] Cf. ibidem, pp. 31-32; C. Roccetta and R. Manes, *La tenerezza grembo di Dio amore*, pp. 131-134.

symbolic interpretation the Church has always seen the Samaritan as Jesus Christ himself, who still today, as the Good Samaritan, comes to the side of every man bent in body and spirit and pours on his wounds the oil of comfort and the wine of hope.[21]

As regards my final image, I would like to emphasize the manifestation of the deep feeling of merciful tenderness of Jesus towards the widow of Nain (cf. Lk 7:11-17). Here, as well, the verb *splagchnízomai* is used. The Lord sees this woman who is suffering greatly, feels tender compassion and invites her to hope. Certainly, this is not a gesture of comfort alone. It also involves the reassurance that something great is happening: the salvific intervention of God in her history is about to take place here and now. The Lord draws near to the coffin of her dead child, touches it, commands the boy to rise up, and after he awoke Jesus returned him to his mother (vv. 14-15).

As can be deduced from the three passages that have just been examined, the compassionate tenderness of the Lord works salvation in a concrete way in the life of man, a salvation that means re-found and re-established filial dignity (cf. Lk 15:11-32), care for human life in all its aspects (Lk 10:25-37), and resurrection to life as a sign of resurrection to the new life of grace and truth (cf. Lk 7:11-17).

2.3. *The Remission of Sins and Salvation: The Great Positive Results of the Mercy of God*

We have seen how the merciful tenderness of the Lord for man is manifested in some important images in Holy Scripture, in which the feeling of "visceral" compassion of God is followed by His immediate action which provides solutions and salvation. Salvation itself is the first of the positive results of the mercy of God and this begins and takes place first of all with the forgiveness of sins. Zechariah sings in the *Benedictus*: "to give his people knowledge of salvation through the forgiveness of their sins" (Lk 1:77) and from this emerges awareness of the forgiveness offered by God through the redemption achieved by Jesus Christ. This salvation, willed by the Father and achieved by Christ, should not be understood as a promise that is kept only in the eschatological future of man, namely in the eternal life of the world beyond. Instead, this is a reality that already begins in this life, on this earth, that is to say in the present historical existence of man. This is what emerges from the account of Zacchaeus, the chief tax

[21] Cf. *Roman Missal*, Common Preface VIII "Jesus the Good Samaritan."

collector who lived in Jericho (cf. Lk 19:1-10), whose encounter with Jesus brought about his repentance and conversion, *proclaimed* by the words themselves of the Lord: "Today salvation has come to this house." Today, Jesus, through his Body the Church, comes, forgives and saves; the today of the intervention of God, in Christ, in the personal history of each one of us. Today clearly indicates an immediate achievement of the salvation accomplished by Jesus, as took place in the distant past (Lk 2:11): "For today in the city of David a savior has been born for you who is Messiah and Lord"; Lk 4:21: "Today this scripture passage is fulfilled in your hearing." So it is, and so it will be, during the course of time.

The salvation that begins with the forgiveness of sins can be understood in a pre-eminent way in Luke 7:36-50. The context is that of a meal in a home in which Jesus takes part in response to a precise invitation given to him by the owner of that home, a Pharisee named Simon. And it was specifically during this meal that the unthinkable took place: a woman of that city, a "sinner" (as the evangelist is quick to say), comes behind him and at his feet, weeping, she begins to wash his feet with her tears. Then she wiped them with her hair, kissed them and anointed them with a very expensive ointment. This, obviously enough, was an approach of great reverence and great humility, as well as one of loving service, which Christ himself sealed with the words: "Your sins are forgiven." In this way, trusting in the benevolent welcome of Jesus, this woman received from the Lord a great manifestation of his mercy (inherent in the words that sealed the forgiveness of her sins), and was thus able to set out on that newness of life that sprung from her salvation: "Your faith has saved you, go in peace!" One is dealing here, therefore, with a demonstration of great mercy by Christ, which would then find its culmination at the moment of crucifixion[22] when Jesus himself turns to the Father to ask for the forgiveness of the sins of his accusers: "Father, forgive them for they know not what they do" (Lk 23:34).

3. The Church as a "Field Hospital": a Welcoming Mother and a Place of Mercy

A few days after his election to the throne of St. Peter, at the Angelus of 17 March 2013 Pope Francis declared that the face of God is that

[22] Cf. *DM*, n. 3.

of a merciful Father who always has patience and never tires of forgiving us. God is love (cf. 1 Jn 4:8) and His limitless mercy has its foundation in His tender and fatherly heart, to the point that mercy is one of the great attributes of God. This mercy is expressed through concrete signs: the forgiveness of sins, the healing of infirmities, the proclaiming of liberation to prisoners and the oppressed, restoring sight to the blind, raising up those who have fallen, caring for the poor, foreigners, orphans and widows (cf. Ps 146:7-9). We perceive these signs, already proclaimed in the synagogue of Nazareth (Lk 4:18-19),[23] as evident, present and fully embodied in the Face and the work of the Lord Jesus. On that occasion, fulfilling the prophecy of Isaiah, Jesus proclaimed "the Year of grace of the Lord," the great Jubilee, by which God was reconciled with man through a total remission of the guilt caused by the sins that he had committed. This applied to the whole of humanity: the reconciliation of God with man, of man with man, and of man with himself and the creation. This is the great mercy that God used — and uses — for His favorite creature. In his Bull for the indiction of the Jubilee of Mercy, Pope Francis states that the Church of our epoch, involved in the new evangelization, must feel strongly the duty to offer anew the subject of mercy with a new enthusiasm and with renewed pastoral activity.[24] Since this is of determining importance for the credibility of what she proclaims, let us ask ourselves how the Church can, and must, be a witness to the mercy of God: faithful proclamation of the Gospel, the celebration of the sacraments, in particular that of penance, and works of corporal and spiritual mercy. In my analysis I will dwell upon the last two.

3.1. *The Sacrament of Penance and Indulgence: The Face of God's Mercy for Us*

In *Evangelii gaudium* we read: "The Church must be a place of mercy freely given, where everyone can feel welcomed, loved, forgiven and encouraged to live the good life of the Gospel."[25] She is the place from which, and in which, re-echoes the invitation to allow oneself to be reconciled with God (cf. 2 Cor 5:20) and to abandon oneself to the arms of His mercy through the Sacrament of Penance and Reconciliation. We well know, from experience as well, that the gift of new

[23] Cf. ibid., n. 7.

[24] Cf. *MV*, n. 12.

[25] *EG*, n. 114.

life born with Baptism and continuously nourished by the sacrament of the Eucharist does not eliminate the frailty and the weakness of human nature nor the inclination to sin.[26] This sacrament of healing, suitably prepared and celebrated, manifests through the mediation of the Church the tenderness of the face of God, the compassion of the love of Christ in the Spirit. This is because it makes us rise again from spiritual death, creates a new life, heals and assuages the wounds of a heart offended by sin, and binds it and looks after it through the mercy that is received.[27] Thus it is that the Church offers herself, by vocation and mission, as a caring mother who welcomes, heals and takes care of, but also as a setting in which she serves and fosters the coming of the Kingdom of God and the communion-encounter with the God of a paternal and merciful face. Love and mercy, made a concrete act of welcome, forgiveness, sharing and a shared journey, attract and convince the men and women of our time that the Church is an experience (and life) of charity in truth, able and always ready to hold the hands of the poor and the least, those who live at the margins of society, "so they can feel the warmth of our presence, our friendship, and our fraternity."[28] This makes credible and loveable the merciful face of Jesus Christ, his Gospel, his forgiveness and his grace.

One thus understands the invitation of Pope Francis to priests to ensure that the Sacrament of Penance is not a place of torture and notable embarrassment for penitents who want to receive the mercy of God. Instead, it should become a favorable setting in which a priest "receives penitents not with the attitude of a judge, nor with that of a simple friend, but with the charity of God, with the love of a father who sees his son returning and goes out to meet him, of the shepherd who has found his lost sheep. The heart of a priest is a heart capable of being moved by compassion, not through sentimentalism or mere emotion, but through the "bowels of mercy" of the Lord! If it is true that Tradition points us to the dual role of physician and judge for confessors, let us never forget how the physician is called to heal and how the judge is called to absolve."[29] The experience of forgiveness and mercy received from God, with the mediation of the Church,

[26] Cf. *CCC*, n. 1426.

[27] Cf. *MV*, n. 15.

[28] Ibid., n. 15.

[29] Pope Francis, Address to those Taking Part in the Course Organized by the Apostolic Penitentiary, 28 March 2014. Cf. M. Gagliardi, "La riconciliazione con Dio nel segno della sua misericordia," in K. Nykiel, P. Carlotti and A. Saraco (eds.), *Il sigillo confessionale a la privacy pastorale* (Vatican City, 2015), pp. 105-120, see p. 109.

must help the believer or the indifferent person to rediscover and explore the transcendent dimension of life, the meaning of faith in God, for Christ, in the Holy Spirit, and the meaning of belonging first of all to the human family and thus the ecclesial community.

3.2. *For the "Benevolent Disposition" of God and "Benevolence" Amongst Brothers and Sisters: The Gift of Indulgence*

The doctrine and the practice of indulgences in the Church are closely connected to the effects of the Sacrament of Penance.[30] "The aim pursued by ecclesiastical authority in granting indulgences is not only that of helping the faithful to expiate the punishment that sin deserves but also that of urging them to perform works of piety, penitence and charity—particularly those which lead to growth in faith and which favor the common good."[31] Truly the mystery of compassion, which is expressed above all in penitence and indulgences, represents the highest expression of the merciful tenderness of our God. From this point of view, the Extraordinary Jubilee of Mercy constituted a time of grace, not only in order to use and personally appreciate the abundance of the mercy of God and experience its health-giving benefits, but also to be educated in, and live, the meaning at the level of community, communion and charity of an indulgence:

> the faithful when they acquire indulgences understand that by their own powers they could not remedy the harm they have done to themselves and to the entire community by their sin, and they are therefore stirred to a salutary humility. Furthermore, the use of indulgences shows us how closely we are united to each other in Christ, and how the supernatural life of each can benefit others so that these also may be more easily and more closely united with the Father. Therefore the use of indulgences effectively influences charity in us and demonstrates that charity in an outstanding manner when we offer indulgences as assistance to our brothers who rest in Christ.[32]

In order to be able to help each other in the exchange of spiritual goods through prayer and penitential expiation, all members of the

[30] Cf. *CCC*, n. 1471.

[31] *ID*, n. 8.

[32] Ibid., n. 9.

faithful must allow themselves to be educated to believe firmly that their lives as children of God and members of the Church are not only a singular particularity. These lives are also, and even more, "joined by a wonderful link to the life of all ... other Christian brothers in the supernatural unity of the Mystical Body of Christ till, as it were, a single mystical person is formed."[33] This is the reason why Pope Francis exhorts Christians to allow themselves to be reconciled fully with God, to draw near to the mercy of the Father with the certainty that His forgiveness is extended in a full way to the life of believers for the benefit of all their brothers and sisters as well.

"An indulgence is the remission before God of the temporal punishment due sins already forgiven as far as their guilt is concerned, which the follower of Christ with the proper dispositions and under certain determined conditions acquires through the intervention of the Church which, as minister of the Redemption, authoritatively dispenses and applies the treasury of the satisfaction won by Christ and the saints."[34] I have already referred to the fact that the practice of indulgences is linked to the effects of the Sacrament of Penance. Forgiven, reconciled and totally purified, the believer not only receives and experiences the great mercy that the Lord has shown but must also manifest the positive results of this renewed life, according to a movement of receiving and giving, a dynamism of justice and mercy in which these two dimensions are not in the least in opposition but, rather, are part of a single reality that progressively develops until reaching its apex in the fullness of love.[35] As can be seen, there is an inseparable link between conversion, repentance-reconciliation, indulgences and works of mercy. Let us listen on this point to the words of St. John Paul II:

> Jesus Christ taught that man not only receives and experiences the mercy of God, but that he is also called "to practice mercy" towards others: "Blessed are the merciful, for they shall obtain mercy." The Church sees in these words a call to action, and she tries to practice mercy. All the beatitudes of the Sermon on the Mount indicate the way of conversion and of reform of life, but the one referring to those who are merciful is particularly eloquent in this regard. Man attains

[33] Ibid., n. 5.

[34] *ID*, *Normae*, 1; *CCC*, n. 1471.

[35] Cf. *MV*, n. 20.

> to the merciful love of God, His mercy, to the extent that he himself is interiorly transformed in the spirit of that love towards his neighbor.[36]

In the light of these words and in a spirit of faith, we want to accept the appeal of the Holy Father Francis who wanted the Christian people during the Jubilee to reflect upon works of corporal and spiritual mercy, to rediscover the tender and needy face of God in our poor and suffering brothers and sisters, and to live merciful love as a response to, and in harmony with, that Love that loved us first.[37]

Saint John Paul II in his first encyclical expressed himself in a succinct way about the concrete love of mercy, experienced as a concrete manifestation of tender attention to one's neighbor: "Man cannot live without love,"[38] "The Church cannot abandon man";[39] man not as an abstract figure but concrete and historical man who lives here and now, amongst us and in front of us.[40]

Clothing, giving drink to someone, visiting, advising, comforting and forgiving (to cite some of the concrete signs of a renewed life in Christ) are not a suit that we wear and take off according to circumstance and our mood: they are the essence of our lives as children of God and disciples of Jesus; a life redeemed, forgiven and reconciled with God and with our brothers and sisters. The commandment that Jesus gave to his disciples, "be merciful as your Father in heaven is merciful" (Lk 6:36), the motto of the Jubilee, reveals the possibility that each one of us has to share in the mercy of God, to demonstrate through our lives His tenderness and His love, to share the suffering and poverty of our brothers and sisters, so that every man renews his personal and salvific encounter with Christ or takes the decision to allow himself to be encountered by him.[41] The Extraordinary Jubilee of Mercy was thus a singular opportunity to discover the "mysticism" of living together the "new works of mercy": supportive against isolation, together against individualism, sharing against material poverty, including against every

---

36 *DM*, n. 14.

37 "Children, let us love not in word or speech but in deed and truth" (1 Jn 3:18); "If someone who has worldly means sees a brother in need and refuses him compassion, how can the love of God remain in him?" (1 Jn 3:17); "Whoever does not love a brother whom he has seen cannot love God whom he has not seen" (1 Jn 4:20).

38 John Paul II, Encyclical Letter *Redemptor hominis* (4 March 1979), n. 10.

39 Ibid., n. 14.

40 Cf. ibid., n. 13.

41 Cf. *EG*, n. 3.

form of exclusion and marginalization, healing, freeing and generating hope against every offence against human dignity.[42]

4. At the School of the Saints

It is said that one day a young priest, a student of theology, asked an elderly theologian whom he knew: "who is the Virgin Mary according to your learning?" And the old man answered: "the heart of God in female form." This is a fine and true answer which we could paraphrase as: the tender face of the mercy of God manifested with the grace and the sensitivity of a completely pure and completely holy woman. The Virgin, Mother of Tenderness (a particularly appropriate title of popular tradition), personally experienced how great was the mercy of God in her and for her and sang of this in the house of Zachariah when she met her cousin Elizabeth, to whom she had hurriedly gone in order to offer her help — that care and concern, the positive result of mercy, that becomes attention and support for the needs of the other (cf. Lk 1:39-45). But one can also not neglect the episode of the wedding feast in Cana in Galilee where the Holy Virgin appeared as the heart of that feast (cf. Jn 2:1-12). The good sense of her heart led her to see that there was no wine and that the bride and bridegroom could experience the failure of their wedding feast. Moved by compassion she went to her Son and ensured that through her loving intercession Jesus began his miracles, whose hour had not yet come. A heart rich in compassion for her brothers and sisters can do so much with God! Seeing, acting and interceding for the joy of brothers and sisters are certainly expressions of a merciful face that loves and foresees the situation of those who are in need.

At the school of the Virgin Mary we find very many examples of holiness, from the remote to the recent past, in men and women who have made the merciful tenderness of God the heart of their lives and their missionary activity. To give just some examples, one need only think of St. Margaret Mary Alacoque (1647-1690) who, in opposition to a distant and cold God, a terrible severe judge, proclaimed the sweetness of the Heart of Jesus, an open heart, in whose wounds the sinners who turn to him find welcome, refuge and regeneration. It is obvious that the image of the Heart of Jesus was adopted as a

[42] Cf. ibid., n. 87.

living metaphor for the tender and merciful love of the Lord.[43] Saint Thérèse of Lisieux (1873-1897) during her short but intense earthly existence proclaimed with especial dedication and passion the merciful love of God, to which she offered herself as a holocaust victim so that the infinite tenderness of the love of Christ would flow into her soul.[44] In recent times we also find the witness of other great saints who sang of the mercy of God. One need only think of the Polish mystic St. Faustina Kowalska (1905-1938) who was fascinated by, and enveloped in, the great mercy of Jesus. Given that mercy finds its beginning and its full manifestation in love, she was made an ambassador by Christ in the world of his immense mercy: "Every time that you want to obtain a joy for me, speak to the world of my great and incommensurable mercy."[45] In another passage we read: "A weak, sinning, soul should not be afraid of drawing near to me; even if that soul had more sins than there are grains of sand on the earth, everything would fall into the abyss of my mercy."[46]

I will refer again to the illuminating words of Pope Francis: "This is the opportune moment to change our lives! This is the time to allow our hearts to be touched ... God never tires of reaching out to us."[47] This is an invitation that every man, whether a believer or non-believer, should adopt. It often happens in our lives that we encounter a paradox: to be afraid of those who want our wellbeing, the totality of our wellbeing. Each one of us, in not seeing themselves with God and in God, sees only negativity, transgression, inadequacy. It is certainly the case that there are very many failings, of varying degrees of gravity, in people's behavior in relation to the Word of God and Mother Church. However, this must not distract us, it must not convince us, foolishly, not to intercept and welcome this comforting tenderness with which the merciful face of God the Father wants to envelop us. We should never be afraid of this tenderness! We should never be afraid of the comfort of God! When contemplating the pages of the Gospel, we notice that all those who knocked at the merciful heart of Christ or allowed Him to encounter them — Jews, Romans, sinners, thieves, usurers, the hungry and the sick — benefited from His tenderness and His salvific intervention which changed their lives.

---

43 Cf. C. Roccetta and R. Manes, *La tenerezza grembo di Dio amore*, p. 19.

44 Cf. Teresa di Lisieux, *Storia di un'anima. Manoscritto C* (Vatican City, 1997).

45 M. F. Kowalska, *Diario. La misericordia divina nella mia anima*, n. 164.

46 Ibid., n. 1059.

47 *MV*, n. 19.

Mother Church, by showing the face of the tenderness of Christ, can continue with greater impetus and conviction to generate new life, the experience of faith, a journey of communion, a new mentality, and a new sense of belonging to humanity and the Church. This is certainly a challenge and specifically for this reason it is a commitment — to be the voice of every man and every woman in invoking from the depths of the heart: “Remember your compassion and your mercy, O Lord, for they are ages old” (Ps 25:6).

INDULGENCES: THEIR MEANING AND CONTEMPORARY RELEVANCE FOR THE LIFE OF THE CHURCH

It may seem strange, even to many Catholics, to hear indulgences still talked about. As we know, they marked the daily lives of the faithful for many centuries. Yet in more recent years, above all in some countries where the practice of confession has also declined, indulgences have been less practiced and sought after, giving the impression, so to speak, that they are "marking time." The reasons for this disaffection are many in number. Certainly, a certain "accounting" mentality which past discipline seemed to encourage, conceiving of the gift of indulgences as a sort of automatism unconnected with the vital riverbed from which they in fact arose, namely a daily commitment to conversion and the Christian life, does not correspond to an authentically evangelical sensibility.

During the general audience of 30 September 1999, dedicated to the subject of indulgences, St. John Paul II pronounced the following important words:

> In the present ecumenical context, the Church is aware of the need for this ancient practice to be properly understood and accepted as a significant expression of God's mercy ... The starting-point for understanding indulgences is the abundance of God's mercy revealed in the Cross of Christ. The crucified Jesus is the great "indulgence" that the Father has offered humanity through the forgiveness of sins and the possibility of living as children (cf. Jn 1:12-13) in the Holy Spirit (cf. Gal 4:6; Rom 5:5; 8:15-16).[1]

[1] John Paul II, General Audience, 29 September 1999.

And at the end of Proposition 7 of the eleventh Ordinary General Assembly of the Synod of Bishops, convoked by Benedict XVI in 2005 at the end of the Eucharist Year, we read:

> The renewal of Eucharistic spirituality can be an opportunity to deepen the understanding and practice of indulgences. This Synod observes that bishops and parish priests can ask the Apostolic Penitentiary for a plenary indulgence to celebrate various events and anniversaries. The Synod encourages a renewed catechesis of indulgences.[2]

Thus silence in this field cannot be justified for pastoral reasons or for ecumenical reasons.[3] Pastors of souls are invited to respond to this solemn appeal of the Church and to explain to the faithful the meaning and the great spiritual advantages of the practice of indulgences, which St. John Paul II defined as a "total gift of the mercy of God."[4]

At the end of the fifteenth century and at the beginning of the sixteenth century there were certainly preachers of indulgences who engaged in the abuse of indulgences. This was especially the case in Germany where the clash between the preachers of papal indulgences seeking to foster the reconstruction of St. Peter's Basilica and the local powers became bitter. Amongst the latter was Frederick of Wittenberg, the powerful protector of Luther, who had accumulated in his castle as many as 17,413 relics of saints — capable, he said, of obtaining for his visitors 128,000 years of indulgences. Fearing heavy losses, Frederick impeded the preaching of papal indulgences in his States. Nonetheless, his subjects crossed rivers and frontiers to obtain them.[5]

The pastoral response was given by the Council of Trent which, on the one hand, emphasized the highest usefulness of indulgences and recommended their use by the faithful, but, on the other, also recommended that bishops should exercise moderation in granting them. This Council, whereas it solemnly laid down that through the power of the Keys the Church legitimately had the faculty to grant

[2] Sinodo dei Vescovi, XI Assemblea Generale Ordinaria, *Elenco finale delle proposizioni*, *Notitiae*, 41 (2005), p. 442.

[3] Cf. J.-M Gervais, "Profondo significato e scopo pastorale delle Indulgenze," *L'Osservatore Romano*, 31 August-1 September 1998, p. 4.

[4] John Paul II, Bull of Indiction for the Jubilee of the 1950th Anniversary of the Redemption *Aperite portas Redemptori* (6 January 1983), n. 8.

[5] Cf. J. Delumeau, *Naissance et affirmation de la Réforme* (Paris, 1973), p. 83.

holy indulgences, at the same time left open many questions for further exploration.[6] This exploration, four centuries later, had as its principal architects Paul VI and the Apostolic Penitentiary.

1. The Evolution of Responsibility for Indulgences

After the ending of the Council of Trent, Clement VIII as early as 1593 had planned the establishment of a specific body with the specific task of disciplining the granting of indulgences. However, the creation of a permanent dicastery only took place on 6 July 1669 with the creation of the Congregation for Indulgences and Relics by Clement IX.[7] Saint Pius X allocated this responsibility in perpetuity to the Sacred Congregation of Rites on 28 January 1904[8] and then on 29 June 1908 he bestowed it on the Holy Office.[9]

On 25 March 1917 Benedict XV, following the clear evolving approach of Canon Law which was laying increasing stress on the close correlation of sacramental repentance and indulgences, entrusted the Section for Indulgences in a final way to the Apostolic Penitentiary, limiting the responsibility of the Holy Office to the doctrinal aspects of new prayers and devotions.[10] This responsibility of the Apostolic Penitentiary for the use and the granting of indulgences was confirmed by St. Paul VI after the Second Vatican Council[11] and by St. John Paul II in his Constitution *Pastor bonus*.[12]

2. The Apostolic Constitution *Indulgentiarum Doctrina* of Pope St. Paul VI

The Apostolic Constitution *Indulgentiarum doctrina* of Paul VI was published on 1 January 1967, a little more than about fifty years ago.

---

[6] Concilium Oecumenicaum Tridentinum Sess. 25, *Decretum de Indulgentiis* (4 December 1563).

[7] Cf. N. Del Re, *La Curia Romana. Lineamenti storico-giuridici* (Vatican City, 1998, fourth edition), pp. 382-383.

[8] Pius X, Motu proprio *Quae in Ecclesiae bonum* (28 January 1904).

[9] Cf. Pius X, Apostolic Constitution *Sapienti consilio* (29 June 1908), I, 1, 3. Responsibility for most holy relics remained entrusted to the Congregation for Rites.

[10] Cf. Benedict XVI, Motu proprio *Alloquentes proxime* (25 March 1917), nn. 4-5.

[11] Cf. Paul VI, Apostolic Constitution *Regimini Ecclesiae universae* (15 August 1967), n. 113.

[12] Cf. *PB*, art. 120.

In drawing up this important document, the Apostolic Penitentiary was directly involved in both the doctrinal part, which is the densest, and the normative part. This Constitution is a notably valuable document and constitutes perhaps the best summary of the doctrine of indulgences that exists, to such an extent, indeed, as to be repeatedly cited in the *Catechism of the Catholic Church.*

The Constitution *Indulgentiarum doctrina* begins with the following statement: "The doctrine and practice of indulgences which have been in force for many centuries in the Catholic Church have a solid foundation in divine revelation."[13] In fact, this document effected no innovation as regards the doctrine of indulgences because, as Cardinal Ciappi, who participated directly in the reform of Paul VI, observed: "this is a doctrine of faith whose foundations God Himself revealed." This Cardinal also warned: "to reject or diminish the traditional doctrine of indulgences ... would mean to reject or extenuate the dogmas of the solidarity of men redeemed with Christ; of the Communion of Saints; of the infinite value of the merits of Christ ... of the power of the Keys ... of the infallibility of the Ecumenical Councils, of the Roman Pontiff and of the universal ordinary Magisterium."[14]

The doctrine on indulgences is based, essentially, on three truths of faith:

a) A debt, the persistence — even after sacramental confession — of the temporal punishment of a sin to be expiated here on earth or in purgatory.[15]

b) A treasury, of which the Church is the dispenser, created by the expiations and the merits of Christ, as well as by the prayers and the good works of the Blessed Virgin Mary and all the saints.[16]

c) A transfer of these merits, in the communion of saints or supernatural solidarity in the Mystical Body of Christ.[17]

---

[13] *ID*, n. 1.

[14] Cf. L. Ciappi, "Concilio e riforma delle indulgenze," *Vita Religiosa*, 2 (1967), pp. 99-108. Cf. also L. Ciappi, "Tradizione e novità nella riforma delle indulgenze," in *L'Osservatore Romano*, 9-10 January 1967, p. 2.

[15] Cf. *ID*, n. 3.

[16] Cf. ibid., n. 5.

[17] Cf. ibidem.

The definition of an indulgence offered by the Constitution *Indulgentiarum doctrina* has by now become classic: it was subsequently placed in *Enchiridion Indulgentiarum*,[18] in the *Code of Canon Law*,[19] and in the *Catechism of the Catholic Church*:[20]

> An indulgence is a remission before God of the temporal punishment due to sins whose guilt has already been forgiven, which the faithful Christian who is duly disposed gains under certain prescribed conditions through the action of the Church which, as the minister of redemption, dispenses and applies with authority the treasury of the satisfactions of Christ and the saints.[21]

Indulgences, therefore, are very useful in the spiritual lives of the faithful: they help in the struggle against sins and the forces of evil; they stimulate charity and offer valuable help to deceased brothers and sisters; they revive hope of a full reconciliation with God the Father; they strengthen the hierarchical communion of the faithful and pastors, above all with the Vicar of Christ; and they help the Church to be holy and immaculate, united in Christ in the bond of charity.

3. The Norms in Force Relating to Indulgences

The norms in force relating to indulgences follow four principles:[22]

a) To foster the spirit of piety and the fervor of charity, the measure of partial indulgence is by now proportionate to the upright intention of the member of the faithful, with a removal of all reference to the days or years present in ancient canonical penances.

b) To exhort a serious interior preparation, a plenary indulgence is by now limited — for individual members of the

[18] Cf. *MDI*, *Norme sulle indulgenze*, 1.

[19] Cf. *CIC*, can. 992.

[20] Cf. *CCC*, n. 1471.

[21] *ID*, norm 1.

[22] Cf. Sacra Paenitentiaria Apostolica, *Positio de Sacrarum Indulgentiarum recognitione. Relatio super schema de Indulgentiis recognoscendis* (Vatican City, 1965). For the Italian translation see G. Caprile, *Il Concilio Vaticano II. Cronache del Concilio Vaticano II edite da "La Civiltà Cattolica,"* V (Rome, 1969), pp. 354-357; J.-M Gervais, "Paolo VI e la riforma della disciplina delle indulgenze," *Periodica*, 88 (1999), pp. 301-329.

faithful — to once a day, with the necessary performance of three conditions (sacramental confession, Eucharistic communion and prayer according to the intentions of the Supreme Pontiff).

c) To eliminate all danger of superstition as regards the objects of piety, an indulgence depends by now on their pious use and not on the purely material fact of having them with one.

d) To reaffirm the centrality of the celebration of the Eucharist, the indulgence of the privileged altar is abolished;[23] this effected a discrimination not only between altars but also between priests.

All the norms relating to the discipline of indulgences, acts of piety and indulgence prayers of the Church, together with the Apostolic Constitution *Indulgentiarum doctrina*, are brought together in the *Enchiridion Indulgentiarum*, an official text of the Church that may be seen as a compendium of all the rules in force relating to indulgences, applicable both to the Latin faithful and to the Eastern faithful.

In this *Enchiridion*, in addition to the general definition to which reference has already been made, we find first of all the distinction between a plenary indulgence and a partial indulgence: "An indulgence is partial or plenary according to whether it removes either part or all of the temporal punishment due to sin."[24] Whereas a plenary indulgence, therefore, removes all of the temporal punishment due to sin already cancelled as regards guilt and eternal punishment, a partial indulgence removes only a part of this punishment.

Individuals who have been baptized, who are not subject to excommunication and who are in a state of grace, at least at the end of the prescribed works, can gain indulgences. In addition, they must have at least the general intention to acquire them and perform the works in the prescribed time and in the due way, according to the sense of the grant.[25] This is enough for a partial indulgence but not

---

[23] This was a plenary indulgence that was applied by a priest to the soul of the deceased for whom he celebrated the Mass. The privileged altar could be local, personal or mixed; perpetual or *ad tempus*; daily or less than daily (cf. can. 918, § 1 CIC 1917). The Cardinals enjoyed a daily personal privileged altar (cf. ibid., can. 219, § 1, 10).

[24] *MDI*, *Norme sulle indulgenze*, 2; cf. can. 993 *CIC*.

[25] Cf. ibid., 17; cf. can. 996, §§ 1-2 *CIC*.

for a plenary indulgence. Indeed, to gain a plenary indulgence a basic principle applies, suitably recalled by St. John Paul II shortly before the opening of the Great Jubilee: "the spiritual condition for receiving a plenary indulgence is the exclusion 'of all attachment to sin, even venial sin.'"[26]

The practice of indulgences reaffirms the need for the mediation of the Church and taking part in the sacraments, first of all the Sacrament of Penance or Reconciliation. Frequent confession is required for a plenary indulgence and without this there cannot be a real spiritual life.[27] In addition, every plenary indulgence is linked to Eucharistic communion — the source and culmination of all of the Christian life.[28] Lastly, it requires prayer according to the intentions of the Supreme Pontiff.[29] In practicing indulgences, the faithful take part really, mystically and directly in the building up of the Church, in union with the Vicar of Christ.

As regards the faculty of confessors, it is to be remembered that they have the faculty to act for the benefit of the faithful when these are legitimately impeded from performing a condition or completing the work of the indulgence.[30] The *Enchiridion* declares: "Confessors can commute either the prescribed work or the conditions in favor of those for whom these are impossible because of a legitimate impediment."[31] This faculty can be exercised outside sacramental confession. The most frequent commutation is certainly that of communion for the sick. Since it is not a dispensation but a commutation, it is sound policy to advise spiritual communion to the sick or elderly.

"The faithful can obtain plenary or partial indulgences for themselves, or they can apply them to the dead by way of suffrage."[32] Before the reform of St. Paul VI, only indulgences granted by the Supreme Pontiff could be applied to the dead.[33] According to the

---

[26] John Paul II, General Audience, 29 September 1999.

[27] Cf. *MDI*, *Norme sulle indulgenze*, 20, § 3: the confession can take place either on the same day as the work or some days beforehand (up to 20) or, if the member of the faithful is in a state of grace, some days afterwards (up to 20). Cf. also Apostolic Penitentary, "Il dono dell'Indulgenza," *L'Osservatore Romano*, 10 February 2000.

[28] Cf. ibid., 20, § 2.

[29] Cf. ibidem.

[30] Cf. J.-M. Gervais, "L'acquisto dell'indulgenza giubilare da parte dei malati e degli altri fedeli legittimamente impediti," *L'Osservatore Romano*, 11 February 2000.

[31] *MDI*, *Norme sulle indulgenze*, 24.

[32] Ibid., 3; cf. can. 994 *CIC*.

[33] Cf. can. 913, § 2 *CIC* 1917.

contemporary rules, all indulgences can be applied to the dead by way of suffrage, that is to say for intercession, as when a Holy Mass is celebrated for the dead.

A member of the faithful, however, cannot apply an indulgence to another living member of the faithful. The reason for this is a consequence of the link between the Sacrament of Penance and indulgences which is always emphasized by doctrine and canon law. Indeed, an indulgence for the living is obtained by way of absolution. We cannot receive sacramental absolution in the place of other people, confessing their presumed sins. In other words, an indulgence for the living depends on an act of will as well on the performance of other conditions.

With respect to diocesan or eparchial bishops or ecclesiastical authorities equivalent to them, these can grant a partial indulgence in their own territories or even outside them for their faithful.[34] In addition, they can "impart in their respective eparchies or dioceses, according to the prescribed formula, the Papal Blessing with a plenary indulgence three times a year on solemn feasts that they have designated, even if they only assist at the Mass."[35]

As regards, instead, the granting of plenary indulgences, application must be made to the Apostolic Penitentiary which acts on the mandate of the Roman Pontiff, to whom has been entrusted by Christ the Lord the distribution of all of the spiritual treasure of the Church.[36]

As regards requests for plenary indulgences, these reach the Apostolic Penitentiary from various countries of the world.[37] As well as the grants envisaged in the *Enchiridion Indulgentiarum*, which concern all the faithful, the Apostolic Penitentiary deals with grants for special groups of the faithful. Indeed, bishops, religious Superiors, parish priests, rectors of sanctuaries, moderators of pious associations or movements, habitually implore the gift of indulgences from the Holy Father, often through the good offices of the nuncios, for certain celebrations or special events.

---

[34] Cf. *MDI*, *Norme sulle indulgenze*, 7, § 1.

[35] Ibid., 7, § 2.

[36] Cf. ibid., 5, §§ 1-2; can. 995, §§ 1-2 *CIC*.

[37] A large part of the requests come from Germany where indulgences were a pretext for the beginning of the Lutheran Reformation and from countries of the Far East, for example Vietnam, where the Church has suffered and still suffers because of persecution and people display a fervent and courageous faith.

4. The Meaning and Contemporary Relevance of Indulgences for the Life of the Church

As has been observed, to receive the gift of a plenary indulgence — and I specifically use the term "gift" and not "purchase" precisely to emphasize what has been said above — the work prescribed by the plenary indulgence has to be performed and three conditions have to be met: sacramental confession, Eucharistic communion and prayer according to the intentions of the Supreme Pontiff,[38] by which is expressed at the same time the filial love of every Catholic for the successor to St. Peter and for the source itself of the indulgence. The Holy Father, as the Vicar of Christ and holder of the keys of St. Peter, grants the gift of an indulgence through *plenitudo potestatis*, the very high and consummately spiritual power that Christ transmitted to his Church.[39] In addition, the exclusion of any affection for sin, of a venial kind as well, is required for the gift of a plenary indulgence.

From what has been said hitherto, one can clearly see how an indulgence is a gift and not a purchase: detachment from sin, indeed, can only be the work of grace. God Himself who loved us first, frees man from the snares and the negative conditioning effects that a disordered use of freedom involves. This confirms us in our assessment that the "punishment" of sin is not a vindictive punishment, which in fact no longer exists in the form of ancient repentance, not even as a consequence of an abstract theological-moral order, a sort of "atonement" in a geometrical sense, as if an excess could be remedied by another excess of an opposite kind to re-establish a kind of balance or equality. But above all else it confirms us in our understanding of the punishment of sin in an existential-personal sense, as for that matter the most elementary psychology teaches us. In simple terms, we can say that the use of indulgences points out to us that we should learn to love God and our neighbor. This is the positive result of grace, but it is also the work of an aware and voluntary conscience and individual freedom that themselves work with grace.

In this way, following Jesus through faith and works of mercy grows and develops, reinvigorated by the sacraments and supported

[38] Cf. *ID*, norm 7.

[39] Cf. K. Nykiel, *La natura della potestà della Chiesa nella concessione delle Indulgenze* (Rome, 2002), pp. 112, 114; U. Navarrete, "Unità della "Potestas Sacra" e molteplicità dei "munera Christi et Ecclesiae," in *Winfried Schulz in memoriam. Schriften aus Kanonistik und Staatskirchenrecht*, II (Frankfurt am Mein 1999), p. 587.

by the communion of saints. In this way, the "treasury" of the Church is revealed, the merits of all the saints: not a strongbox or the *caveau* of a bank, full of money and precious stones, but the effective action of good which by its nature is "*diffusivum sui*,"[40] so that the "yes" of Jesus Christ to God the Father, offered in the Holy Spirit, becomes ours, since he himself lives in us and flows into us. Furthermore, the "here I am" of the Blessed Virgin Mary and all the saints sustains our freedom, it supports it, heals it, liberates it, and makes us truly their fellow citizens and family relatives. Thus in daily life, above all at the beginning of spiritual life, partial indulgences work in us and erode the space that evil still has in our souls; they act progressively, like medicines that are taken constantly, until achieving complete healing. Thus healed, the soul will achieve true liberation, complete regeneration, a full experience of the mercy of God. In other terms, the vivifying paschal experience of the Lord will lie not only in rites but in our own lives. In this sense, between a plenary indulgence and a partial indulgence there is a difference akin to that between a fruit and a flower: they both spring from the charity of Christ, but one of them, after a certain fashion, foreshadows it, and the other completes it. In ontological terms, there is certainly no difference between them because one always has the remission of the temporal punishment for sin. But between "less" and "everything" there is not only a quantitative difference. For that matter, in spiritual realities quantity is a category that is rather difficult to use.

Therefore, as St. John Paul II put it: "indulgences, far from being a sort of 'discount' on the duty of conversion, are instead an aid to its prompt, generous and radical fulfilment."[41]

God can only love because "God is love," as Benedict XVI stressed in his encyclical *Deus caritas est.* "Since God has first loved us (cf. 1 Jn 4:10), love is now no longer a mere "command"; it is the response to the gift of love with which God draws near to us."[42]

In man's relationship with God, therefore, the initiative is always with God who always offers us His forgiveness every time that we have not been able to imitate His love. The Church, in ringing out in time the proclaiming of forgiveness and reconciliation proclaimed by Jesus, reminds us that our Christian journey is a journey of conversion and repentance that must lead all Christians with their burden of sins

---

[40] T. Aquinas, *Summa Theologiae*, I, q. 5 a. 4, ad 2.

[41] John Paul II, General Audience, 29 September 1999.

[42] Benedict XVI, Encyclical Letter *Deus caritas est* (25 December 2005), n. 1.

to obtain the mercy of God, the forgiveness of guilt, the purification of the evil that is in them, the remission of temporal punishments through the gift of indulgences, and the carrying out of works of repentance and charity so as to grow in love of God and their brothers and sisters.

The fullness of the mercy of the Father who sent His son Jesus, who died and rose again for us, offers believers the possibility of experiencing the joy of forgiveness taken to its extreme consequences, as an ultimate sign of the love of God for sinners. The Christian life is born and develops in this love.

As St. John Paul II stated in his Bull of Indiction for the Holy Year of 2000, an indulgence specifically "discloses the fullness of the Father's mercy, who offers everyone his love, expressed primarily in the forgiveness of sins." And he went on: "It is precisely through the ministry of the Church that God diffuses his mercy in the world, by means of that precious gift which from very ancient times has been called 'indulgence.'"[43]

One may justifiably end this section by observing that although the use of indulgences is one of the factors that has contributed to divisions amongst Christians, an ecumenical concern is an important part of the present discipline. Thus various prayers of the Eastern traditions have been made a part of indulgences[44] and the centrality of the word of God in mental prayer, which has been very much emphasized by the most recent grants, is especially felt in the ecclesial communities that came out of the Reformation. This, together with a less juridical and more existential view of the journey of repentance and conversion of each person, could be a good point of encounter.

[43] John Paul II, Bull of Indiction for the Great Jubilee of the Year 2000 *Incarnationis mysterium* (29 November 1998), n. 9.

[44] Cf. *MDI*, *Concessioni*, 23.

THE GIFT OF INDULGENCES AND THE JOY OF FORGIVENESS

By the Apostolic Constitution *Indulgentiarum doctrina* of 1 January 1967, Paul VI completely updated the entire field of indulgences in order to adapt them to the "renewal" called for by the Second Vatican Council. Amongst other things, he abolished the traditional measurement in days, months and years of the partial indulgence, something that could be a source of misunderstanding amongst less informed people. In its place he established that this gift of the Church (namely indulgences) was proportionate to the expiatory value of the action engaged in by the member of the faithful. Paul VI also eliminated the distinction between "personal," "real" and "local" indulgences so that the role of personal commitment of the penitent would emerge more clearly and, as a consequence, the members of the faithful would be more stimulated in their sense of belonging to the communion of saints, their fervor as regards charity (especially towards deceased members of the faithful), and their spirit of prayer, rebirth and sacrifice.

Subsequently St. John Paul II decreed new grants, some of which were indicated in the Bull of Indiction of the Great Jubilee of the year 2000, as well as others of a general character to which I will return below. Thus the Apostolic Penitentiary, by the decree of 16 July 1999, promulgated the fourth edition of *Enchiridion Indulgentiarum* (the last reprint of which goes back to January 2008) in which, indeed, are to be found all the norms on the discipline of indulgences.

1. Between History and Pastoral Care

As is well known, indulgences were born in the ancient discipline of repentance of the Church when bishops gave authentic absolution to public penitents at the end of a long journey of contrition. The aim was to shorten this journey, which was from many points of view arduous and uncertain, and this explains the mention of years, months and years in relation to indulgences. These were, in effect, periods of time that were eliminated in order to arrive at the celebration of reconciliation.

With the modification of the discipline of repentance, making private confession prevail over public confession, the removal of the ancient "priced" repentance envisaged in books on repentance, and, lastly, granting absolution immediately (before, that is, the actual "penance" was performed), indulgences did not disappear. Instead, they were understood in a more profound way. It began to be realized that they involved not the remission of the temporal punishment envisaged by the ancient canons but, rather, the temporal punishment that every sin itself involves before divine justice, to be expiated on earth with penance and good works, or before God, in that state that we habitually call "purgatory" (on which authoritative historians have written very interesting essays). In this way, indulgences have since accompanied the piety of the entire Christian people, albeit at times even falling into abuse and ingenuousness. The Council of Trent emphasized their use and legitimacy: hence their arrival to our times, more precisely to the changes effected in the years after the Second Vatican Council, to which I referred above.

It is now appropriate to go into the details of the norms, in an exposition that does not seek to be primarily juridical or theological but, rather, prevalently pastoral and spiritual in character — definitions that are, for that matter, specific to the subject under discussion.

First of all, let us examine the general grants of indulgences decreed by Paul VI. As has been observed, they replaced the whole field, which had become very muddled and reduced to interminable lists of works of piety involving indulgences carried out in days, months and years, with a partial indulgence — its breadth proportionate to the fervor of the member of the faithful — granted in three spheres, or essential moments, of the Christian life. I quote: "partial indulgence is granted to the Christian faithful who, while carrying out their duties and enduring the hardships of life, raise their minds in humble trust to God and make, at least mentally, some pious invocation."[1] It is very clear that the Church in this way intended to encourage the members of the faithful to engage in constant and trusting prayer, the offering of their own trials and selves to Christ, conforming themselves to Jesus praying,

[1] *MDI*, p. 35.

offering himself up and being obedient to the will of the Father. All can see that this means having before one the Face of Christ: with constant and trusting prayer we go beyond, so to speak, the clouds of life, which is at times so harsh and at times tragic, to draw light and strength from that Face which is the very origin of light and strength. "May God ... make his face to shine upon us," says the psalmist (Ps 67:1) — an invocation often repeated, even in the metal small image of the Holy Face that is so providently widespread — and in essential terms one can say that the above-cited grant is nourished by this. We are invited to live in front of the Face of God, of His presence, in familiarity and daily intimacy with our Savior: our prayers, for example, are nothing else but a response to the light of that Face because "When thou hidest your face" all the living "are dismayed ... they die and return to their dust" (Ps 103:29). In "your light, Lord, we will see the light," declares a fine antiphon of the Liturgy of the Hours.

A second grant of a general character is as follows: "A partial indulgence is granted to the faithful who, led by the spirit of faith, give compassionately of themselves or of their goods to serve their brothers in need."[2] Here the Face of Jesus is in front us, incarnated in those who could rightly be called his legitimate representatives, in those whom he loved so much as to say that whatever we did to them, he would hold that it had been done to him — the poor. Every kind of poverty reflects the Face of Christ, spiritual poverty as well as material poverty. Lack of money, in fact, dispenses nobody from the observance of the great precept of charity. Almsgiving is one of the works that is most praised in Holy Scripture. It does not involve making our wallet alone available. It also, and above all else, involves making ourselves available and to such an extent that one can say that where there is no real self-giving there is no almsgiving, however great the offerings may be (the famous example of the widow's mite applies to us all). We are dealing, therefore, with making our own time available, our own ability to welcome, our own patience, and not only our money. We can thank God that in our times many people act in this way in various forms of voluntary work and care that have multiplied in number. For that matter, in the past, as well, members of the faithful, from the humblest levels to princes and queens, served the poor in hospitals and soup kitchens or such places, specifically as expiation for their sins and as comfort for Christ himself.

[2] Ibid., p. 38.

A third general grant declares: "A partial indulgence is granted to the Christian faithful who, in a spirit of penance, voluntarily abstain from something that is licit for and pleasing to them."[3] To deprive oneself of something and place oneself and one's possessions at the service of one's neighbor are two sides of the same coin — charity. Indeed, the value of fasting and abstinence (from meat or something else (television, cinema or any kind of entertainment) does not lie — according to the teaching of St. Gregory the Great — in self-mortification but, rather, in charity, of which mortification is an end and therefore a cause. In this way, a member of the faithful is continuously encouraged to engage in penance but not in a spirit of fear or sadness: on the contrary, in the joy of an offered gift. Saint John teaches that we love God because He has loved us first (1 Jn 4:19). Thus we can well say that this kind of activity is born from beholding the Face of Christ, from the experience of his love for me, and thus to the desire to respond to love with other love, as is taught by the saints. From the Face of Christ in front of men, beheld in silence and prayer, to the Face of Christ in front of men in his poor children, for whom I can chose what Christ chose and wished for himself, namely sharing my life and my possessions. The inevitable sacrifice involved here does not find its source in a kind of "Christian stoicism," in demonstrating to ourselves that we can live with less than what we are accustomed to, nor even in an unhealthy contempt for the pleasures of live. It finds its source, rather, in the joy of being loved which activates in us the dynamic of supernatural free-giving, that is to say charity, by which, having received mercy, we ourselves give charity.

I will end this section with the fourth grant of a general character, suitably introduced in 1999 into the new edition of the *Enchiridion*: "A partial indulgence is given to the Christian faithful who, in the particular circumstances of daily life, voluntarily give explicit witness to their faith before others."[4] Here we are all invited to be the Face of Christ that shines forth for others, the city on the hill that one can but see: Christ and his Face are in front of us in prayer, in front of us in charity, in the charity of witness. There is nothing improper, indiscreet or arrogant in this. Pope Francis loves to remind us of a phrase of Francis of Assisi: "Proclaim Christ in all ways: if necessary, with words as well." In essential terms, the witness of the Christian life is only making him shine forth: whoever lives in symbiosis with

---

[3] Ibid., p. 41.

[4] Ibid., p. 44.

him in prayer and the exercises of devotion, whoever is gripped by his Spirit of charity, can only be a mirror in which is reflected a light that is not their own. Witness to Christ is that much truer the more it involves the disappearance of our own person. It is not witness to ourselves, or to our way of thinking, even if religious. It does not involve being raised up before a public audience. On the contrary, it involves Christ being raised up because it is we who serve him and not he who serves us. It is also true that an extremely important apostolic work is direct witness to him and his Word, in a world that appears to have forgotten his Word and in circumstances in which respect for the other can hinder our impetus.

2. Observations of a Pastoral Character

It is therefore evident that an indulgence, as understood by the Church, is not in the least a kind of mechanism or automatism of which the Christian life avails itself. Instead, it is the Christian life itself. It is its expression and one of its culminating points and thus one can well say that what leads to the fervor of charity and prayer, or is its fruit, is in some way enriched by an indulgence. The particular grants themselves bear witness to this. To refer to only some of them: the granting of a plenary indulgence for pious meditation on Holy Scripture, for at least half an hour; for the adoration of the Most Holy Sacrament; for the pious exercises of the *Via Crucis* and the Marian rosary.[5] It is clear that the intention of Mother Church is precisely that of leading the faithful to ever greater intimacy with her Lord, from which can only spring ever more generous actions of readiness to help their neighbor and true supernatural charity.

One could say that the gift of an indulgence is a "supplement of mercy" of the Father of all goodness received through the mediation of the Church. Indeed, since we have received mercy we become merciful; the charity received by us flows into our hearts, making us participants in the life itself of God. In this sense, the punishment of sin — that is to say those influences on, those forms of tiredness and fatigue of, the will and the intellect, those psychological and physical bonds, that sin involves (any sin, because it is true that sin brings with it its own punishment, just as a poison has toxic principles) — is alleviated and in the end absorbed by the new life of grace, which is nothing else but the new man, Christ the Lord, who takes habitual

[5] Cf. ibid., *Norme*, nn. 7, 13, 17, 30.

possession of our faculties and of the whole of ourselves until we can say: "yet I live, no longer I, but Christ lives in me" (Gal 2:20). Let us now see how it is possible, indeed a matter of duty, to understand the "punishment" of sin in a less and more existential-personal sense. In other terms, the disorder generated by every sin, as an evil and thus a privation of good, is a wound to the person and to the mystical body of Christ — the Church. Faith and charity, which are expressed in the actions required by an indulgence, heal and repair our hearts — and the Church herself — of such wounds, feeing us from the snares and the bonds in which, because of own free will, we become entangled.

In this sense, indulgences are inconceivable without an intense sacramental life, of which they are the crown. The sacraments, and in particular the Eucharist and reconciliation, are the ordinary channels by which we obtain grace and thus are conditions to "purchase" — as was once said, or also "earn" (terms that today sound totally unsuitable) — a plenary indulgence. They are not in themselves required for an indulgence. When they are, as in the case of taking part in one's first Holy Mass or first Holy Communion, or for the renewal of one's baptismal promises on the anniversary of one's Baptism or on the solemn Easter Vigil,[6] they are because of the fact that we are invited to pray for men who have just become priests and to thank the Lord for the sacraments themselves. This absence of being necessarily required is because they signify much more: incorporation in Christ and the Church, source and origin of the remission of every punishment due to sin. Thus the sacraments have greater importance than indulgences, but the latter lead us to the former, at least from a practical and pastoral point of view, albeit with their continued autonomous existence from a theological and ontological perspective. And thus it should be enough to remember that a partial indulgence is granted to a member of the faithful who is preparing devotedly for confession with an examination of conscience or an act of contrition, or who piously thanks God for the offered and received Eucharist.[7]

3. Further Observations

I have already observed that to obtain the gift of a plenary indulgence a member of the faithful must perform the work required by the

[6] Cf. ibid., *Norme*, nn. 8 § 1, 27 and 28 § 1.

[7] Cf. ibid., *Norme*, nn. 8 § 2 and 9.

indulgence and meet the usual conditions envisaged by the Church: sacramental confession, Eucharistic communion and prayer according to the intentions of the Pope. For the indulgence to be plenary, that is, for it to free completely from the temporal punishment, exclusion of any affection for sin, even of a venial character, is required.[8]

The condition of full and complete detachment from sin well expresses the dimension of an indulgence being first of all a gift, before it being an acquisition by a member of the faithful or a result of a personal and voluntary effort. Indeed, the exclusion of sin is a grace, attainable through the free and freely given intervention of God who is the first to bend down lovingly to man to redeem him from sin. This is because human nature on its own is not sufficient in itself to avoid sin, even though the followers of Pelagius argued in antiquity, and some neo-Pelagian currents of thought appear to argue today, that it is. Pope Francis on a number of occasions has warned us about this error.[9]

Understanding an indulgence as a gift helps us to clarify at the same time the concept of "temporal punishment." This is not a "vengeance" inflicted on sinners because of their guilt, but, rather, a consequence itself of sin, an "unhealthy attachment to creatures, which must be purified."[10] This purification is, once again, the positive result of grace, which certainly requires the cooperation of human freedom.

Lastly, the concept of *thesaurus Ecclesiae* deserves some commentary. This famous "treasury" of the Church is not made up of precious goods of some kind or secret funds available to the Pope. It is made up (and much more) of the infinite merits of Christ, applicable to removing the punishments due to sins through indulgences. To the sacrifice of Jesus offered up on the cross in the Holy Spirit to the Father, are also united the "yes" of Mary and the merits of all the saints that have followed one another down the centuries. Here we have the communion of saints, the exchangeable bond of charity that links the members of the heavenly and earthly Church.

---

[8] Cf. *ID*, norm 7.

[9] Cf. for example: "Ultimately, the lack of a heartfelt and prayerful acknowledgment of our limitations prevents grace from working more effectively within us, for no room is left for bringing about the potential good that is part of a sincere and genuine journey of growth": Pope Francis, Apostolic Exhortation *Gaudete et exsultate*, 19 March 2018, n. 50.

[10] *CCC*, n. 1472.

In this sense, therefore, we can say that the practice of indulgences, made possible by faith, nourished by works of mercy, nurtured by taking part in the sacraments and sustained by the communion of saints, is a privileged pathway in following Christ.

From what has been expounded hitherto, one can see clearly that the remission of temporal punishments due to sins that have already been forgiven in confession as regards guilt is truly a great gift and the full manifestation of the mercy of the Father, "the total gift of the mercy of God" to use a happy phrase of St. John Paul II.[11]

---

[11] John Paul II, Bull of Indiction for the Jubilee of the 1950th. Anniversary of the Redemption *Aperite portas Redemptori* (6 January 1983), n. 8.

EDUCATING CONSCIENCES TODAY: EXPECTATIONS, CHALLENGES AND IMPLICATIONS

An analysis of the education of consciences means addressing one of the most delicate and complex issues of the mission of the Church at this stage in history. This is because the term "conscience" refers to that deep interiority of the human person that the Second Vatican Council well described as "the most secret core and sanctuary of a man"[1] and, at the same time, because nowadays this interior dimension can easily be defined in individualistic terms, thereby withdrawing it *de facto* or *de iure* from the need for formation.

Those who are involved at a pastoral or educational level in the Church community well perceive this malaise. Never before, probably, has "the conscience" and its inviolable rights been so spoken about in society, but the subject of "education of the conscience" seems to provoke much suspicion and to belong to the past. In other words, it is forgotten that the conscience, in addition to claiming rights, establishes first of all a fundamental obligation — its own formation. The conscience has the right to be respected, just as it has the right to truth. In an epoch such as ours, when "spiritual desertification" has inexorably advanced, as Benedict XVI pointed out,[2] the task of education to make people rediscover the religious character of the conscience has become urgent, and this so that it becomes truly a "sanctuary of a man" where "he is alone with God, Whose voice echoes in his depths" and where he "detects a law which he does not impose upon himself, but which holds him to obedience."[3]

[1] Second Ecumenical Vatican Council, Pastoral Constitution on the Church in the Modern World *Gaudium et spes* (7 December 1965) (hereafter *GS*), n. 16.

[2] Cf. Benedict XVI, Homily at the Holy Mass Opening the Year of the Faith, 11 October 2012.

[3] *GS*, n. 16.

In this analysis I will therefore examine three fundamental aspects that seek to illustrate the question that has just been referred to: 1) the task of educating the conscience in the face of the hopes of nowadays; 2) some cultural challenges connected to the subject of conscience; and 3) the pastoral implications, especially from the educational point of view.

1. Educating the Conscience Given the Expectations of the Contemporary Context

The evocative image of a desert, which was used on a number of occasions by Benedict XVI, is an effective means by which to interpret the modern world and its crisis.[4] At first sight, it could appear to be pessimistic because it sadly highlights the great contradictions of our epoch, which, indeed, is going through an evident spiritual void, an authentic "spiritual desertification,"[5] as though God did not exist (*etsi Deus non daretur*). However, when we go deeper into this image of the teaching of Benedict XVI we see that it is not in the least pessimistic. Instead, we find in it a healthy realism that leads us to look with confidence at this spiritual, moral and educational emergency because "it is in starting from the experience of this desert, from this void, that we can again discover the joy of believing."[6]

Indeed, in a desert, as Benedict XVI points out, "we rediscover the value of what is essential for living; thus in today's world there are innumerable signs, often expressed implicitly or negatively, of the thirst for God, for the ultimate meaning of life. And in the desert people of faith are needed who, with their own lives, point out the way to the Promised Land and keep hope alive."[7]

In Biblical wisdom a desert is an experience of trial and suffering, but it is also the place where one experiences that God is the educator of His people. In the theological interpretation of the painful experience of the desert, Israel learns, as Deuteronomy observes, that only a society that listens to the word of God and puts it into practice is a

---

[4] Cf. Benedict XVI, Homily at the Holy Mass for the Beginning of the Petrine Ministry of the Bishop of Rome, 24 April 2005.

[5] Cf. Benedict XVI, Homily at the Holy Mass Opening the Year of the Faith, 11 October 2012.

[6] Ibidem.

[7] Ibidem.

society that can have life and a future. A personal and social existence constructed without reference to God, entrusted only to its own forces, is an incomplete and sick life that sooner or later will destroy itself: "He therefore let you be afflicted with hunger, and then fed you with manna, a food unknown to you and your fathers, in order to show you that not by bread alone does man live, but by every word that comes forth from the mouth of the Lord ... So you must realize that the Lord, your God, disciplines you even as a man disciplines his son" (Dt 8:3-5).

A desert thus becomes a propitious opportunity for purification, for spiritual growth — an obligatory passage, we may say, to becoming aware of reality with all its limitations. Deserts, therefore, are also hopes that often remain implicit and require deciphering in order to be transformed into opportunities. Behind the void of our time, behind the gravest problems that we can observe in the practice of pastoral care, are frequently concealed profound needs of the heart, aspirations and hopes for a more sensible and human life. The deserts of our time reveal a great thirst for truth and good as well.

But what are these deserts from the point of view of the moral conscience? In what sense are they implicit hopes addressed to the ecclesial community? Analyses of current problems are always difficult because they involve us from near to hand and often do not allow that sufficient and necessary distance required for their comprehension. However, it seems that one can identify at least one strong symptom of this "spiritual desertification" around the moral conscience that could, however, also become an opportunity to rediscover what is essential for moral life, understood as fullness of life (cf. Jn 10:10).

This symptom of spiritual desertification around the moral conscience can be recognized in its radically individualistic interpretation. If today we often hear people proclaim the idea that a choice is good simply because it has been "decided autonomously," because it is an expression of a person's "individual conscience," this is undoubtedly the outcome of a subjectivist anthropology that defines the individual in terms of a closed and self-sufficient individuality. The roots of this way of thinking go back in time and may be identified in the spirit of the modern epoch. Indeed, modern culture has been characterized, ever since its origins, by the reduction of the person to an individual, to the detriment of their personal dimension with reference to neighbor, community and God. The Enlightenment, which at a political level found expression in particular in the French Revolution, strongly contributed to an exaltation of the freedom of conscience — understood as an affirmation of individual rights — amongst the various forms of freedom. Industrialization and the rise of capitalism strengthened what was a concept of freedom based upon an essentially individualistic and egoistic premiss. Thus the subsequent spread of the democratic system also placed the recognition of the rights of the individual conscience at its basis.

The primacy of the conscience, which as an advance is in itself to be appreciated and is also highly important for the humanization of civil society, thus acquired the connotation of subjectivism. As a decisive criterion of morality, already previously recognized in the best tradition of theology (as is shown by St. Thomas Aquinas[8] and St. Alphonsus Liguori[9]), the conscience became an exclusive criterion — if not the only criterion — of moral decision-making. The absolutization of the conscience and the individualist relativism that follows from it were highlighted in the encyclical *Veritatis splendor* of St. John Paul II (1993). The ultimate question is the relationship between freedom and truth, a relationship that plays out in the conscience.[10]

The peril spread by various subjectivist currents of thought have had a worrying impact on the behavior of people. The dependence of freedom on truth has been weakened or even systematically denied,[11] to the point of exalting "*freedom to such an extent that it becomes an absolute.*"[12] This development, in the analysis of St. John Paul II, should be interpreted as "the consequence, manifestation and consummation of *another more serious and destructive dichotomy, that which separates faith from morality.*"[13]

The absolutization and the unilateral exaltation of the conscience constitutes a great pastoral concern of our time. Where the link with truth is obscured, the conscience ceases to be a witness to objective good, a judgment that reflects the truth about good.[14] But behind the affirmation of the fundamental value of the conscience of the individual we can also see an appeal to the ecclesial community and an implicit hope of nowadays — the retrieval of personhood reminds

---

[8] Cf. T. Aquinas, *Summa Theologiae*, I-II, q. 19, a.5; *De Veritate*, 17, 3, resp.

[9] Cf. A.M. De' Liguori, *Theologia moralis*, lib. I, tract. I.

[10] Cf. John Paul II, Encyclical Letter *Veritatis splendor* (6 August 1993), n. 84.

[11] Cf. ibid., n. 34.

[12] Ibid., n. 32.

[13] Ibid., n. 88.

[14] Cf. ibid., n. 61.

us that the conscience is the unitary center around which revolves the moral experience of the person. The formation of the conscience is thus an inescapable requirement.

To recognize the absolute primacy of the conscience for moral life also means educating it in listening to the voice of God and making it mature in a truly personal sense. It is not sufficient to transmit only values and normative contents — one has to foster a sort of connaturality between the person and true good.[15] How can this take place? The encyclical *Veritatis splendor* observes that "Such a connaturality is rooted in and develops through the virtuous attitudes of the individual himself: prudence and the other cardinal virtues, and even before these the theological virtues of faith, hope and charity."[16] Only in true and profound personal encounter with the Lord Jesus can there take place conversion to the truth and objective good, which, indeed, protect the conscience against folding in on itself. Familiarity with the Lord in personal prayer, like listening to, and meditating on, His Word, as an intimate conversation that places life in a relationship with the law of God, helps the conscience to become truly personal and an authentic expression of the self.

This "vertical" meaning of the conscience was described well by the great theologian Romano Guardini:

> The conscience is the organ for good; it is the organ for God. As soon as we peer a little deeply into the feeling of duty, our awareness that there are obligations, our stances and what else we call the moral conscience, we reach a religious terrain. What on the surface signifies the moral conscience, in its ultimate roots is the "bottom of the soul," the "spark of the soul." We can also take an inverse direction and say: what at its base signifies the moral conscience, at its top is the "tip" or the "blade" of the spirit.[17]

The primacy of the conscience, together with a strong awareness of personhood and freedom, thus refer, even if in an implicit way, to a "base," digging in which we discover God. In a certain sense, subjectivism and the mistaken use of freedom are also indicators of a troubled and unsatisfied person: who can satisfy the aspiration to life and fullness

---

[15] Cf. T. Aquinas, *Summa Theologiae*, II-II, q. 45, a. 2.

[16] John Paul II, *Veritatis splendor*, n. 64.

[17] R. Guardini, *La coscienza* (Brescia, 1997), pp. 38-39.

if not God alone? One is dealing, therefore, with intercepting in the contradictions of our time the real needs that emerge as a deep thirst of the heart. On this point, Pope Francis in his apostolic Exhortation *Evangelii gaudium* reminds us that: "We also evangelize when we attempt to confront the various challenges which can arise."[18] In this sense, the spiritual desertification of our time is not a reason for pessimism or resignation but, rather, an appeal to offer he who truly has the power to make the dry earth bloom: the Lord Jesus who makes himself a neighbor to everyone and makes the individual truly a person.

2. The Denial of the Personal Dimension: a Contemporary Challenge for the Moral Conscience

Side by side with the strong subjectivization of the conscience I have just discussed as a symptom of the spiritual void that surrounds us and at the same time as an appeal to the ecclesial community, we must also remember another challenge that has arisen today in connection with the question of the conscience. We are dealing here with a tendency diametrically opposed to the first — denying that the conscience has any character relating to personhood and reducing it to a simple biological function of the brain.[19]

In recent years this radical reduction of the moral conscience has witnessed a powerful propagation in some areas of the scientific community and in common mentalities (especially amongst the young) through the mass media. In the wake of some fascinating examples of research into the brain, the conscience has been reduced to a function of the brain or a phenomenon that can be explained at a purely biological level. The magisterium of the Pope Emeritus also observed this tendency, which, indeed, expresses the technological logic of our time. In neurological reductionism "man's interiority is emptied of its meaning and gradually our awareness of the human soul's ontological depths, as probed by the saints, is lost."[20] The self of the person is reduced to the brain and the soul is confused with cerebral activity intended for rational calculation or the emotions.

[18] *EG*, n. 61.

[19] Cf. L. Renna (ed.), *Neuroscienze e persona: interrogativi e percorsi etici* (Bologna, 2010); P. Legrenzi and C. Umiltà, *Neuromania. Il cervello non spiega chi siamo* (Bologna, 2009).

[20] Cf. Benedict XVI, Encyclical Letter *Caritas in veritate* (29 June 2009), n. 76.

What we habitually call freedom and the conscience are said to be nothing else but an illusion and a phenomenon that can be explained at a mechanistic level.[21]

When observing this reduction closely, other challenges come to mind experienced by the subject of the conscience in the past, with evident consequences for common mentalities and for education as well. Theological thought and Christian pedagogy in recent decades have amply entered into debate with some tendencies within psychology (especially psychology with a psychoanalytical approach) which have reduced the conscience to a paternal voice or a voice of institutions that we internalized during the years of our childhood, with all of its commands and prohibitions from the outside. Thus the social sciences, where they express a functionalist anthropology, have also often interpreted the conscience as a superstructure of society, of the customs and lifestyles imposed on the individual by a dominant class or group. In these currents of thought, as well, the conscience has been emptied of its character relating to personhood and morality has lost its terrain of connection: in emptying man of his interior principle, one comes to deny morality itself; freedom and ethical choices are presented as illusory. Every form of education of the moral conscience loses its meaning because ethical decisions have been withdrawn from that personal and interior unitary center that we call the conscience.[22]

The challenge that has been posed in recent years by the neurosciences does not, however, only amount to a dangerous reduction of the conscience and the possibility of forming it in an adequate way. Specifically from the scientists of the brain there have also emerged stimulating perspectives for the task of the Church of educating at a moral level. Just as the psychological and social sciences have increased the awareness in Christian pedagogy of influences on the conscience (impulses, educational figures, social models), so recent studies on the human brain have offered pieces by which we can understand its complexity in a better way. We should bear in mind this complexity of the moral conscience so that moral education adheres more to reality and is more effective in the lives of people. The various sciences, if cultivated honestly and without ideological

[21] Cf. *Siamo davvero liberi? Le neuroscienze e il mistero del libero arbitrio*, edited by M. De Caro, A. Lavazza, and G. Sartori (Turin, 2010).

[22] Cf. E. Combi, *Educazione morale cristiana. Il ministero ecclesiale per la costruzione della personalità morale* (Milan, 2002).

prejudices, are never enemies of the faith because, as the Second Vatican Council teaches when addressing scientific knowledge, "earthly matters and the concerns of faith derive from the same God."[23]

Thus the neurosciences remind us, for example, that in moral education the affective component is fundamental. Deciding is strictly linked to the affections and the emotions, as a certain spiritual tradition had already wisely intuited — one may think, for example, of the dynamics of the *Spiritual Exercises* of St. Ignatius of Loyola which are especially attentive to this empathetic and also emotional dimension in moral and spiritual discernment.[24] Too often in the past the formation of the conscience has been seen above all as a question of the transmission of normative elements: in the background there was a conception of the conscience that was prevalently cognitive, as a result of which formation was understood as the transmission of knowledge.[25]

Dialogue with the empirical sciences, on the other hand, has encouraged us to take more seriously the dimension of the affections, the emotions and needs in the attempt to educate the moral lives of believers. Moral decision-making is much more than the application of a syllogism — it is discernment that involves both reason *and* the heart. Educators and confessors are called upon to be convinced that it is no longer sufficient to proclaim moral truth. This truth must be offered in a meaningful way so that it encounters the mind and the affective and emotional resources of a person. From this point of view, the rediscovery of the ethics of virtue, which has recently obtained new attention and contemporary relevance, is of great significance. The virtues, because they are habitual and steady dispositions to do good, highlight how this disposition is profoundly linked to all the dimensions of the human person and not only to the cognitive dimension. What we have before us is the idea of the integral formation of the moral personality: thinking, feeling and deciding are intertwined in an inseparable way and exercise an influence on each other, mutually completing each other.

---

[23] *GS*, n. 36.

[24] Cf. Ignazio di Loyola, *Esercizi spirituali. Ricerca sulle fonti*, edited by P. Schiavone (Cinisello Balsamo, 1995); F. Imoda, *Esercizi spirituali e psicologia. L'altezza, la larghezza e la profondità (Ef 3,18)* (Rome, 2000).

[25] Cf. S. Majorano, *La coscienza. Per una lettura cristiana* (Cinisello Balsamo, 1994), pp. 128-131; G. Gatti, "La personalità morale cristiana," in G. Coffele and G. Gatti (eds.), *Problemi morali dei giovani oggi* (Rome, 1990), pp. 105-119.

As the *Catechism of the Catholic Church* observes, a virtue "allows the person not only to perform good acts, but to give the best of himself. The virtuous person tends towards the good with all his sensory and spiritual powers; he pursues the good and chooses it in concrete actions."[26] The overall promotion of formation of the conscience requires especial care to be paid to this unitary aspect of the person. Indeed, virtue is the *habitus* that dwells in the faculties of the soul, involving not only the cognitive and volitional dimension but also the affective dimension of the person. To pay attention to these unitary and overall features of the moral dimension means being aware of the complex psychological dynamisms and the biological structures that support moral life itself. At the same time, it allows going beyond the minimalist approach of a moral proposal only built around the observance of norms. For a believer, moral life is an experience of "the loftiness of the calling of the faithful in Christ" and it is thus called to holiness in order to bear "fruit in charity for the life of the world."[27] In the context of the sacramental practice of confession, it is thus important not only to enunciate moral truth and uproot sin but also to strive to plant theological life in the conscience of penitents.

3. The Formation of the Conscience: Pastoral Implications

The various reductions of the conscience and the spiritual deserts of our age call into question the very possibility of a moral education, understood as an introduction to the right relationship between freedom and truth and as formation in theological life, which is a life of grace and conformation to Christ. Reference is rightly made to an "educational emergency" to indicate the difficulty that parents, teachers and agents of pastoral care have in taking on the task of shaping the moral personality of the new generations. Whereas scientific knowledge and technological achievements have grown, one can observe a steady disappearance of the meaning of what is done and the objectives of a fully human life. The image of a liquid society[28] is one of the most accredited that exists to interpret what we can observe in

[26] *CCC*, n. 1784.

[27] Second Ecumenical Vatican Council, Decree on Priestly Training *Optatam totius* (28 October 1965), n. 16.

[28] Cf. Z. Bauman, *Modernità liquida* (Rome/Bari, 2002).

the practice of pastoral care. The absence of stable reference points, a sense of loss and the growth of uncertainties seem already to torpedo at the outset any attempt at education.

The "Orientations" for pastoral care of the Italian bishops for the second decade of the third millennium put this question at the center of their concerns and acutely describe the situation as it is perceived:

> People encounter increasing difficulty in giving a profound meaning to their existence. The symptoms of this are disorientation, closing in on oneself and narcissism, an insatiable desire for possessions and consumption, the search for sex detached from the affections and a life commitment, anxiety and fear, an inability to hope, the spread of unhappiness and depression. This is also reflected in the loss of an authentic meaning of educating and a recognition of the inextinguishable need for it.[29]

However, the ecclesial community has not resigned itself in the face of the difficulties. Instead, it emphasizes with conviction the need to form consciences. Indeed, the *Catechism of the Catholic Church* observes that this formation has a continuity that lasts the whole of human existence: "The education of the conscience is a lifelong task."[30]

It is no exaggeration to state that it is precisely the nexus between education and morality that is most urgent nowadays. Indeed, the moral dimension is not a reality placed at the side of other experiences of life. Rather, it is a dimension that incorporates the entire human experience. At its center is the conscience as the most secret core of man, his own interiority that commands at the right moment doing good and avoiding evil, becoming a judgment of reason.[31] As well as being an "organ"[32] by which a person becomes aware of good and responds to it, the conscience is also a "door by which the eternal enters time," as Romano Guardini wrote, "a window open on eternity and at the same time on the course of time and daily events."[33]

However, we must also make an admission: it is not enough to reaffirm the need for the formation of the conscience. There is also

---

[29] Conferenza Episcopale Italiana, *Educare alla vita buona del Vangelo. Orientamenti dell'Episcopato italiano per il decennio 2010-2020* (4 October 2010), n. 9.

[30] *CCC*, n. 1784.

[31] Cf. ibid., nn. 1776-1782.

[32] R. Guardini, *La coscienza* (Brescia, 1997), p. 25.

[33] Ibid., p. 29.

the question of how this can take place. To educate has never been easy but today it seems to be especially complex, in particular when the subject of truth and good is involved. "The task of educating seems to have become increasingly difficult," observed Benedict XVI, "because, in a culture which all too often makes relativism its creed, the light of truth is lacking; indeed it is even considered dangerous to speak of truth, thereby sowing doubt on the basic values of personal and community life."[34]

What, therefore, should be our approach to the education of the conscience? The question is a major one and it would be dishonest to offer easy prescriptions. However, there is an aspect on which Benedict XVI placed great emphasis and which various pastoral projects, like that of the Italian bishops for the second decade of the third millennium, have highlighted: there cannot be education without the presence of authentic educators.

The enunciation of good or the denunciation of evil is not sufficient. Something much greater is needed: the figure of the educator who is first and foremost a witness to what he wishes to transmit at the level of contents — the educator-witness. "This witness becomes a proper reference point to the extent that the person can account for the hope that nourishes his life (cf. I Pt 3:15) and is personally involved in the truth that he proposes. On the other hand, the witness never refers to himself but to something, or rather, to Someone greater than he, whom he has encountered and whose dependable goodness he has sampled."[35] In this sense, it seems to me important to understand formation not principally as the transfer of something but as a relationship and activity that take place between individuals who are different but linked by a deep alliance. The education of the conscience is not therefore a technique but, rather, an art that passes by way of the human qualities of he who educates. More than contents, it is the relationship and love themselves that form the conscience of the other. Only the certainty of being heard, understood and loved makes possible the effective work of education. For that matter, the patron saint of educators, St. John Bosco, loved to observe that "education is something of the heart and God alone is its master."[36] To educate thus

[34] Benedict XVI, Address to those Taking Part in the Plenary Session of the Congregation for Catholic Education, 7 February 2011.

[35] Benedict XVI, Address at the Opening of the Ecclesial Conference of the Diocese of Rome, 6 June 2005. See also for the same idea Conferenza Episcopale Italiana, *Educare alla vita buona del Vangelo*, nn. 29-30.

[36] G. Bosco, *Epistolario*, edited by F. Motto, IV (Rome, 2003), p. 209.

means accompanying towards a personal relationship that offers an opportunity to experience first of all the love that welcomes with joy and trust. One brings into play above all one's own person, without meaning by this the exaggerated putting forward of one's own self or self-exhibition, but, rather, the offering of the person of Christ through the humble and authentic testimony of a witness who has experienced the liberating love of Christ, the beauty of the Gospel, the truth that makes men free (cf. Jn 8:31-42), as well as the frailty that is forgiven, if entrusted to the mercy of the Father.

If we apply this way of understanding formation of the conscience in a more specific way to the context of the Sacrament of Penance, there come to mind the words that St. John Paul II used in his apostolic Exhortation *Reconciliatio et paenitentia* to emphasize the human and spiritual qualities of a confessor who is also always an educator of consciences:

> the confessor must necessarily have human qualities of prudence, discretion, discernment and a firmness tempered by gentleness and kindness. He must likewise have a serious and careful preparation, not fragmentary but complete and harmonious, in the different branches of theology, pedagogy and psychology, in the methodology of dialogue and above all in a living and communicable knowledge of the word of God. But it is even more necessary that he should live an intense and genuine spiritual life. In order to lead others along the path of Christian perfection the minister of penance himself must first travel this path. More by actions than by long speeches he must give proof of real experience of lived prayer, the practice of the theological and moral virtues of the Gospel, faithful obedience to the will of God, love of the church and docility to her magisterium.[37]

One thus understands that in the context of confession as well, formation, as Romano Guardini, suggests, is first of all a question of "self-formation,"[38] in the sense that a good confessor is called to "care for himself," to promote the maturation of his own conscience, and to exercise his own relationship with God through the exercise of

[37] *RP*, n. 29.

[38] Cf. R. Guardini, *Lettere sull'autoformazione* (Brescia, 1994).

thought and analysis in order to be aware of himself and of good, in the eyes of God.[39]

Indeed, just as faith is transmitted through the faith of those who bear witness to it, so the conscience is formed through the consciences of those who live habitually in a dynamic of discernment, engaged in with the Lord and with the help of grace in understanding truth and good, and in assessing and making decisions about reality and situations. Wise pastoral activity is guided by this awareness. In the sacramental context as well, for the formation of the conscience the theological life of those who have the task of educating is central. Personal friendship with Jesus, prayer and spiritual discernment applied to one's own interior world and to relationships and experiences all emerge in an inevitable way in the person of the confessor.

The experience of the free giving and nearness of God in this way animates the ministry of a priest, especially when he welcomes the penitent in the confessional. Precisely because he has encountered the Lord and experienced His love, he can be a father who welcomes, a physician who cures, a teacher who educates and a judge who employs mercy.[40] Being a judge who employs mercy, a father who welcomes, a physician who cures and a teacher who educates — all these characteristics are fundamental in the art of confessing and at the same time in educating the conscience of man.

As is well known, Pope Francis lays much emphasis on communicating the fact that God is infinite mercy because he wants to provoke in the hearts of men and women of good will the trust and the hope that in life changes are always possible — there is always time for conversion and salvation. His Holiness wants the Church to show herself to the world as a mother and teacher of mercy, as a "house for everyone, where all can be renewed, transformed, sanctified by his love, the strongest and the weakest, sinners, the indifferent, those who feel discouraged or lost."[41]

This is why when the Sacrament of Reconciliation is administered the confessor is offered a valuable and propitious opportunity to evangelize, to proclaim the good news, and to engage in the moral education of the conscience of every member of the faithful who turns to him. At the same time, for the confessor as well the confessional

[39] Cf. R. Guardini, *La coscienza* (Brescia, 1997), pp. 31-73.

[40] Cf. A.M. De' Liguori, *Pratica del confessore per ben esercitare il suo ministero.*

[41] Pope Francis, General Audience, 2 October 2013.

becomes a reason for spiritual growth and conforming to Christ, the priest and physician of souls.

Benedict XVI expressed this concept in an evocative way in 2012 on the occasion of the course on the internal forum organized by the Apostolic Penitentiary. At that event, the Pope Emeritus observed to those taking part that the new evangelization starts from the confessional but only to the extent that he who proclaims the news of the Gospel has allowed himself to be evangelized by Christ:

> The minister of the Sacrament of Reconciliation collaborates with the New Evangelization in the first place by renewing himself, his own awareness that he is a sinner and is in need of receiving sacramental pardon. In this way may be renewed the encounter with Christ, which was begun in Baptism and has found its specific and definitive form in the sacrament of Orders.[42]

In this process of the formation of the conscience of the faithful, confessors are instruments to the utmost because through their activity God embraces, heals and saves all those who knock at the door of the confessional, the only and privileged place from which springs the source of mercy and true peace. The pastors of the Church, therefore, are not mere jurists who ascetically analyze Scholastic problems. Rather, they are pastors who wish to help their faithful — brethren in the faith and in following the Lord — to live communion with the Church intensely, to conserve it, to make it grow, and to recover it when it is wounded. Confessors, who are ministers of mercy and educators of the conscience, should always bear in mind that in the exercise of this sensitive ministry one is not only dealing with a case in hand but also with people, with real cases, with individual men and women, remembering the words spoken by the Lord Jesus: "there will be more joy in heaven over one sinner who repents than over ninety-nine righteous people who have no need of repentance" (Lk 15:7).

[42] Benedict XVI, Address to those Taking Part in the Course on the Internal Forum Organized by the Apostolic Penitentiary, 9 March 2012.

EDUCATING IN MERCY: THE SACRAMENT OF PENANCE AS WITNESS TO A RECONCILED LIFE

Educating in mercy is one of the most important aspects of the Christian life and is located in the broadest horizon not only of the pastoral care provided by the Church but also in the challenges that characterize our time. We live in a cultural context that is complex, plural, strongly secularized and from certain points of view not definable: a society that has lost its sense of God and consequently has lost its dynamic towards the supernatural. In this socio-cultural panorama, with everything that it involves, man no longer knows who he is, whence he comes and whither he is directed. Having lost the compass that directs him towards the God of Jesus Christ, the first and last reference point of man, of the creation and of history itself, he lives with reference to himself, his own sensations, in a malaise that presents him as an individual without a vocation to the transcendent. The self, the emotions and affectivity without truth, seasoned with everything and immediately, clearly highlight the frailty of people and at the same their false idea of autonomy. Without going beyond this, in these few lines I have attempted to summarize the features that describe the contemporary world. All of this is known because it is taking place before everyone's eyes.

In this context is located the emergency of education to which the Italian Church has addressed itself. The basic choice of the pastoral "Orientations" for the decade 2010-2020, entitled "Educating in the Good Life of the Gospel," emerges as a point of convergence of three guidelines: 1) Continuity with the "Orientations" of the previous decade ("Communicating the Gospel in a Changing World"); 2) The National Conference of Verona which was celebrated on 2006; and 3) The distant in time but always relevant decree of the Second Vatican Council, *Gravissimum educationis.*

These "Orientations" seek to deepen the educational role of the Church in history. But there is a relevant phrase which — amongst many others — it is advisable to stress because in it are to be found some of the fundamental themes of my analysis: "To educate in the good life of the gospel means first of all making ourselves the *disciples* of the Lord Jesus, the Teacher who never ceases to *educate* for a new and full humanity. He always speaks about intelligence and *warming the hearts* of those who *open themselves* to him and *welcome* the company of our brothers and sisters so that they may *experience* the beauty of the gospel."[1]

My analysis unfolds in two parts. The first part is entitled "Educating in Penance and Mercy" and outlines the efforts of priests who are confessors (even better if catechists-educators) to take penitents — who practice Catholicism to varying degrees — by the hand according to a pathway of illumination and awareness of the real possibilities of encounter with the salvific mercy of Jesus Christ, in the logic of discipleship. The second, entitled "Educated by Penance and Mercy," addresses the believer who, after experiencing the merciful love of God in Christ in the Sacrament of Penance, opens up to bearing witness and attesting to that gift that destroys evil and builds up good, that rises up and vivifies. Only the person who has experienced and experiences true and real reconciliation with God and their brothers and sisters becomes a credible witness to an authentically reconciled life.

1. Educating in Penance and Mercy

This first part seeks to identify possible educational dynamics of the faith, and the conditions that allow them, within the context of a renewed educational commitment of the Church. To do this, it is essential, firstly, to ask the following question: is it possible to educate in mercy outside the general framework of the education of the Christian life? It is certainly the case, given the enormous breadth of the subject, that we must engage in a selection of the criteria that help us to provide an adequate answer and one that is as exhaustive as possible. However, we should not lose sight of the fact that this

[1] Conferenza Episcopale Italiana, *Educare alla vita buona del vangelo. Orientamenti dell'Episcopato italiano per il decennio 2010-2020* (4 October 2010). In the quotation I have put in italics those key terms that refer to the important subjects of my analysis.

proposal as regards education in mercy is offered to believers, namely to those who intend to continue their journey of faith that has been begun in the community, and to those who decide to recommence — after losing it — their authentic experience of the Christian life. These are the targets we are aiming at, without forgetting that unfortunately we are witnessing, even in the believing parts of our ecclesial communities, various forms of the secularization of faith, believers who are areligious or who flee from their baptismal commitments. This is no small challenge! After making this clear, let us now see the horizon in which, and from which, an education in mercy is possible which finds in the celebration of the Sacrament of Penance its point of arrival and at the same time of departure, in order to achieve an authentic "reconciled" witness to life.

1.1. *The Unitary Character of the Educational Discourse of Faith*

In his apostolic Exhortation *Evangelii gaudium*, in the third chapter on the proclaiming of the Gospel, Pope Francis observes that evangelization must take every person and the project that the Lord has for them seriously, producing a journey of formation and maturation[2] and accompanying the faithful in their personal processes of growth.[3] The educational challenge that calls upon us lies specifically in the adoption of this task. We understand immediately that educating *per se*, and above all educating in the faith and as a consequence in mercy, is not easy. Above all else, nothing should be taken for granted. The education that is offered — in continuity with the basic points of Pope Francis and the "Orientations" of the Italian Episcopate — must demonstrate that what Christianity offers accompanies the processes of growth of a person and, like the gradual welcoming of faith, also opens believers up to a supernatural vision of their existence. The educational question of faith, the horizon in which education in mercy and in the Sacrament of Penance finds meaning and opportunity, should be addressed in a dual direction: as a unitary proposal of education involving Christian initiation and as a proposal that educates in a new anthropology. What are we talking about here?

First of all, it is advisable to clarify that the very term "education" has down the years undergone expansions in its meaning. Often it

---

[2] Cf. *EG*, n. 160.

[3] Cf. ibid., nn. 24, 51, 169.

has been seen as synonymous with development, growth, formation, socialization, inculturation and updating. From this it emerges that the idea of education has always been understood as having multiple aspects, with stress on one dimension rather than another according to the context. Beyond the meanings with which the term "education" has been enriched in the post-modern age,[4] I would like to emphasize one thing: in the educational activity of faith and the Christian life the understanding has advanced that educational action can no longer be a matter of the action of one individual (the parish priest, confessor, catechist, mother, father). Rather, it is an interaction of individuals who work in a "network" in line with a logic of real cooperation. In addition, there are some basic assumptions about the educational activity of faith. It is always relational and it is always carried out through interpersonal relationships and in structures that foster relationships (in our case: the ecclesial community, the confessional ...). To this should be added the limitations of an approach that is no longer sufficient, such as that which for a very long time highlighted only the objective fact of faith and saw as the sole principle of Christian education the doctrinal side of things to the detriment of other dimensions. It is clear that between knowledge of doctrine and personal adherence to what is offered as regards education in faith, the whole provocation of subjective perception is at work. We are face to face with a turning point: from concern with doctrine alone (although this is absolutely necessary as a single whole in every proposal relating to education in the Christian life) to an analysis of the credibility of what is being offered. The documents of the Magisterium on catechesis, understood as a prominent feature of education in the Christian life, have always attempted this synthesis.

1.2. *The Itinerary of Christian Initiation: A Fundamental Educational Experience*

Knowing and understanding the world in which we live, its hopes, its aspirations and its dramatic character, is important. However, it is not sufficient. As Paul VI observed, being passive observers of the phenomena of the lives of young people and people in general is not a good educational service offered to consciences. The educator is a teacher, a friend, a physician and a father, one for whom the

[4] Cf. C. Nanni, "Educazione," in C. Nanni (ed.), *Dizionario di Scienze dell'Educazione* (Leumann, 1997), pp. 340-341.

life of a person is truly important.[5] These are the criteria that must always preside over every journey of Christian initiation: an educational journey in which every individual initiative in education in faith must find inspiration, light and support. Christian initiation, far from being a mere preparation for the sacraments, must, rather, be seen as an itinerary of education in faith and the Christian life through the sacraments which are certainly its constituent and essential stages. In their "Orientations" for 2010-2020, the Italian bishops define Christian initiation not as one of the many activities of the Church but that which "defines the self-expression of the Church in being invited to generate faith and fulfil herself as a mother. It has gradually acquired a catechumenal inspiration that leads people towards a gradual awareness of faith through differentiated itineraries of catechesis and experience of the Christian life. The celebration of the sacraments of Christian initiation, followed by a suitable mystagogy, constitutes the completion of this journey towards full Christian maturity."[6]

I am aware that in itself the Sacrament of Penance does not belong to the sacramental triad of initiation. However, I am equally convinced that good education in the sacramental experience of forgiveness cannot avoid being located in a broader horizon of education in and for faith, in which every particular experience of the Christian life finds its right motivation, expression and meaning. In essential terms, it is not enough to establish and set in motion educational itineraries on some aspect of the Christian life in order to solve the problem of its appreciation and its meaning in the life of a believer. To be clear: I do not know whether it is really useful to plan journeys of education in mercy, penance or marriage taken individually, outside or parallel to (at times even replacing) the broader processes of education. In these, a number of realities interact and give greater theological-liturgical-experiential weight to the celebration of the Sacrament of Penance (and through it to the experience of mercy). Motivating and leading believers to have a vision in line with faith in the mercy of God and the importance of the Sacrament of Penance, in which experience of merciful love is almost palpable, is certainly a challenge for pastoral care that is of no small import. An adequate

[5] Cf. Paul VI, Address on the XL Anniversary of the Movement of Aspirants of Catholic Youth, 21 March 1964.

[6] Conferenza Episcopale Italiana, *Educare alla vita buona del vangelo*, n. 40; Cf. also Ufficio Catechistico Nazionale, *La formazione dei catechisti per l'iniziazione cristiana dei fanciulli e dei ragazzi* (4 June 2006), n. 6.

response can be made to it if the itineraries of Christian initiation, at various levels, advance a proposal of faith located on the front of the truth of revelation that best identifies the truth about man. I will now clarify what I have just argued.

For very many years the itineraries of Christian initiation have been increasingly shaped to achieve the integration of the knowledge-dimension of faith (for example catechesis, etc.) and the other dimensions of the Christian life, such as the liturgical, ecclesial, ethical and witness dimensions. We can say with certainty that this educational approach to faith has had positive results but ones perhaps not in line with the wishes and hopes of the ecclesial community. Indeed, although, on the one hand, we have experienced that this discourse is based upon a knowledge of faith that includes celebration and witness, as well as a sense of belonging to the Church,[7] on the other, we have witnessed a certain cooling of believers towards sacramental penance and as a consequence towards the positive results that mercy produces in men's hearts. Here we already have one of the many difficulties that we now have to address: how many believers, of varying levels of religious observance, feel that they belong to the Church to such an extent as to perceive the celebration of penance as a transcendent force that gives vigour, incisiveness and a new direction to their spiritual lives? This is one of the very many questions that can be posed. We can also ask how many manage to associate the sign of reconciliation with the human reality of daily life? As I have already observed, unfortunately the terrain in which we locate our activity relating to education in faith very often is outside the specific context of faith. In essential terms, this is a matter of overcoming a certain secularized vision of Christian belief.

The instruments of education in faith, although they keep alive the knowledge-dimension of faith, which is a guarantee of a good spiritual journey in this epoch of relativism, are called to situate knowledge itself in a journey of life that has the person in his or her totality at the center of things, the "sacred ground" in front of which every educator must always learn to remove his sandals, in respect and nearness.[8] In large measure, we are dealing with giving a more spiritual direction to our educational itineraries of faith. At this point, I believe that it is important to ask in which horizon, and according to

[7] Cf. F. Placida, *La catechesi missionaria e la nuova evangelizzazione nell'Europa post-cristiana* (Assisi, 2013), p. 129.

[8] *EG*, n. 169.

which categories, the proposal of faith of our educational itineraries can generate, motivate and mature a wish — or to express it better a nostalgia — for the merciful love of God through the experience of sacramental penance. Given this context, I will seek to offer a possible path forward.

1.3. *Education in Penance and Mercy in the Truth of Revelation*

To develop this analysis, I will refer once again to the pastoral "Orientations" of the Italian bishops for the decade 2010-2020. In chapter five, which presents recommendations for the planning of pastoral care, we read as follows: "Today care needs to be given in particular to relationships involving listening, recognizing, the stability of ties and free-giving. This means understanding the wish for deep relationships that dwell in the heart of every man, directing people to the search for truth and witness to charity; placing gift at the center of what is offered at the level of education as the achievement of the maturation of a person; and bringing out the educational strength of faith as a dynamic towards the fullness of a relationship with Christ in ecclesial communion."[9] As can be observed, the key category of these recommendations is relationships and their qualities in the educational itineraries of faith. A relationship means welcome, reciprocity, gift, freedom and responsibility. These words say even more if we read them in the light of the dynamics of the revelation of God.

In the dynamic of revelation, God's initiative to communicate Himself encounters man, looks for him and calls him. The Word of God is more than law — it is a gift to be welcomed, a gift that is offered by He who is not looked for (by us) but who looks for us. It is precisely this dynamism that makes us become aware of our freedom and conscious of our limitations, of being touched, of being looked for first. God's initiative is followed by the initiative of man who is not only the recipient of a Word but is also an individual who interacts so that a relationship of faith and love may begin. This is the experience of great figures in the Bible, Abraham, Jacob, Moses, the prophets, and the people of the Old and New Covenant. In essential terms, they were sought, reached and touched by the loving mercy of God who made them participants — through a gift — in His love, in His liberation and in His forgiveness. Thus while the Lord reaches us, we make ourselves be reached; while He speaks to us, we allow Him to

[9] Conferenza Episcopale Italiana, *Educare alla vita buona del vangelo*, n. 53.

speak to us; while He forgives us, we allow ourselves to be forgiven: He looks for us and we allow ourselves to be found and loved. In this relationship of God who searches and gives Himself, and man who allows himself to be sought and answers, is constructed the relationship between truth and freedom, gift and responsibility, and experience and awareness of an experience that has been lived.

This relationship thus puts to the forefront an appeal to conversion, to entrusting oneself, that precedes an understanding of the mystery of mercy and forgiveness that is experienced and lived, specifically following the example of the great stories in Holy Scripture. In them the experience of liberation, first, and of forgiveness, subsequently, in the light of the Spirit, are understood, interpreted and narrated to the new generations.

What does everything that I have said hitherto mean for our educational itineraries of the faith and its multiple expressions? How can we live the educational relationship in relation to forgiveness and mercy, in the horizon of the widest educational action of the Church, according to the paradigm of revelation?

2. Educated by Penance and Mercy: A Renewed Life

In this second part, I would like to emphasize that the dynamic of revelation, inside an itinerary of initiation and education in faith, moves the believer towards becoming aware of the gift of the Sacrament of Penance as a sign of the merciful love of God who calls to conversion and gives a renewed life of grace. The narratives of revelation themselves introduce us to knowledge of the divine pedagogy of a patient and merciful God. On this point, I believe that it is advisable to refer, albeit briefly, to some episodes of the New Testament that seem to me to be paradigmatic of forgiveness received and Divine Mercy experienced, and which set in motion a reconciled life that in its turn became a reason for proclaiming and witness. Usually, in these contexts, some texts of the Magisterium also present the parable of the merciful father and the prodigal son.[10] Instead, I would like here to go back to the salient moments of the story of Zacchaeus (cf. Lk 19:1-10) and the witness of the forgiveness received from Paul (cf. 1 Tm 1:12-16).

[10] Cf. *DM*, nn. 5-6; *RP*, nn. 5-7.

2.1. *The Merciful Look of Christ: The Experience of Zacchaeus (Lk 19:1-10)*

I have said that it is always God that looks for man because forgiveness, salvation and a renewed life arise from a personal encounter between God and man. Because God sent his only Son, Jesus Christ, now it is he who encounters a person. It is the encounter with the gaze of Jesus that changes the history of a person, transforms him or her and gives him or her a new course. In essential terms, it is not so much us seeing Jesus — through the quick thinking of going up the nearest tree — that ensures encounter with the forgiveness and the mercy of God, as being looked for and identified by the gaze of the Lord. Presence as a pre-condition and the curiosity of seeing Jesus pass by, although important, do not assure a health-giving encounter. The thing that amazes one is that Jesus does not say to Zacchaeus "your sins are forgiven," as in other contexts, but simply expresses to him the wish to go to his house. Certainly, the joy of Zacchaeus is felt not only because he will have the Lord as his guest. It is also, and above all else, because the loving look of Jesus had moved something in his heart; it is as though in that encounter he had demolished and rebuilt him, because he felt forgiven and reborn. In essential terms, that look was an authentic grace. What Zacchaeus subsequently says to the Lord attests to, and reveals, a life reconciled with God, his brothers and sisters, and things. His was a true change, a true conversion, because he gave a half of what was his and returned to the unfortunate people he had defrauded four times what he had taken. We convert because the Lord with his forgiveness and mercy creates a new heart and a new life.

2.2. *The "Confession" of Merciful God: The Experience of Paul (1 Tim 1:12-16)*

Another wonderful story of experience of the mercy of God in Christ, which is transformed into witness and confession of faith in the goodness of God, is that of Paul, the Apostle of the Nations. This experience could also be paradigmatic for education in the mercy of God every time that God's forgiveness is experienced through the Sacrament of Penance. To educate starting with one's own forgiven and renewed history is a true act of witness to the merciful love of God. To go back in time, to read one's life anew in the light of the encounter with the mercy of God who put one's heart back in movement, giving that life a dimension of transcendent and believing life, is possible in the experience of confession. God is recognized as the source of all the good that there is in the world, good which He performs through us as well. Paul well knew that he was a blasphemer because he had dishonored the person of Jesus and fought his truth and his grace, his body — the Church. He knew that he had also been a persecutor of Christ, that he had approved the death of Stephen and that he wanted to injure the life of Christ in his disciples. In him there was a desire for truth but not knowledge of truth; his conscience, and therefore his knowledge, were deformed. But something special happened in his life which meant that his story was transformed into a proclaiming of faith, a profession of faith. From his situation of spiritual death, which generated other forms of death, Paul emerged thanks to the grace of Christ and the mercy of God. If through his forgiveness and mercy the Lord saved Paul, a sinner, this means that he wants to save every sinner, without distinction. Sinners are called to conversion and salvation, on the condition that they allow themselves to be reconciled and saved by him. What salvation does Paul speak about? The salvation that will take place in eternity? Certainly not. He speaks about the salvation that is a passage from darkness into the light of the gospel, from judging and condemning to patient and grateful love, from inaction to evident mission. Unfortunately, many Christians do not have this concept of salvation. Christ came to achieve salvation in time through his death and resurrection, in this time, in this life, in this history, placing in the law of hatred the law of love, in the law of death the law of life, in the law of falsehood the law of truth, in the law of violence the law of meekness and humility of the heart.

It is evident that these two experiences (but how can we not also remember that of the Samaritan woman!) well show how people are educated by Divine Mercy that is experienced, lived and the subject of awareness, that becomes a force for conversion and witness of a life that is truly reconciled in the forgiveness of God, achieving a credible and fertile proclaiming. In the stories of Zacchaeus and Paul we discern the essential elements of what the celebration of the Sacrament of Penance should be, at least at the level of a seed, in the heart of penitent believers. Thus, whereas the itineraries of education in the faith must work to provoke and generate the desire for the merciful love of God through sacramental forgiveness, the celebration of this sacrament must bring about encounter with the merciful Christ —

a living and true encounter. From this lived experience springs the beginning of a renewed and reconciled life; the Sacrament of Reconciliation acquires an existential meaning of faith because the sign of reconciliation is not in dissonance with the daily life of the believer.

I chose to refer to these two stories of redemption (Zacchaeus and Paul) because it seemed to me that one can see in them elements that are useful and pertinent both for the confessor — a witness to the forgiveness and mercy received — and for the penitent. In addition, it appears that they also enable us to identify some criteria that help in restoring greater dignity, a greater approach of faith and greater relevance to the celebration of the Sacrament of Penance. One should certainly always bear in mind that the crisis of penance, both recently and today, is always a consequence of a general crisis of faith that generates a loss of a sense of God, of man and of sin.[11] Thus the crisis of the identity of penance seems almost to be almost placed in the second row compared to the indifference and non-faith that surrounds this great gift of mercy and love. What is absent, and this is to be observed every day, is awareness of sin and its consequences: a fracture of the covenant of love with God, refusing to feel and see that we are creatures, children, disciples, fathers, and loved by God Himself. One often hears: "but why should I confess? I have not killed anyone, I have not stolen, I have not blasphemed," as well as: "Why I should I confess that I have had sexual relations with my girlfriend? If we love each other, there is no sin … sins are other things." This way of thinking clearly expresses the crisis of a sense of sin and of journeying according to the requirements of the gospel.

How can this difficulty be overcome? What should we aim at in the educational itineraries of faith; which evangelical approaches should we rediscover and relive in the experience of the celebration of penance?

2.3. *At the School of Mercy for an "Educated" and Reconciled Life*

I would like, at this point, to outline some practical routes that appear to be feasible relating to how one should understand the educational pathways intended to achieve a maturation of a living sense of forgiveness and mercy.

---

[11] Cf. *RP*, n. 18; Conferenza Episcopale Italiana, *Evangelizzazione e Sacramenti della Penitenza e dell'Unzione degli infermi* (12 luglio 1974), nn. 13-14.

To adapt a phrase of Pope Francis, the celebration of the Sacrament of Penance, like the Church herself, "must be a place of mercy freely given, where everyone can feel welcomed, loved, forgiven and encouraged to live the good life of the Gospel."[12] The style of accompanying and nearness, taking seriously the lives of believers and directing their choices in the horizon of faith to the gospel, valuing the human and its universe,[13] in the context of the spiritual journey of education, seem by now to be points of no return. Starting from the truth of revelation and its human meaning, we experience the fact that faith and its expression, for example the sacraments of the Church, are approached in terms of the relationship they have with what they say and express about the meaning of living, the dignity of the person, and the possibility of having an experience of a life that is reconciled in hope.[14] Education in faith, the importance of the sacraments and the meaning of penance pass by way of the litmus test of the meaning of living of our contemporaries, whether believers or not. One often witnesses the fact that the educational proposal of faith is not welcomed because of the authoritativeness of the proposal itself. The encounter with faith depends, rather, increasingly on the reasons for hope and the merciful love of God that the Christian message is able to offer, on encountering a person and their concrete history; on the educational proposal of faith and experience of the sacraments being perceived as experiences of forgiveness, conversion and rebirth that expand and dwell in the hearts of people and enable them to live their lives with dignity and truth.

Thus it is that the educational experience of faith can help the meaning of faith dwell in the Sacrament of Penance by following itineraries of education in the faith whose aim is certainly experience and knowledge of faith but which also allow a person to experience faith as a resource of true humanity. From the point of view of method, we could speak about guidelines that from a certain point of view intersect, namely pathways directed towards encounter with God that at the same time enable people to follow with God the pathways of life, of the human. As a result, life and its events are not simply the premiss or consequence of a maturation of faith but privileged "settings" in which faith and the sacraments can be understood

[12] *EG*, n. 114.

[13] Cf. ibid., nn. 169-171.

[14] Cf. S. Currò, *Perché la Parola riprenda suono. Considerazioni inattuali di catechetica* (Turin, 2014), p. 51.

in terms of their true meaning. In this dynamic, the Sacrament of Penance and the phrase "mercy of God," which would otherwise be incomprehensible because they do not perceive the specific loss of a concrete sense of living, find their meaning. These recommendations, read in the light of the experience of revelation, offer confessors and penitents points of thought for their own spiritual lives: the more we discover that we are children and disciples in need of forgiveness and the mercy of God, the better do we live the dimensions of penance and reconciliation. This is something that Zacchaeus and Paul can tell us a great deal about.

2.4. *The Sacrament of Penance as a "Place" of Conversion and Reconciliation*

Although it does not form a part of the sacraments of Christian initiation, penance is nonetheless essential to the Christian life precisely because, as a result of concupiscence and sin, the new life received from the sacraments of initiation can weaken or even be lost.[15] Here we cannot but refer to the *Catechism of the Catholic Church* in which the Sacrament of Penance is also called the "sacrament of conversion" because it fulfills, sacramentally, Jesus' appeal to conversion, the journey of return to the Father, from whom we distance ourselves through sin.[16] To this meaning the *Catechism* adds another two which express the essence and the efficacy of the Sacrament of Penance — that of penance and that of reconciliation. The first refers to the personal and community journey of repentance and conversion that the penitent has to engage in; the second refers to the proclaiming of witness because he "who lives by God's merciful love is ready to respond to the Lord's call: 'Go, be first reconciled with your brother'."[17]

Pope Francis in *Evangelii gaudium* reminds priests that the confessional should not be a torture chamber but a place of the mercy of the Lord that stimulates us to do the good that we can.[18] Consequently, the celebration of the Sacrament of Penance must be a school, a place of apprenticeship as regards mercy and reconciliation. The confessor must foster conditions by which the penitent meets

[15] Cf. *CCC*, n. 1420.

[16] Cf. ibid., n.1423.

[17] Ibid., n. 1424.

[18] Cf. *EG*, n. 44.

the loving gaze of Jesus who reads, touches and converts; the place in which the penitent has the same sensations that Zacchaeus and Paul had. Thus the celebration of this sacrament becomes a setting in which one discovers and one feels personally the greatness of the love of God which shakes our hearts away from the horror and the burden of sin, makes them aware and directs them ever more to the Gospel. One hopes that this will take place. It can really occur as long as it follows on from a journey of education in faith, as I have already observed, in which Jesus is shown to be not only present but also at work in our lives, the Love that turns to man and embraces everything that makes up his humanity.[19] This merciful love that welcomes and forgives is encountered, indeed allows us to be encountered and looked at, in the celebration of this sacrament so that one may experience how much the heart of God is greater than our sin: the confessional becomes the sycamore tree that we clamber up to attract the attention of Christ who converts and renews.

To end this section, I will quote an evocative phrase of St. Leo the Great quoted in the exhortation *Reconciliatio et paenitentia* of St. John Paul II. This is a sentence that we can well adapt to our subject: "Everything that the Son of God did and taught for the reconciliation of the world we know not only from the history of his past actions, but we experience it also in the effectiveness of what he accomplishes in the present."[20] Every penitent coming out of the confessional should, with Paul, proclaim and remember, place anew in his own heart and the hearts of his brethren, this great truth.

[19] Cf. *DM*, n. 3.

[20] *RP*, n. 8.

RECONCILED WITH GOD, RECONCILED WITH THE CREATION: RELEVANT SUBJECTS FOR AN ECOLOGY OF THE SPIRIT

When it was published, the national Press in Italy defined the encyclical *Laudato si'* as the "green" encyclical of Pope Francis, hoping that it would have a capillary dissemination and be carefully read. This wish was based on the fact that the ecological question, and thus care for our common home, is an obviously transversal subject that interests public opinion and raises serious questions for the whole of global society, but in particular the political classes. Indeed, in paying special attention to the sub-title of this papal document one could legitimize a reading of it that is principally "environmentalist." However, with the right approach such is not really the case. Although, on the one hand, this encyclical seeks to foster a dialogue with all people about safeguarding our common home (the earth) by trying to make its own political-environmental motivations that are universally shared in order to support a promotion of ecology at all levels, on the other, from its first lines onwards a theological-Christological argument is highlighted, as is an anthropological argument, and this makes up the foundation of the whole document. The earth "protests" because of the evil that is done to it every day by man, the Pope observes, because of the irresponsible use and the abuse of the goods that God has placed in it; because the violence that exists in the heart of man, who is wounded by sin, is expressed in all its dramatic colors as exploitation and maltreatment of the earth, which, indeed, the Supreme Pontiff holds up as the "among the most abandoned and maltreated of our poor."[1]

Faced with this desolating reality, Pope Francis offers an integral ecology of justice and charity, presenting it as the outcome of a

[1] Pope Francis, Encyclical Letter *Laudato si'* (24 May 2015) (hereafter *LS*), n. 2.

conversion and a reconciliation that define the exact profile of a new order for the fundamental relationships of man with God, with himself, with other people and with the creation: "an approach to ecology which respects our unique place as human beings in this world and our relationship to our surroundings."[2] But this is possible only as long as man is brought back to a true and authentic relationship with God, with Christ and with the Spirit; a relationship of listening to and welcoming the Word, a relationship of repentance, conversion and reconciliation that places man anew in his original vocation to be a "keeper and tiller" of the creation. This itinerary, which seeks to offer an integral ecology for the full development of man, should be explored starting from those "convictions"[3] of faith that underlie the so-termed theology of creation. These are convictions that spring from accounts of the history of salvation, in particular the accounts of Holy Scripture in *Genesis* 1-2, which assert that human existence is based upon the three fundamental and strictly connected relationships that have been discussed above. It is specifically these accounts that express the benevolence of God who is not closed up in Himself but, rather, acts in a merciful way towards "His" creation; a God who relates and is open to man and the creation. I intend to argue precisely from these theological perspectives in order to try to identify in the dynamism of the conversion-reconciliation of man with God the fundamental criterion by which it is possible to perceive the transcendent dimension of faith of the relationship God-man-creation, the horizon of a new and important integral ecology, of the Spirit and with the Spirit.

1. Ecology as a Theological Question: God and Man in the Garden of Eden

It is not my intention at this point to offer general or specific guidelines for the exploration of a theology of nature or the creation. Despite this, I am persuaded that to refer to the great subjects of the creation of the world and the new creation of man and of all things is fundamental in solidly supporting the subject of this analysis. In the first chapter of *Laudato si'* Pope Francis analyzes the current situation of our common home, highlighting that theological or philosophical

---

[2] Ibid., n. 15.

[3] Ibid., nn. 62, 64.

thought on the contemporary situation of humanity and the world must not be seen as ancient canticles that repeat empty or repetitive music and messages. On the contrary, the presentation of what man is doing to the creation — whose keeper and tiller man was made by divine will — as an outcome of his sinful selfishness and loss of any reference to the Word of God must lead us to a serious examination of conscience so that a real Christian vision of man, of the creation itself and of their mutual relationship can be developed. This is necessary for man, and in particular Christian man, to retrieve that noble vocation and vision of himself which certainly sees him at the margins of the universe but at the same time at the center of the creation[4] as a collaborator of God and His project of love, since it is specifically the love of God that is the fundamental reason for the whole of the creation.

I would like to stress, as indeed emerges from the accounts of the creation in *Genesis*, that God creates from His almighty Word, that He creates the world in the diversity of its elements, that He creates man in His image and likeness, working an absolute novelty, as an element of fracture with the previous mode of creation, to indicate the dignity and the singularity of man in relation to God, to himself and to the creation itself, of which he is an integral part. After creating, God sees that it is a good thing and sees man as a very good thing; the presence of this adverb, as the *Catechism of the Catholic Church* observes, indicates that human beings have in themselves a great special dignity because man "is not just something, but someone. He is capable of self-knowledge, of self-possession and of freely giving himself and entering into communion with other persons."[5] God put man in the Garden of Eden so that he would till it and keep it, a garden that the Lord Himself had planted and that indicates in theological terms not a physical space that can be located but a condition of harmony in which man finds himself — that order that involves a friendly relationship and communion between God, man and the creation. However, this is a relationship that has its foundation and its continuity in listening and obedience to the Word of God. To till and to keep can also indicate that God is not looking for someone (a collaborator) to complete the work of creation — He

[4] Cf. Benedict XVI, Post-Synodal Apostolic Exhortation *Verbum domini* (30 October 2010), n. 9; F. Brancaccio, *Ai margini dell'universo, al centro del creato. L'uomo e la natura nel dialogo tra scienza e fede cristiana* (Cinisello Balsamo, 2016), pp. 270-271.

[5] *CCC*, n. 357.

is searching for a particular recipient to whom to entrust it as a gift and promise of life.[6]

Yet one should not forget that the accounts of the creation assert that the task of man in relation to the creation of God is not only to till and to keep[7] — it is also to subdue and to have dominion. The two terms mean that in essential terms man has a certain "power" over the creation, a power of "enslavement" to do good with a view to a greater good, both for man and for the creation itself. In essential terms, we can define man as a "created god," however one in perennial dependence on the only God, Creator and Lord, because "We are not God. The earth was here before us and it has been given to us."[8] The fact that the terms "subdue" and "have dominion" follow the blessing of God on man, created male and female, means that man is ready to take possession of the creation and to lead it, with the help of God, towards its goal.

As one can see, everything in the creation of God — trees, animals and man — receives its own place, its own order, each knows what to do and what not to do, because everything is admirably predisposed and ordered. We should also observe that after the creation no word or decision was pronounced and taken by man. Everything had been said and disposed by God because He is always the Lord of the creation who must "say" and to whom the creation must constantly look.[9] However, man receives the power to name animals, as a result of which he is not a passive being without anything to say. Rather, he begins to cooperate with the work of God, exercising his "lordship" in His name over the whole of the creation.[10] Although it is true that man is the end of the creation, it is equally true that he cannot live without the creation. He needs it to achieve the purpose of his existence, of being created, because without the creation itself he would be useless to God and God would certainly have received a very limited glory. We can therefore say that where God is the Lord, man in a certain sense is as well but certainly not in an absolute way.

[6] Cf. A. Bonora, "L'uomo coltivatore e custode del suo mondo in Gen 1-11," in A. Caprioli and L. Vaccaro (eds.), *Questione ecologica e coscienza cristiana* (Brescia, 1988), pp. 162ss.

[7] Cf. J. Moltmann, *Uomo, terra, creazione* (Venice, 2016), pp. 21ss.

[8] *LS*, n. 67.

[9] Cf. P. M. Haffner, *Verso una teologia dell'ambiente. L'eredità ecologica di Papa Giovanni Paolo II* (Rome, 2007), pp. 108-117.

[10] Cf. C. Boureaux, *Dio è anche giardiniere. La Creazione come ecologia compiuta* (Brescia, 2016), pp. 24-31.

Indeed, the creation is entrusted to his responsibility and although the creation is governed and moved by its own laws, human intelligence and wisdom can ensure that the creation itself is at the service of the authentic good of every man. In this way, man "has dominion" over the creation and inclines it to his true good, "subduing it."[11] However, he is a keeper and tiller. The garden does not belong to him; it belongs to God. Man must beautify it, keep it ordered and usable, for all those who come after him as well. Obviously, if man remains faithful to the Word of God, to the creative Word that supports the common home with its wisdom, then the creation will be served with love and according to truth: reconciliation and peace with the creation require reconciliation and peace with God the Creator. If, instead, man rejects God and His Word and raises himself to be the only "lord," then he will increasingly abuse — in a worse way — the creation with falsity and selfishness. Here the teaching of St. John Paul II is still very pertinent and of notable contemporary relevance.[12]

Albeit briefly, I have touched on some fundamental themes of the accounts of the creation that point out to us that in *Genesis* human existence is based fundamentally on four relationships that are strictly connected and interdependent: man's relationship with God, with himself and with other humans, and with the creation.[13] The Christian vision of faith of the creation, and in particular of man, helps us to see and assess our common home as God sees it and assesses it: as a space of union and interpersonal communion between God and man. This generates a new salutary responsibility on the part of man towards our natural environment. In this balance lies the question of integral ecology which the encyclical *Laudato si'* speaks so much about. Pope Francis finds the leitmotif of the whole of his encyclical in the fact that we are all interconnected and thus interdependent. In essential terms, such is the integral ecology advanced by the Supreme Pontiff: every man is in a relationship with the rest of the human family and the truth of this relationship is based upon the truth of the relationship that every man has with the God of Jesus Christ: "These ancient stories, full of symbolism, bear witness to a conviction which we today share, that everything is interconnected, and that genuine

---

[11] Cf. G. De Luca, *Egli ci ha fatto e noi siamo suoi. Antropologia cristiana tra grazia e responsabilità* (Soveria Mannelli, 2009), pp. 40-41.

[12] Cf. John Paul II, Message for the XXIII World Day of Peace. Peace with God the Creator, Peace with all of Creation (8 December 1989).

[13] Cf. *LS*, n. 66.

care for our own lives and our relationships with nature is inseparable from fraternity, justice and faithfulness to others."[14] This assumption must spur us to consider that "Together with our obligation to use the earth's goods responsibly, we are called to recognize that other living beings have a value of their own in God's eyes: "by their mere existence they bless him and give him glory," and indeed, "the Lord rejoices in all his works" (Ps 104:31). By virtue of our unique dignity and our gift of intelligence, we are called to respect creation and its inherent laws."[15] The ultimate theological foundation that justifies the interdependence and inter-relationship of the whole of reality and every form of life, as of social structures, is the union, the love and the communion of the Trinity. In the Trinity and for the Trinity every living being tends to God as its ultimate end and while it tends to God forms constant relationships with other living things.[16] However, it is certain that we are community beings and the more we grow in justice and holiness, the more we move out of our own selfishness and enter into a relationship of communion with God, our fellow men and all creatures.[17]

2. From the *Cosmos* to *Chaos*: Man East of Eden

In number 238 of *Laudato si,'* the Holy Father, to demonstrate how the Most Holy Trinity is the first and last cause of the relationship between creatures, including man, writes as follows:

> The Father is the ultimate source of everything, the loving and self-communicating foundation of all that exists. The Son, his reflection, through whom all things were created, united himself to this earth when he was formed in the womb of Mary. The Spirit, infinite bond of love, is intimately present at the very heart of the universe, inspiring and bringing new pathways. The world was created by the three Persons acting as a single divine principle, but each one of them performed this common work in accordance

[14] Ibid., n. 70.

[15] Ibid., n. 69.

[16] Cf. J.I. Kureethadam, "Va' e ripara la mia casa che, come vedi, è tutta in rovina" in J.I. Kureethadam, *Cura della casa comune. Introduzione a* Laudato si' *e sfide e prospettive per la sostenibilità* (Rome, 2015), pp. 43-46.

[17] Cf. *LS*, n. 240.

> with his own personal property. Consequently, "when we contemplate with wonder the universe in all its grandeur and beauty, we must praise the whole Trinity."

Our common home and the entire universe were therefore led to existence, and are perennially maintained in being, by the One and Triune God: creation belongs to the very order of the love of God. This ordered love of God has its roots in the intra-Trinitarian truth of the Christian God. According to Biblical tradition and even more Patristic tradition, from this ordered love comes through creation not *chaos* but the *cosmos*, that is to say a world on which God has impressed his seal. Indeed, in the light of God the Trinity, the Love that is harmonious and loves what He created (cf. Wis 11:24-6), we can also see that all the subjects of the creation have an order and an unrepeatable character.

Unfortunately, in the garden, in this climate of ordered and harmonious love in which man and God lived a perfect communion, and in which the rest of the creation was involved and reflected this communion, something dramatic happened that marked for ever the relationship of God, man and the creation. Indeed, the harmony between the Creator, humanity and the creation was destroyed by the sin of pride of man because he sought to be like God and take His place, refusing to recognize that he was a humble creature who was dependent on God and limited in his being. The move was from the *cosmos* to *chaos* because the result of this act of insubordination transformed the original relationships: from being obedient and in communion with God, man became disobedient and falsely autonomous. Man's relationship with the creation, one of keeping and tilling, became a relationship of conflict, the selfish exploitation of resources and a pitiless dominion of the elements.

It is true that the creation was entrusted to the responsibility of man and for this reason God from the outset showed that He was open to a relationship of life with man and with the creation. However, the difference from the rest of the creation is that man must want, as an act of freedom, a true relationship with God.[18] For this reason, after sin things change for man but they do not change for God. Man draws away from God, he hides and is then banished from the Garden of Eden towards a land that offers thistles and thorns;

[18] Cf. D. Concolino, *Il Dio trinitario. La sua identità la nostra differenza* (Vatican City, 2013).

a land, in essential terms, that turns against man and in relation to which man advances his "rights" of absolute dominion. Yet God never ceases to show to man that He is present, He who continuously looks for him to offer him His friendship anew, His communion. Paradoxically, this loving presence of God is a reality that awakens His absence in man's sinful heart. Thus, rather than being a reason for the return of man, it becomes a reason for a further flight from God, a flight to East of Eden, a flight that expresses a certain "malaise" in front of God, manifesting how the relationship of man with God has been broken and dragging into this laceration man's relationship with the creation as well.

To summarize, the account of the creation and sin in *Genesis* can be summed up by the three following themes: the creation, including man, goes from non-being to being, from non-existence to existence. A theological vision is incomprehensible if one does not recognize creation with reference to God the Trinity. As in-depth Patristic theological analysis brought out, the creation of God is in and for Christ, the Wisdom of God, and in the Spirit. Together with the truth of the existence of good, of unity, of complementariness and of interdependence, we also find the birth in man of evil, of rebellion, of selfishness and rejection — in essential terms of spiritual and physical, social and moral death. Yet God, who created the universe and man, did not abandon man to his spiritual and moral misery. As the end of His creation, God was with him to love him and teach him the law of life and communion. Thus from the first moment of his sin, God was always next to man in order to achieve in him a rebirth, that second "genesis" or second creation, both physical and spiritual, and in it to retrieve a salutary and loving relationship with the whole of the creation. But with a difference: the first creation cost God a few words: "Let us make man in our image, after our likeness" (Gen 1:26). The second creation cost Him the blood of His only begotten Son who came to free us from sin and the snares of death and thus to make all things new.

3. Ecological Conversion: Restoring to God What is God's

The title of this sub-section seeks to emphasize a fundamental aspect of the relationship of God, man and the creation, which finds in Christological mysticism its deepest reason, convinced as I am that the conversion of man to the Gospel, as well as the commitment to ecological conversion, finds in the gift of reconciliation with God its foundation and its ultimate meaning. We well know that reconciliation is a gift of God and His initiative, a gift that takes concrete form in the mystery of Christ the reconciler and liberator of man from sin in all its forms. As St. John Paul II observed: "St. Paul likewise does not hesitate to sum up in this task and function the incomparable mission of Jesus of Nazareth, the word and the Son of God made man."[19] Specifically through the mystery of the Incarnation, the Word of God became flesh, came to dwell amongst us and entered the history of the world. As we pray in the *Preface of Christmas II*, he appeared visibly in our flesh to take upon himself the whole of the creation and to raise it up from its fall, thereby reintegrating the universe into the design of God, and to lead dispersed humanity back to Him. It is evident that these phrases are an echo of the reconciling mission of Christ through his cross about which the Apostle John speaks in his gospel (cf. Jn 11:52). The same may be said of the vision of the work of Christ of a cosmic dimension[20] described by Paul in his Letter to the Colossians. There he writes that Christ is the firstborn of the whole of the creation because in him and in looking forward to him all things were created and subsist, and for him and looking forward to him all things, creatures in heaven and earth, were reconciled (cf. Col 1:15-22). Thus through the incarnation, death and resurrection of Christ, the reconciliation of man is defined in its dual aspect: liberation from sin, communion of grace with God and respect for our brethren and the creation. However, to be reconciled with God or to allow oneself to be reconciled with Him means detaching oneself with free will from sin, which, as took place in the Garden of Eden, rejects love of God, man and the creation itself.

As a consequence, the question of ecology before being a moral problem or an anthropological issue is, I believe, first and foremost a Christic question which speaks of a deeper definition of the Christian anthropological identity. This term has an exclusively theological meaning because it derives from the word "Christ" — the title that the confession of Christian faith gave to Jesus of Nazareth. Jesus is the Christ of God but also His only begotten Son who, as we know from revelation, is located by God Himself at the origins, at the center and at the summit of His salvific design realized in history. Thus the whole of the salvific action of God, actuated by the Spirit, reaches man and the creation through Christ with a view to his glory. For this reason,

[19] *RP*, n. 7.

[20] Cf. ibidem.

Jesus Christ is not only the center of the history of salvation — he is also he who comes from God and is the only way that leads to God. To say the question of integral ecology is a Christic question means to understand the ecological question according to two approaches. Firstly, the lives of men, of the human family and of the creation are so united to the "event of Jesus Christ" that one can recognize in them a Christic relationship and dimension in the sense that their lives and their relationship (man-men-creation) are not comprehensible and are not to be understood in the truth of their being and their interaction and interdependence if they are not related to the mystery of Jesus. Secondly, the life of man and with it the whole of the creation, animal and vegetable, like fundamental choices to live in justice and peace, can only be referred to, assessed in relation to and led back to, Jesus Christ, the way, the truth and the life of God. In this sense, God must "re-appropriate" what is His and what man in his pride and his sin has, in a certain sense, robbed and stolen from Him. However, God wants to achieve this "re-appropriation" of man and the creation, seeking and asking for the collaboration of man as His partner, keeper and tiller, as He had once seen him.

At this point, it is right to ask by which ways one can collaborate with God in the work of the re-appropriation of man and the creation. Is there only a rational way, made up of good intentions and perhaps political-financial agreements based on eco-sustainable projects, or is it the case that one can perceive a personal and community journey of new relationships built on solid bases of faith that relocate man in the heart of God and *vice versa*, so that in recognizing that God is his Father and Creator man puts an end to raising himself up to being his own master and the master of his brethren and the creation?

4. A New Relationship between Man and God and Man and the Creation: the New Ecology

The two key words of this analysis are "relationship" and "reconciliation." As the Biblical references that have already been cited indicate, the relationship between God and man is bi-directional in the sense that it flows out of God as a relationship of creation but returns from man towards God as a relationship of knowing and love. Indeed, "the relationship itself of knowing and love does not have its origins in man because it is first of all God who perfectly knows and loves man, and man, as the image of God, can respond according to the ways of a creature."[21] Indeed, in Holy Scripture the relationship of man with God is first of all a relationship of God towards man: it is not man who discovers God but God who through His initiative speaks to man, looks for him, calls him and invites him to the covenant. Since the relationship of man with God is a constituent part of his being, man lives and fulfills himself only within this relationship. The creation, on the other hand, takes part in something that is of God but does not turn to Him to be. Man, however, is truly himself only in a relationship of communion with God. The relationship of lordship that marks out the relationship of man with the creation finds its foundation in the fact that the Lord God created man specifically as lord of the creation, as the only creature willed for its own sake. As God has no other being above Him, man in the creation has no other being above him. This lordship of man is expressed in his rationality, in his freedom and in his will. In the exercise of these faculties, man fulfills his being in the image of God the Lord. When, therefore, the lordship of man over the creatures of the world is affirmed, that superiority of man is affirmed that is not only the outcome of a greater created dignity: the lordship in itself is the consequence of the superiority of the nature of God over created nature in which man participates. Such lordship is exercised in history thanks to the openness of man as a creature to the perfections of God: will, intelligence, conscience and freedom are the possibilities that man realizes, in his relationship with God, with "the other" and with creatures — the fulfillment of the nature specific to man.

However, the relationship of man with the creation, which is based on a difference of being, cannot be valid in interpersonal relationships between individuals. If we want to use the same lexicon, respect for the lordship of man as the image of divine lordship imposes, rather, a relational character of union, communion and social equality, above all of justice and charity, of such a kind that "superiority" in functional terms does not become a superiority of being, which would be a lie towards man as man. If all of this applies to every man, it particularly applies to Christians who through the sacraments are associated with the paschal mystery, configured to the dead Christ, and on a journey towards resurrection. Every day Christians fulfill themselves by carrying out the new law of love, something they are made capable

[21] F. Brancaccio, *Antropologia di comunione. L'attualità della* Gaudium et Spes, (Soveria Mannelli, 2006), p. 47.

of thanks to the gift of the Spirit: "equal in being and dignity, men through the commandment of love pursue their common ultimate end — God Himself. The law of love for neighbor is therefore theocentric not only because love for neighbor cannot be disjoined from love for God but also because in love for neighbor is achieved the journey towards the end of man, which is God Himself."[22] I believe that this is the heart of a new ecology which, to employ the words of Pope Francis, must lead to the adoption of new lifestyles that find their source in that "personal transformation that is expressed in the solid cultivation of the virtues"[23] which make possible the dynamic of self-giving in an integral ecological commitment.

In essential terms, this is a new approach to human ecology[24] that points to a vital passage that the Church must become convinced of and take responsibility for in her educational processes of faith. This involves going from an education in ecological values to an education in the cardinal virtues. Obviously, we are not dealing here with underestimating the educational processes in those values, in the ecological field as well, that are universally valid and recognized, which the Pope calls "environmental education."[25] I believe simply that this educational approach is not sufficient to educate men in a right relationship with God, each other and the creation. After all, the subject of integral ecology is a question of faith which, if we understand things aright, can be sustained only in a vision of faith. To act first from the cardinal virtues means to want to recognize the Christian way as an important approach to the ecological crisis. Since this crisis calls on us to engage in a deep interior conversion, the virtues offer themselves as a pathway or better a way of living the relationships that have always characterized human existence.[26]

It seems that in the sixth chapter of *Laudato si'*, entitled "Educational Spirituality and Ecology," Pope Francis addresses himself directly to believers and invites them to live their vocation to be, after a certain fashion, keepers of the work of God as an integral part of

---

[22] D. Tettamanzi, *La comunità degli uomini*, in *Commento alla Costituzione pastorale sulla Chiesa nel mondo contemporaneo "Gaudium et Spes," Quaderni di orientamento pastorale*, 10, (Milan, 1967), p. 202.

[23] Cf. *LS*, nn. 206, 211.

[24] For some aspects of this see A. Carioti, *La pace: dono di Dio e impegno dell'uomo. Riletture bibliche, prospettive magisteriali e implicazioni teologico-pastorali* (Soveria Mannelli, 2009).

[25] *LS*, n. 210.

[26] Cf. ibid., n. 66.

Christian spirituality, living an essentially virtuous life, the outcome of a personal encounter with Jesus and of the gift of the Spirit. It could not be otherwise given the fact that a virtuous life is possible only if we live with the wisdom of God. When reading the wisdom books of the Bible (cf. Wis 7-8), we notice that the virtues, which are necessary to the life of man as a relational being, are the outcome neither of human efforts nor of an intelligence that often places its fullest trust in the body. They are directly connected to the wisdom of God; they are His gift to be asked for and welcomed. This wisdom became in our history incarnated Wisdom: Jesus Christ. The believing life, directed according to the cardinal virtues, allows us to diminish — almost to the point of elimination — exterior deserts, because these virtues diminish first of all interior deserts.[27] As a result, a new ecology pre-supposes an ecological conversion, as the Holy Father affirms, and for this reason men need do nothing else than live the virtues.[28]

One need only think of the virtue of justice, a virtue that refers to otherness and leads existence to a fundamental order. According to the Thomist tradition, the specific feature of justice compared to the other virtues is that it orders the relationship of man with everything connected to others; it is giving to God what is God's, to man what is due to him, and to the creation the respect that it deserves. It is a virtue necessary for the spiritual edification of man: "justice is always born as love for the order of things, from knowledge of their nature and their appreciation."[29] Prudence is understood as the virtue of upright action; it governs times and moments, decides the advisability and/or the need to engage or not to engage in an act; it does not look directly at the achievement of the ends (whether natural or supernatural) of human life but, rather, at the ways by which such ends can be achieved. It always teaches the best way to construct a project and achieve a goal. Since this involves an assessment, one must have the greatest wise knowledge of things. As regards ecological conversion, prudence helps a person in the choice of suitable means, ones that are worthy and commensurate to the end and respect the nature of things.

Temperance may be seen as the ecological virtue to the utmost. A virtue of balance and an upright use of the things of this world,

[27] Cf. Benedict XVI, Homily at the Holy Mass for the Beginning of the Petrine Ministry of the Bishop of Rome, 24 April 2005; *LS*, n. 217.

[28] Cf. G. De Luca, *Egli ci ha fatto e noi siamo suoi*, pp. 254-263.

[29] L. Valera, *Ecologia umana. La dimensione antropologica e le sfide etiche del rapporto uomo/ambiente* (doctoral thesis, Rome, 2010), pp. 312-3.

it promotes action that re-establishes order within man and in the "common home" as well. We can say that this virtue is a divine force in man to ensure that man does not degrade himself and what surrounds him, disposes his heart towards otherness, and in a balanced way uses the resources of the creation that are available to him.

Lastly, there is fortitude, a virtue which — paradoxically — pre-supposes a sense of limits and human frailty. It refers to accepting one's own wounds and a sense of sacrifice. In essential terms, fortitude, like the other virtues, requires an adequate knowledge of things, their correct appreciation, and constant prayer. As regards the new ecology, this virtue teaches man to act when the trial of being wounded takes place and to forgo a good (perhaps one's own) for a greater good (for others and the creation). Because of all of this, all of us, and especially those who have political positions, should repeat with the author of the Book of *Wisdom*: "Her [Wisdom] I loved and sought after from my youth; I sought to take her for my bride and was enamoured of her beauty" (Wis 8:1-2).

5. A Penitential Spirituality for an Ecology of the Spirit

Christian spirituality, of which the Church is the treasury and from which she continually draws her resources, can only be a penitential spirituality, that is, a spirituality of conversion that is able to offer important impulses of interior renewal for the benefit of humanity. It does not seem to me out of place, therefore, to refer, lastly, to some fundamental stages of the pathway that the Church proposes, above all during the period of Lent; a penitential journey that is well located in the context of our subject, since we can point to it as a pre-condition to being able to live an integral ecology according to the Spirit. This pathway brings on stage the realities of prayer, of almsgiving and of fasting, which Christian faith and theological thought have always connected to the fundamental relationships of man with God, with others, with the creation and with himself.[30] As an icon of this itinerary, designed to create a "universal communion"[31] in which our fellow men and the creation are seen and received as a gift of God, Pope Francis offers from the first numbers of his encyclical onwards St. Francis of Assisi, who paid special attention to the creation of God and the

[30] Cf. *LS*, n. 66.

[31] Ibid., n. 220.

poorest and abandoned. His life in harmony with God, other people and the creation found its foundation and its motivation specifically in an existential choice based on a life of prayer and fasting, a prophetic lifestyle following the model of Jesus, which is offered without doubt as an alternative to an existence lived as self-absorption, selfishness, concupiscence, abuse of power and idolatry.

Saint John Paul II himself defined this penitential journey in the following terms: "The principal effort of penitence consists in … entering this dimension of one's own humanity in which, in a certain sense, God is waiting for us,"[32] as conversion to God and rejection of every form of falsehood that distances us from Him and from everything that He loves. However, this ascetic effort itself must not end in man himself. Indeed, it must lead to a deeper opening of the human heart to others than him and beyond him. This is the meaning of prayer as communion of the heart of man with the heart of God as an always present moment when in front of God is placed the history of every man. Precisely in prayer, one confesses first of all the lordship of God over man and the creation, recognizing our nature as creatures and our finitude. With the prayer of man the creation is recognized as such and one returns to living the harmony established by God. Indeed, in prayer, above all in the celebration of the Eucharist, the creation finds its greatest elevation:

> In the Eucharist, fullness is already achieved; it is the living centre of the universe, the overflowing core of love and of inexhaustible life. Joined to the incarnate Son, present in the Eucharist, the whole cosmos gives thanks to God. Indeed the Eucharist is itself an act of cosmic love: "Yes, cosmic! Because even when it is celebrated on the humble altar of a country church, the Eucharist is always in some way celebrated on the altar of the world." The Eucharist joins heaven and earth; it embraces and penetrates all creation. The world which came forth from God's hands returns to him in blessed and undivided adoration.[33]

The sign of almsgiving "under the one name of 'mercy,' embraces many good works"[34] because its field is immense. Almsgiving may be

[32] John Paul II, General Audience, 28 February 1979.

[33] *LS*, n. 236.

[34] Benedict XVI, General Audience, 9 March 2011.

understood as a free disposition of the heart to forgo and to engage in generous deeds but not only as charitable deeds for the benefit of those who are closest to one but also as an expression of universal fraternity, which involves recognition of the fundamental rights of the person, the fight against injustice and poverty, the valuing of human life at all its stages and in all its expressions, a capacity to live together, sharing the resources of the earth: in a few words feeling responsible for each other. I acknowledge that this may appear utopian, but despite this it necessarily belongs to that ecological conversion so much called for by the Holy Father.

Lastly, there is fasting which according to the Christian tradition is closely connected to almsgiving. Fasting does not only mean abstinence from food — it involves other forms of privation to obtain a more sober life. It must be the external sign of an interior reality, of commitment, with the help of God, to abstaining from evil and living by the Gospel; privation, therefore, whose only foundation is great charity and solidarity to be lived with our brothers and sisters. One does not fast for oneself but, rather, to take the place of the other, and in the place of the other one perceives poverty, nakedness, loneliness, hunger, thirst and every form of misery. Almsgiving and fasting emerge as a true and authentic antidote to indifference and diffidence towards a new ecology.

The four cardinal virtues, and the ascetic practice of prayer, of almsgiving and of fasting, represent the stars that must direct the journey of an authentic ecological conversion. When referring to the Gospel, I stated that one should give back to God what is God's — above all man — and by this I expressed, in my judgment, the keystone of the whole of human ecology. In essential terms, what is the ecological crisis, which has arisen from a form of idolatry, if not the theological consequence of man who tries every day to remove God from the heart of the creation (including man) and to raise himself up to being the "creator," with the right of life and death over the work of God? Human efforts, political-economic compromise and environmental policies can do nothing with man who has obscured God, lost himself and compromised the creation, which flees from man every day.

CONCLUSION

I was profoundly impressed by the words spoken by the Holy Father Francis when, in his speech to those taking part in the twenty-eighth course on the internal forum organized by the Apostolic Penitentiary, he observed that one cannot improvise being good confessors because "the confessional is a 'lifelong school.'"[1] His words were a clear invitation, for those of us who were present and for all those in the Church who dedicate themselves in a particular way to the service of the ministry of reconciliation, to rediscover the spiritual dimension of this service and to immerse themselves in it with ever greater force. Rediscovering this dimension certainly does not mean putting the theological-pastoral dimension in the second row. To understand matters aright, indeed, in all the recommendations that the Pope made to the Apostolic Penitentiary, and every time that he speaks about the importance of the experience of Divine Mercy to be lived and internalized in the celebration of reconciliation, a determining approach emerges, an authentic ascetic-theological-pastoral itinerary.

To live a relationship of discipleship and friendship with Jesus the Good Shepherd, to go to the school of the Holy Spirit to become men of the Spirit, men of prayer, and to achieve good and fertile discernment in order to "demonstrate" the loving face of the Father, who with care and concern waits for His children to return to Him with penitent and sincere hearts, is an imperative that a confessor cannot neglect. In the light of this gospel experience, he can really perceive the impulses of the heart that spring from the act of welcoming penitent brothers and sisters who, moved by grace, wish to be welcomed in the benedictory embrace of the merciful Father. We then realize, as Pope Francis asserts, that no confessor is placed in this ministry because of his own merits, because of his own theological and juridical expertise. A knowledge of this leads priests, in their turn,

[1] Pope Francis, Address to those Taking Part in the XXVIII Course on the Internal Forum Organized by the Apostolic Penitentiary, 17 March 2017.

to allow themselves to be evangelized, to be educated by the merciful love of God, through the celebration itself of the Sacrament of Reconciliation during which the Lord often makes us witness simple and poor souls who trust the Church and thereby lead confessors themselves to a greater motivation by faith.

At the same time, however, priests who are confessors, as pastors, teachers and witnesses, must feel the impelling need to evangelize and educate in mercy, in the love of Christ, through reconciliation. Words of the Gospel one can, and one must, always say; words that illuminate and direct a heart on the pathways of a real conversion and an authentic journey of discipleship. Words and grace together so that reconciliation becomes a privileged experience of loving encounter between a wounded heart and the Father who is rich in mercy.

In writing this volume, the outcome of experience in the field and in-depth thought, I have wanted to make the reader take part in my experience as a confessor but also as a disciple of the Lord and a brother amongst brethren. This was the initial intention and I hope that in some ways I have been successful in my endeavor.

It is clear to everyone that today emphasis is placed on what is connected to the senses, the immediate, the palpable, the easily felt. I hope that in our priestly service in favor of the ministry of reconciliation, with that pastoral charity that must mark us out and animate us, we will manage to make people perceive, see and learn through touching that the "confessional," more than a physical place, is a setting in which the "open heart" of God the Good Father is experienced. A place of evangelization and formation in the love of Christ and the Church, a place in which the children of God are welcomed, taken by the hand and accompanied to their encounter with the real Face of God, which the Lord Jesus himself revealed to us.

LIST OF ABBREVIATIONS

AAS — *Acta Apostolicae Sedis*, Vatican City, 1909 *et sequentes.*

CCC — *Catechism of the Catholic Church*, Vatican City, 1992.

CCEO — *Codex Canonum Ecclesiarum Orientalium Auctoritate Ioanni Pauli PP. II Promulgatus*, Vatican City, 1990.

CIC — *Codex Iuris Canonici Auctoritate Ioanni Pauli PP. II Promulgatus*, Vatican City, 1983.

CIC 1917 — *Codex Iuris Canonici Pii X Pontificis Maximi Iussu Digestus Benedicti Papae XV Auctoritate Promulgatus*, Rome, 1917.

DM — John Paul II, Encyclicaal Letter *Dives in Misericordia* (30 November 1980).

EG — Francis, Apostolic Exhortation *Evangelii Gaudium* (24 November 2013).

EV — *Enchiridion Vaticanum*, Vatican City, 1962 *et sequentes.*

GS — Second Vatican Ecumenical Council, Pastoral Constitution on the Church in the Modern World *Gaudium et Spes* (7 December 1965).

ID — Paul VI, Apostolic Constitution *Indulgentiarum Doctrina* (1 January 1967).

LF — Francis, Encyclical Letter *Lumen Fidei* (29 June 2013).

LG — Second Vatican Ecumenical Council, Dogmatic Constitution on the Church *Lumen Gentium* (21 November 1964).

LS — Francis, Encyclical Letter *Laudato Si'* (24 May 2015).

MDI — *Manuale delle Indulgenze. Norme e Concessioni*, Vatican City, 1999, fourth edition.

MM — Francis, Apostolic Letter *Misericordia et Misera* (20 November 2016).

MV — Francis, Bull *Misericordiae Vultus* (11 April 2015).

PB — John Paul II, Apostolic Constitution *Pastor Bonus* (28 June 1988).

PDV — John Paul II, Post-Synodal Apostolic Exhortation *Pastores Dabo Vobis* (25 March 1992).

PL — *Patrologiae Cursus Completus*, accurante J.-P. Migne, Paris, 1844–1864.

RP — John Paul II, Post-Synodal Apostolic Exhortation *Reconciliatio et Paenitentia* (2 December 1984).

SC — Second Vatican Ecumenical Council, Constitution on the Sacred Liturgy *Sacrosanctum Concilium* (4 December 1963).

SST — John Paul, Apostolic Letter in the form of a *motu proprio, Sacramentorum Sanctitatis Tutela* (30 April 2001), with an updating by Benedict XVI of 21 May 2010.

BIBLIOGRAPHY

Acta Apostolicae Sedis (Vatican City, 1909 *et sequentes*).

A. Amato, "Paternità-maternità di Dio. Problemi e prospettive," in A. Amato, *Trinità in contesto* (Rome, 1994), pp. 273-296.

Ambrose, *Apologia Prophetae David*, in *PL* 14 (Paris, 1845).

Ambrose, *Epistulae*, in *PL* 16 (Paris, 1845).

Apostolic Penitentiary, "Il dono dell'Indulgenza," *L'Osservatore Romano*, 10 February 2000.

Augustine, *Enarrationes in Psalmos*, in *PL* 36 (Paris, 1865).

Augustine, *In epistolam Joannis ad Parthos tractatus decem*, in *PL* 35 (Paris, 1864).

Augustine, *In Evangelium Ioannis tractatus centum viginti quatuor*, in *PL* 35 (Paris, 1864).

G. Barbaglio, *Il pensare dell'apostolo Paolo* (Bologna, 2004).

Basil, *Trattato sullo Spirito Santo*, éd. B. Pruche (Paris, 1969^{2}) (*Sources Chrétiennes*, n. 17bis).

Z. Bauman, *Modernità liquida* (Rome-Bari, 2002).

Benedict XV, Motu proprio *Alloquentes proxime* (25 March 1917), in *AAS* 9 (1917), p. 167.

Benedict XVI, Address at the Opening of the Ecclesial Conference of the Diocese of Rome (6 June 2005).

Benedict XVI, Address at the Sanctuary of the Holy Face of Manoppello (1 September 2006).

Benedict XVI, Address to those Taking Part in the Course Organized by the Apostolic Penitentiary (11 March 2010).

Benedict XVI, Address to those Taking Part in the Course Organized by the Apostolic Penitentiary (25 March 2011).

Benedict XVI, Address to those Taking Part in the Course on the Internal Forum Organized by the Apostolic Penitentiary (9 March 2012).

Benedict XVI, Address to those Taking Part in the Plenary Session of the Congregation for Catholic Education (7 February 2011).

Benedict XVI, Encyclical Letter *Caritas in veritate* (29 June 2009).

Benedict XVI, Encyclical Letter *Deus caritas est* (25 December 2005).

Benedict XVI, General Audience (9 March 2011).

Benedict XVI, Homily at the Holy Mass for the Beginning of the Petrine Ministry of the Bishop of Rome (24 April 2005).

Benedict XVI, Homily during the Holy Mass Opening the Year of Faith (11 October 2012).

Benedict XVI, Message for the XX World Day of the Sick (20 November 2011).

Benedict XVI, Post-Synodal Apostolic Exhortation *Sacramentum caritatis* (22 February 2007).

Benedict XVI, Post-Synodal Apostolic Exhortation *Verbum domini* (30 October 2010).

Bernard of Clairvaux, *Sermones in Cantica Canticorum*, in *PL* 183 (Paris, 1862).

A. Bonora, "L'uomo coltivatore e custode del suo mondo in Gen 1-11," in A. Caprioli and L. Vaccaro (eds.), *Questione ecologica e coscienza cristiana* (Brescia, 1988), pp. 155-166.

G. Bornkmamm, "Mystérion," in *Grande Lessico del Nuovo Testamento*, VII (Brescia, 1971), coll. 643-715.

G. Bosco, *Epistolario*, edited by F. Motto, IV (Rome, 2003).

C. Boureaux, *Dio è anche giardiniere. La Creazione come ecologia compiuta* (Brescia, 2016).

F. Brancaccio, *Ai margini dell'universo, al centro del creato. L'uomo e la natura nel dialogo tra scienza e fede cristiana* (Cinisello Balsamo, 2016).

F. Brancaccio, *Antropologia di comunione. L'attualità della* Gaudium et Spes (Soveria Mannelli, 2006).

R. Bultmann, "Éleos", in *Grande Lessico del Nuovo Testamento*, III (Brescia, 1967), coll. 399-424.

A. Calabrese, *Diritto penale canonico* (Vatican City, 2006, third edition).

G. Caprile, *Il Concilio Vaticano II. Cronache del Concilio Vaticano II edite da "La Civiltà Cattolica"*, V (Rome, 1969).

A. Carioti, *La pace: dono di Dio e impegno dell'uomo. Riletture bibliche, prospettive magisteriali e implicazioni teologico-pastorali* (Soveria Mannelli, 2009).

Catechism of the Catholic Church (Vatican City, 1992).

Caterina da Siena, *Lettere*, edited by G. Di Ciaccia, I (Bologna, 1996).

L. Ciappi, "Concilio e riforma delle indulgenze", in *Vita Religiosa*, 2 (1967), pp. 99-108.

L. Ciappi, 'Tradizione e novità nella riforma delle indulgenze', in *L'Osservatore Romano*, 9-10 January 1967, p. 2.

M. Cimosa, "Il linguaggio biblico (ebraico, greco e latino) dell'amore e della misericordia divina," in M. Marin and M. Mantovani (eds.), *Eleos: "L'affanno della ragione" fra compassione e misericordia* (Rome, 2002), pp. 197-213.

P. Coda, "Il volto come metafora," in *Nuova Umanità*, 149 (2003), pp. 509-518.

Codex Canonum Ecclesiarum Orientalium auctoritate Ioanni Pauli PP. II promulgatus (Vatican City, 1990).

Codex Iuris Canonici auctoritate Ioanni Pauli PP. II promulgatus (Vatican City, 1983).

Codex Iuris Canonici Pii X Pontificis Maximi iussu digestus Benedicti Papae XV auctoritate promulgatus (Rome, 1917).

E. Combi, *Educazione morale cristiana. Il ministero ecclesiale per la costruzione della personalità morale* (Milan, 2002).

Conciliorum Oecumenicorum Decreta. Edizione bilingue, edited by G. Alberigo *et al.* (Bologna, 2002, second edition).

Concilium Oecumenicum Tridentinum, Sess. 25, *Decretum de Indulgentiis* (4 December 1563), in *Conciliorum Oecumenicorum Decreta*, pp. 796-797.

D. Concolino, *Il Dio trinitario. La sua identità la nostra differenza* (Vatican City, 2013).

Conferenza Episcopale Italiana, *Educare alla vita buona del Vangelo. Orientamenti dell'Episcopato italiano per il decennio 2010-2020 (4 ottobre 2010)* (Bologna, 2010).

Conferenza Episcopale Italiana, "Evangelizzazione e sacramenti della Penitenza e dell'Unzione degli infermi (12 luglio 1974)," in *Enchiridion*

CEI. Decreti, dichiarazioni, documenti pastorali per la Chiesa Italiana, II (Bologna, 1985), nn. 1351-1550.

Conferenza Episcopale Italiana, Ufficio Catechistico Nazionale, *La formazione dei catechisti per l'iniziazione cristiana dei fanciulli e dei ragazzi* (4 June 2006).

Y. Congar, *Spirito e libertà* (Turin, 1969).

Congregation for Catholic Education, *Directives on the Preparation of Seminary Educators* (4 November 1993).

Congregation for Catholic Education, *Ratio fundamentalis institutionis sacerdotalis* (19 March 1985).

Congregation for the Clergy, *Directory for the Ministry and the Life of Priests* (Vatican City, 2013).

Congregation for the Doctrine of the Faith, *Rescriptum ex audientia SS.mi*, (7 February 2003).

S. Currò, *Perché la Parola riprenda suono. Considerazioni inattuali di catechetica* (Turin, 2014).

Cyprian, *Epistulae*, in *PL* 4 (Paris, 1844).

F. D'Ostilio, *Prontuario del Codice di Diritto Canonico* (Vatican City, 1995).

M. De Caro, A. Lavazza and G. Sartori (edd.), *Siamo davvero liberi? Le neuroscienze e il mistero del libero arbitrio* (Turin, 2010).

H. De Lubac, "La costituzione *Lumen gentium* e i Padri della Chiesa," in J.M. Miller (ed.), *La teologia dopo il Vaticano II. Apporti dottrinali e prospettive per il futuro in una interpretazione ecumenica* (Brescia, 1967).

H. De Lubac, *Meditazione sulla Chiesa* (Milan, 1993).

G. De Luca, *Egli ci ha fatto e noi siamo suoi. Antropologia cristiana tra grazia e responsabilità* (Soveria Mannelli, 2009).

V. De Paolis, "Il Libro I del Codice," in *Il diritto nel mistero della Chiesa*, 1, *Il diritto nella realtà umana e nella vita della Chiesa*, edited by the *Gruppo Italiano Docenti di Diritto Canonico* (Rome, 1982), pp. 374-401.

N. Del Re, *La Curia Romana. Lineamenti storico-giuridici* (Vatican City, 1998, fourth edition).

J. Delumeau, *Naissance et affirmation de la Réforme* (Paris, 1973).

Dio Padre di misericordia, published by the *Commissione Teologico-Storica del Grande Giubileo dell'Anno Duemila* (Milan, 1998).

Enchiridion Indulgentiarum. Normae et concessiones (Vatican City, 1999, fourth edition). For the Italian edition see *Manuale delle Indulgenze. Norme e concessioni* (Vatican City, 1999; reprint 2012). For the English edition see *Manual of Indulgences. Norms and Grants* (Washington DC, 1994).

G. Fitzer, "Sfraghis," in *Grande Lessico del Nuovo Testamento*, XII (Brescia, 1979), coll. 378-418.

Francis, Address before the *Regina Coeli* (26 April 2015).

Francis, Address to the Parish Priests of Rome (6 March 2014).

Francis, Address to the Poor and the Prisoners of the City of Cagliari (22 September 2013).

Francis, Address to those Helped in the Centre for Re-education of Santa Cruz di Palmasola (10 July 2015).

Francis, Address to those Taking Part in the Course Organized by the Apostolic Penitentiary (28 March 2014).

Francis, Address to those Taking Part in the Course Organized by the Apostolic Penitentiary (17 March 2017).

Francis, Apostolic Exhortation *Evangelii gaudium* (24 November 2013).

Francis, Apostolic Exhortation *Gaudete et exsultate* (19 March 2018).

Francis, Apostolic Letter *Misericordia et misera* (20 November 2016).

Francis, Bull *Misericordiae vultus* (11 April 2015).

Francis, Encyclical Letter *Laudato si'* (24 May 2015).

Francis, Encyclical Letter *Lumen fidei* (29 June 2013).

Francis, General Audience (2 October 2013).

Francis, General Audience (20 November 2013).

Francis, General Audience (19 February 2014).

Francis, General Audience (10 September 2014).

Francis, General Audience (9 December 2015).

Francis, Homily during the Penitential Liturgy and the Rite of Reconciliation (13 March 2015).

Francis, Homily for the Petrine Ministry of the Bishop of Rome (19 March 2013).

Francis, *Il nome di Dio è misericordia. Una conversazione con Andrea Tornielli* (Vatican City-Milan, 2016).

Francis, *Letter of His Holiness Pope Francis According to which an Indulgence is Granted to the Faithful on the Occasion of the Extraordinary Jubilee of Mercy* (1 September 2015).

Francis, Morning Meditation in the Chapel of the *Domus Santae Marthae* (1 April 2014).

Francis, Morning Meditation in the Chapel of *Domus Sanctae Marthae* (7 April 2014).

Francis, Press Conference on the Return Flight from Brazil (28 July 2013).

M. Gagliardi, "La riconciliazione con Dio nel segno della sua misericordia," in K. Nykiel, P. Carlotti and A. Saraco (eds.), *Il sigillo confessionale a la privacy pastorale* (Vatican City, 2015), pp. 105-120.

G. Gatti, "La personalità morale cristiana," in G. Coffele and G. Gatti (eds.), *Problemi morali dei giovani oggi* (Rome, 1990), pp. 105-119.

J.-M. Gervais, "L'acquisto dell'indulgenza giubilare da parte dei malati e degli altri fedeli legittimamente impediti," in *L'Osservatore Romano* (11 February 2000).

J.-M. Gervais, "Paolo VI e la riforma della disciplina delle indulgenze," in *Periodica*, 88 (1999), pp. 301-329.

J.-M. Gervais, "Profondo significato e scopo pastorale delle Indulgenze," in *L'Osservatore Romano* (31 August-1 September 1998).

R. Guardini, *La coscienza* (Brescia, 1997).

R. Guardini, *Lettere sull'autoformazione* (Brescia, 1994).

P.M. Haffner, *Verso una teologia dell'ambiente. L'eredità ecologica di Papa Giovanni Paolo II* (Rome 2007).

Ignazio di Loyola, *Esercizi spirituali. Ricerca sulle fonti*, edited by P. Schiavone (Cinisello Balsamo, 1995).

F. Imoda, *Esercizi spirituali e psicologia. L'altezza, la larghezza e la profondità (*Ef *3,18)* (Rome, 2000).

John XXIII, Address before the Opening of the Second Ecumenical Vatican Council (11 October 1962).

John Paul II, Address to the Penitentiaries of the Patriarchal Basilicas of Rome (20 March 1989).

John Paul II, Apostolic Constitution *Pastor bonus* (28 June 1988).

John Paul II, Apostolic Constitution *Universi dominici gregis* (22 February 1996).

John Paul II, Apostolic Letter in the form of a motu proprio *Sacramentorum sanctitatis tutela* (30 April 2001); with update by Benedict XVI of 21 May 2010.

John Paul II, Apostolic Letter *Tertio millennio adveniente* (10 November 1994).

John Paul II, Bull of Indiction for the Great Jubilee of the Year 2000 *Incarnationis mysterium* (29 November 1998).

John Paul II, Bull of Indiction for the Jubilee of the 1950th Anniversary of the Redemption *Aperite portas Redemptori* (6 January 1983).

John Paul II, Encyclical Letter *Dives in misericordia* (30 November 1980).

John Paul II, Encyclical Letter *Redemptor hominis* (4 March 1979).

John Paul II, Encyclical Letter *Veritatis splendor* (6 August 1993).

John Paul II, General Audience (28 February 1979).

John Paul II, General Audience (29 September 1999).

John Paul II, Homily during the Holy Mass for the Canonization of the Blessed *Maria Faustina Kowalska* (30 April 2000).

John Paul II, Message for the XXIII World Day of Peace. Peace with God the Creator, Peace with all of Creation (8 December 1989).

John Paul II, Post-Synodal Apostolic Exhortation *Pastores dabo vobis* (25 March 1992).

John Paul II, Post-Synodal Apostolic Exhortation *Reconciliatio et Paenitentia* (2 December 1984).

K. Köster, "Splágchnon," in *Grande Lessico del Nuovo Testamento*, XII (Brescia, 1979), coll. 903-934.

M.F. Kowalska, *Diario. La misericordia divina nella mia anima* (Vatican City, 2007, eleventh edition).

J.I. Kureethadam, "'Va' e ripara la mia casa che, come vedi, è tutta in rovina," in J.I. Kureethadam, *Cura della casa comune. Introduzione a* Laudato si' *e sfide e prospettive per la sostenibilità* (Rome, 2015).

P. Legrenzi and C. Umiltà, *Neuromania. Il cervello non spiega chi siamo* (Bologna, 2009).

Leo the Great, *Sermones*, in *PL* 54 (Paris, 1846).

A.M. De' Liguori, *Pratica del confessore per ben esercitare il suo ministero.*

A.M. De' Liguori, *Theologia moralis*, cura et studio L. Gaudé, I (Romae, 1905).

S. Majorano, *La coscienza. Per una lettura cristiana* (Cinisello Balsamo, 1994).

Manuale delle Indulgenze. Norme e concessioni (Vatican City, 1999, fourth edition; reprint 2012).

J. Moltmann, *Uomo, terra, creazione* (Venice, 2016).

G.P. Montini, "La tutela penale del Sacramento della Penitenza. I delitti nella celebrazione del Sacramento (cann. 1378; 1387; 1388)," in *Le sanzioni nella Chiesa. XXIII Incontro di Studio, 1 luglio-5 luglio 1996*, edited by the *Gruppo Italiano Docenti di Diritto Canonico* (Milan, 1997).

C. Nanni, "Educazione," in C. Nanni (ed.), *Dizionario di Scienze dell'Educazione* (Leumann, 1997), pp. 340-341.

U. Navarrete, "Unità della 'Potestas Sacra' e molteplicità dei 'munera Christi et Ecclesiae,'" in *Winfried Schulz in memoriam. Schriften aus Kanonistik und Staatskirchenrecht*, II (Frankfurt am Mein, 1999), pp. 569-603.

K. Nykiel, *Foro interno*, in *Peccato Misericordia Riconciliazione. Dizionario Teologico-Pastorale* (Vatican City, 2016), pp. 185-189.

K. Nykiel, "Il Foro interno e le materie di competenza della Penitenzieria Apostolica," in C. Papale (ed.), *I delitti contro il sacramento della penitenza riservati alla Congregazione per la Dottrina della Fede* (Rome, 2016) (= Quaderni di Ius Missionale, 7), pp. 33-56.

K. Nykiel, "Il Sigillo Confessionale in prospettiva canonica," in K. Nykiel, P. Carlotti and A. Saraco (eds.), *Il sigillo confessionale e la privacy pastorale* (Vatican City, 2015), pp. 39-54.

K. Nykiel, "Indulgences. Their meaning and ongoing actuality," in *Commentarium pro religiosis et missionariis*, 97 (2016), pp. 197-212.

K. Nykiel, *La natura della potestà della Chiesa nella concessione delle indulgenze* (Rome, 2002).

K. Nykiel, "Las indulgencias: significado y actualidad para la vida de la Iglesia," in *Prawo Kanoniczne*, 59/3 (2016), pp. 52-72.

K. Nykiel, "'Misericordiae vultus': il magistero di papa Francesco," in K. Nykiel *et al.* (eds.), *Il Sacramento della Riconciliazione "porta santa" della misericordia* (Rome, 2017), pp. 17-38.

K. Nykiel, "Significado y Finalidad de las Censuras y Irregularidades en el Derecho Canónico," in *Prawo Kanoniczne*, 60 (2017), pp. 117-134.

A. Oepke, "Kryptô," in *Grande Lessico del Nuovo Testamento*, V (Brescia, 1969), coll. 1161–1169.

E.M. Palma, "La misericordia: sigillo del vero uomo e del cristiano autentico," in *La misericordia e le sue opere. Atti del Convegno, a cura dell'Arcidiocesi Metropolitana di Catanzaro-Squillace* (Catanzaro, 2013), pp. 29-41.

Paul VI, Address on the XL Anniversary of the Movement of Aspirants of Catholic Youth (21 March 1964).

Paul VI, Apostolic Constitution *Indulgentiarum doctrina* (1 January 1967).

Paul VI, Apostolic Constitution *Regimini Ecclesiae universae* (15 August 1967).

Patrologiae cursus completus. Series latina, accurante J-P. Migne, 221 voll. (Paris, 1844-1864).

Pio da Pietrelcina, *Epistolario*, II (San Giovanni Rotondo, 1987).

Pius X, Apostolic Constitution *Sapienti consilio* (29 June 1908), in *AAS* 1 (1909), pp. 7-19.

Pius X, Motu proprio *Quae in Ecclesiae bonum* (28 January 1904), ed. in *Pii X Pontificis Maximi Acta*, I (Rome, 1905), pp. 141-144.

F. Placida, *La catechesi missionaria e la nuova evangelizzazione nell'Europa post-cristiana* (Assisi, 2013).

P. Rattin, "'Non ha apparenza né bellezza.' Il rovescio della bellezza," in *Parola Spirito e Vita*, 2 (2001), pp. 67-77.

Regolamento generale della Curia Romana (1° luglio 1999), in *AAS* 91 (1999), pp. 630-699.

L. Renna (ed.), *Neuroscienze e persona: interrogativi e percorsi etici* (Bologna, 2010).

C. Rocchetta and R. Manes, *La tenerezza grembo di Dio amore. Saggio di teologia biblica* (Bologna, 2015).

Sacra Paenitentiaria Apostolica, *Positio de Sacrarum Indulgentiarum recognitione. Relatio super schema de Indulgentiis recognoscendi* (Vatican City, 1965).

Second Ecumenical Vatican Council, Constitution on the Sacred Liturgy *Sacrosanctum Concilium* (4 December 1963).

Second Ecumenical Vatican Council, Decree on Priestly Training *Optatam totius* (28 October 1965).

Second Ecumenical Vatican Council, Decree on the Ministry and Life of Priests *Presbyterorum Ordinis* (7 December 1965).

Second Ecumenical Vatican Council, Decree on the Mission Activity of the Church *Ad gentes* (7 December 1965).

Second Ecumenical Vatican Council, Decree on the Pastoral Mission of Bishops in the Church *Christus Dominus* (28 October 1965).

Second Ecumenical Vatican Council, Dogmatic Constitution on Divine Revelation *Dei Verbum* (18 November 1965).

Second Ecumenical Vatican Council, Dogmatic Constitution on the Church *Lumen gentium* (21 November 1964).

Second Ecumenical Vatican Council, Pastoral Constitution on the Church in the Modern World *Gaudium et spes* (7 December 1965).

A. Serra, "Tenerezza: tema biblico orchestrato a più voci," in *Servitium. Quaderni di ricerca spirituale*, 183 (2009/III).

A. Spadaro, "Intervista a Papa Francesco," *La Civiltà Cattolica*, 3918 (2013/III), pp. 449-477.

H.J. Stoebe, "Hesed," in E. Jenni and C. Westermann (eds.), *Dizionario Teologico dell'Antico Testamento*, I (Turin, 1978), coll. 520-539.

H.J. Stoebe, "Rḥm," in E. Jenni and C. Westermann (eds.), *Dizionario Teologico dell'Antico Testamento*, I (Turin, 1978), coll. 685-692.

Synod of Bishops, *XI Ordinary General Assembly* (2-23 October 2005), *Final List of Propositions.*

Synod of Bishops, *XIII Ordinary General Assembly* (7-28 October 2012). *Final List of Propositions.*

Teresa di Lisieux, *Storia di un'anima. Manoscritto C* (Vatican City, 1997).

Tertullian, *De carnis resurrectione*, in *PL* 2 (Paris, 1844).

D. Tettamanzi, *La comunità degli uomini*, in *Commento alla Costituzione pastorale sulla Chiesa nel mondo contemporaneo "Gaudium et Spes,"* in *Quaderni di orientamento pastorale*, 10 (1967).

E. Tiedtke, "Volto," in L. Coenen, E. Beyreuther and H. Bietenhard (eds.), *Dizionario dei concetti biblici del Nuovo Testamento* (Bologna, 1976, seventh edition), p. 2013.

T. Aquinas, *Summa Theologiae.*

L. Valera, *Ecologia umana. La dimensione antropologica e le sfide etiche del rapporto uomo/ambiente* (Doctoral thesis, Rome, 2010).

R. Virgili, "Misericordia di Dio e conversione nella tradizione profetica," in *Credere Oggi*, 202 (2014/4), pp. 17-28.

ABOUT THE AUTHOR

Monsignor Krzysztof Jozef Nykiel, born in 1965 in Osjaków, Poland, was ordained a priest in 1990 in the Archdiocese of Łódź. After obtaining a degree in theology at the Theological Academy of Warsaw, in 2001 he was awarded a doctorate in canon law at the Pontifical Gregorian University in Rome. Since 1995 he has worked for the Holy See and since 2012 he has been the Regent of the Apostolic Penitentiary. He teaches canon law at the Faculty of Canon Law of the Pontifical Gregorian University and is involved in pastoral activity at the Parish of St. Anne of Passoscuro.

Monsignor Nykiel is Postulator of the causes of beatification and canonization of the Venerable Servant of God Wanda N. Malczewska of the Archdiocese of Łódź (Poland), and of the Venerable Sister Mary Julitta Ritz of the Diocese of Würzburg (Germany). He has published numerous scholarly and pastoral articles, edited collections of essays, and has been a speaker and moderator at many symposiums, seminars and conferences.

Essential Divine Mercy Resources

Diary of Saint Maria Faustina Kowalska:
Divine Mercy in My Soul

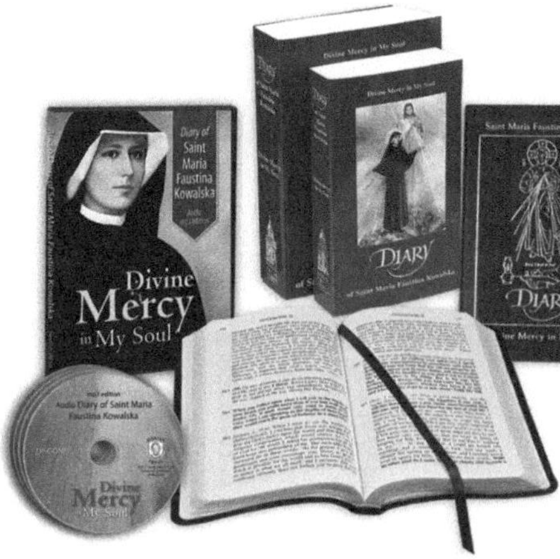

The *Diary* chronicles the message that Jesus, the Divine Mercy, gave to the world through this humble nun. In it, we are reminded to trust in His forgiveness — and as Christ is merciful, so, too, are we instructed to be merciful to others. Written in the 1930s, the *Diary* exemplifies God's love toward mankind and, to this day, remains a source of hope and renewal.

Large Paperback: Y117-NBFD
Compact Paperback: Y117-DNBF
Deluxe Leather-Bound Edition: Y117-DDBURG
Audio *Diary* MP3 Edition: Y117-ADMP3
e Also available as an ebook – Visit ShopMercy.org

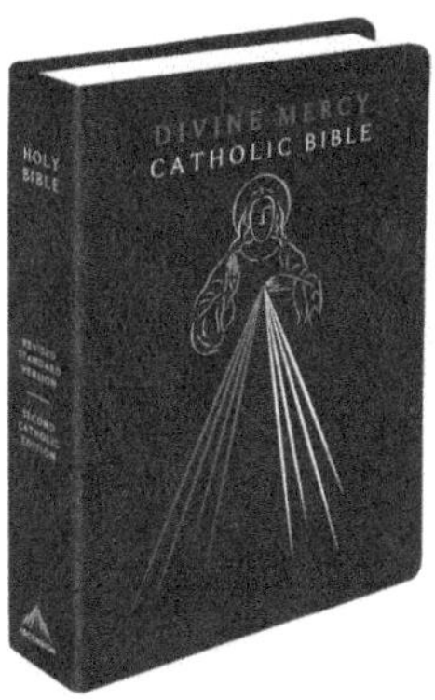

Divine Mercy Catholic Bible

Many Catholics ask what version of the Bible is best to read. In the Revised Standard Version Catholic Edition (RSV-CE) you have the answer.

The *Divine Mercy Catholic Bible* clearly shows the astounding revelation of Divine Mercy amidst the timeless truths of Sacred Scripture. This Bible includes 175 Mercy Moments and 19 articles that explain how God encounters us with mercy through His Word and Sacraments. Leather-bound. 1,712 pages. Y117-BIDM

Explaining the Faith Series

Understanding Divine Mercy

by Fr. Chris Alar, MIC

The entire Divine Mercy message and devotion is summarized in one, easy-to-read book! Explaining the teaching of Jesus Christ as given to St. Faustina, *Understanding Divine Mercy* by Fr. Chris Alar, MIC, has it all. Written in his highly conversational and energetic style, this first book in his *Explaining the Faith* series will deepen your love for God and help you understand why Jesus called Divine Mercy "mankind's last hope of salvation." Paperback. 184 pages.

Y117-EFBK e

For our complete line of books, prayer cards, pamphlets, Rosaries, and chaplets, visit ShopMercy.org or call 1-800-462-7426 to have our latest catalog sent to you.